PENGUIN BOOKS

# RIGHTEOUS GENTILE

John Bierman is a journalist who, over a lengthy career, has covered trouble spots in many parts of the world for major news organizations in Britain, the USA and Canada. For ten years he was a BBC Television News and World Service staff correspondent, much of that time in the Middle East. In addition to the Wallenberg book, first published in New York in 1981, he is the author of major biographies of the French emperor, Napoleon III, and the African explorer, Henry Morton Stanley. He now lives in Cyprus, where he undertakes freelance journalistic assignments when he is not swimming, fishing, indulging his passion for jazz and classical music, and catching up on all the books he never before found time to read.

D1036601

JOHN BIERMAN

# Righteous Gentile

*The Story of Raoul Wallenberg,*
*Missing Hero of the Holocaust*

**Revised Edition**

**PENGUIN BOOKS**

PENGUIN BOOKS

Published by the Penguin Group
Penguin Books Ltd, 27 Wrights Lane, London w8 5tz, England
Penguin Books USA Inc., 375 Hudson Street, New York, New York 10014, USA
Penguin Books Australia Ltd, Ringwood, Victoria, Australia
Penguin Books Canada Ltd, 10 Alcorn Avenue, Toronto, Ontario, Canada m4v 3b2
Penguin Books (NZ) Ltd, 182–190 Wairau Road, Auckland 10, New Zealand

Penguin Books Ltd, Registered Offices: Harmondsworth, Middlesex, England

First published by Allen Lane 1981

Published in Penguin Books 1982
Revised edition 1995
1 3 5 7 9 10 8 6 4 2

Copyright © John Bierman, 1981, 1995
All rights reserved

Typeset by Datix International, Bungay, Suffolk
Printed in England by Clays Ltd, St Ives plc
Set in 10/12.5pt Monophoto Ehrhardt

*For Jonathan,*
*so that*
*he should know the best there is to know —*
*and the worst.*

# *Author's Note*

The fiftieth anniversary of the end of World War II and the tenth anniversary of the effective end of the Cold War (with the accession to power of Mikhail Gorbachev, who called it off) seems an appropriate time to reissue a book about Raoul Wallenberg, exemplary hero of the first conflict and emblematic victim of the second.

For those – and they must be very few by now – who need reminding, Wallenberg was a pseudo-diplomat who left the safety of neutral Sweden and went to Nazi-dominated Hungary in the summer of 1944 on a seemingly impossible mission. There, he managed, through a combination of courage, determination, guile and cunning, to rescue upwards of 20,000 Jews (some claim as many as 100,000) from the Nazi gas chambers. After that, he was taken prisoner by the advancing Red Army and was swallowed up in Stalin's Gulag, never to emerge.

Together with Oskar Schindler, Wallenberg is the best known of that small band of Righteous Gentiles, as the Israelis call them, who stood up to Nazi barbarism and saved significant numbers of Jews from the death camps, thereby demonstrating that lone individuals can, indeed, make a difference.

It would be hard to imagine two individuals more different than Wallenberg and Schindler – the Swede quiet, serious and idealistic, the Sudeten German flashy, lecherous and opportunistic. Yet they had one very important attribute in common: a fundamental decency that made it impossible for them to stand by and let the Nazis get on unimpeded with the ghastly business of genocide. Remarkably, it was only many years after the end of World War II that the names of Wallenberg and Schindler came to the attention of the Western public. Schindler, of course, was made famous by Thomas Keneally's Booker prize-winning novel* *Schindler's Ark* (1983) and by Steven Spielberg's memorable film *Schindler's List* (1993), based on Keneally's book.

In the case of Wallenberg, *Righteous Gentile* – and a television documentary I made on the same subject for the BBC – played a similar if somewhat less emphatic role. When I was researching the book and filming the documentary during 1979–80, Wallenberg's name was virtually unknown, so far as the general public was concerned, outside his native Sweden. I myself had never heard of Wallenberg until, while working as a BBC correspondent in Israel, I chanced across a brief and intriguing reference to him in the *Jerusalem Post* in the summer of 1979.

The subsequent screening of the BBC film in a number of English-speaking countries in 1980 and the publication of the book in Britain and the United States the following year helped to make Wallenberg's heroic deeds during the Holocaust, and his disappearance into the Soviet prison system, known throughout the world.

A closed-circuit showing of the BBC documentary to members of the US Congress in the spring of 1981 helped persuade an overwhelming majority in both the House of Representatives and the Senate to vote for a bill conferring honorary US citizenship on Wallenberg, the only foreigner apart from Sir Winston Churchill ever to receive it. That measure, signed into law by the newly elected president Ronald Reagan in a ceremony at the White House, had a more than symbolic purpose. Its sponsors hoped it would put some diplomatic muscle behind US efforts to get the Kremlin to disclose the truth about Wallenberg's fate. They wanted to know not just the how, when and why of his purported death in Soviet captivity, but to test

* It wasn't really a novel, but essentially a work of non-fiction, but let that pass.

the possibility that he might still be alive somewhere in the Gulag, and if so to secure his release.

Compelling evidence led many people – including myself – to believe it just possible that Wallenberg *could* have survived three and a half decades of incarceration and that even in the intense Cold War atmosphere of the early 1980s it might be possible to rescue him, in however pitiable a condition, to spend his last years in freedom with friends and family.

Another fifteen years on, it is well-nigh impossible to hold on to that belief. After all, if still alive Wallenberg would be eighty-three, which is some ten years longer than the average life span of Western men, even under comfortable conditions. And the collapse of Soviet communism, with the emptying of the prison camps and the admission by the Russians of crimes of far greater magnitude than the wrongful imprisonment of one individual, however noble, have failed to produce a clue to his whereabouts.

None the less, a small band of surviving siblings, old friends and colleagues, and younger admirers not only believe but declare their conviction that he *has* survived and *is* alive – perhaps under an imposed false identity – somewhere in the vastness of post-Communist Russia. Their fervour must be respected, even if it cannot be shared. Certainly, this tireless band of true believers deserves support and encouragement in its unremitting efforts to find out exactly what did happen to this remarkable man while in Soviet captivity. For the tantalizing fact remains that, so far, not one scrap of documentary evidence has surfaced to support the Russians' official assurances that, regrettably, he died in custody during the bad old Stalinist days. Against this, a formidable body of circumstantial evidence exists to suggest that Wallenberg was alive, somewhere in the Gulag, well into the 1970s and perhaps beyond.

For reasons which remain obscure, the Soviet official file on Wallenberg was destroyed and all that remain, scattered here and there throughout the compendious but poorly organized Kremlin archives, opened to investigators since Gorbachev began the process of liberalization which culminated in the collapse of the Soviet Union, are tantalizing hints and ambiguous references.

In some dusty corner of those archives the definitive document may yet be found which discloses when, where, on whose orders and by what means Raoul Wallenberg, the saviour of so many, met his end. Meanwhile, his fate remains one of the most poignant and disturbing mysteries of the Cold War, just as his deeds during the Holocaust remain among the most inspiring achievements of the World War that preceded it.

*Paphos, Cyprus.*
*June 1995*

# *Acknowledgements*

In writing this book I have relied heavily on the original research done immediately after the war by the Austrian-born writer Rudolf Philipp in Stockholm and the historian of the Hungarian holocaust Jenö Lévai in Budapest.

In my own researches, I was especially helped by Wallenberg's half-sister, Nina Lagergren, who opened her family archives to me, adding many hours of personal reminiscence, advice, and invaluable onward contacts. Also in Stockholm, I was generously assisted by, among others, Per Anger, former Swedish ambassador to Canada, Carl-Fredrik Palmstierna, a former official at the Swedish court, and Eric Sjöqvist of the daily newspaper *Expressen*, themselves all authors of books touching on the Wallenberg affair.

In Israel, the Budapest-born journalist Naftali Kraus was unstintingly generous of his time and advice and of his own research files. So was Dr Livia Rothkirchen, the Holocaust historian at Yad Vashem, whose publications – notably the Diary of Eva Heyman – and research facilities were heavily drawn upon. I wish to thank László Szamosi of Haifa for access to his private documents and unpublished memoirs of the period and Hakan Wilkens, counsellor at the Swedish embassy in Tel Aviv during the late 1970s.

Many other individuals and organizations on three continents gave their help and encouragement. Most of them are mentioned in the text and I am grateful to them all. Thanks are especially due to the

BBC, which gave me permission to incorporate material gathered during the filming of my television documentary, *Missing Hero*; to the World Federation of Hungarian Jews in New York for permission to quote from their publications; and to Lars Berg at the Swedish embassy in Brasilia, who allowed me to quote from his memoirs of wartime Budapest. Thanks are also due to the Raoul Wallenberg Committee of the United States and its president, Rachel Haspel-Osterreicher.

Finally, I must acknowledge a couple I never met – Wallenberg's mother and stepfather, Maj and Fredrik von Dardel. They died within two days of each other in February 1979, before I had begun my research – in fact, before I had ever heard of Raoul Wallenberg. Their steadfast loyalty to their son, and to each other, over the long and bitter years following his disappearance shines through the darkness that envelops the Wallenberg affair.

# PART ONE

*Holocaust*

# *Prologue*

Early in March 1944, Obersturmbannführer Adolf Eichmann was supervising the construction of a hostel for Gestapo officers on a site some fifty miles from Berlin. The work was being carried out by a group of Jews brought in from the 'model' concentration camp at Theresienstadt, and Eichmann, who knew almost nothing of building or construction, had not much to do apart from keeping an overall eye on the work force and ensuring that the Jewish engineers and their labourers performed their task with appropriate zeal.

Eichmann was disgruntled. This was not the kind of work for which he had joined the SS and clambered up through the ranks to achieve the status of lieutenant-colonel in charge of Department IV-B-4 of the Reichssicherheitshauptampt (RSHA), better known as the Gestapo and SD. Nor was it the proper work of his department, which was responsible for 'Jewish Affairs and Deportation,' a euphemism for the concentration, deportation, and extermination of the Jews of occupied Europe and the satellites and allies of the Nazis. That task, however, was virtually completed and life had subsequently lost some of its sparkle for Adolf Eichmann. He had already, with great efficiency and dispatch, cleared as many Jews as could be found alive from Germany and Austria, from France, Belgium, Holland, and all the other countries Germany had overrun, and from the satellite and allied states such as Rumania and Bulgaria. To his chagrin he had been denied access to the areas of most densely concentrated Jewish population under Nazi rule – Poland and the occupied areas of the Soviet Union. And now, it seemed, there was nothing fulfilling for him to do.

However, there was still one country within the Nazi sphere of influence which had a substantial Jewish population. In Hungary, more than three-quarters of a million Jews still lived in comparative safety, thanks to the vacillation of the regent, Miklós Horthy. Though he had little love for them, Horthy could not quite bring himself to allow 'his' Jews to be subjected to Hitler's Final Solution – especially since he now believed that his Nazi allies were bound to lose the war.

The secret instructions brought to Eichmann that day by his immediate boss, SS Gruppenführer Heinrich Müller, were to change all that. Bearing the signature of SS Reichsführer Heinrich Himmler himself, these instructions told him to leave the building site forthwith and ready himself and a Sondereinsatzkommando, a special action group, to leave for Hungary on short notice. That country was about to be taken over by the Germans to enforce the total obedience of Horthy, their increasingly reluctant ally. A matter of top priority was Horthy's compliance with the demands for the Final Solution of the Jewish problem. Eichmann and the Kommando, which he would personally lead, were to organize the concentration and deportation of the Hungarian Jews in the quickest possible time.

Eichmann was elated. This was the 'big job' that would re-establish his reputation in the Nazi hierarchy as an organizational genius – perhaps bringing him his long-awaited promotion to the rank of full colonel, and a decoration besides. It would also give him a chance to outshine in speed and volume the achievement of his fellow-SS Obersturmbannführer, Hans Hoffle, who had organized the deportation to the death camps of Warsaw's five hundred thousand Jews.

On a less exalted level, it would give him the opportunity for a brief reunion with his wife, Vera, and their three small sons – Klaus, Horst, and Dieter – for he had to proceed first to the Gestapo concentration camp at Mauthausen, not far from his home in Linz. Although relations with Vera were not good, mainly because of his relentless womanizing, Eichmann enjoyed the company of his two older boys. He could also look forward to the good fellowship of a big reunion with his departmental assistants, now dotted about Europe, who were all coming to Mauthausen to be briefed on the forthcoming operation in Hungary.

That spring of 1944, Raoul Gustav Wallenberg also felt discontent. At thirty-one, he had lost his way. A gifted descendant of a rich and influential dynasty, a man brought up in the assurance that he had the background and personal qualities to do great things, he nevertheless found himself focusing his considerable talents on the importation of goose breasts and pickled cucumbers and the exportation of smoked salmon and cods' roes – this at a time when the Great Powers were locked in combat and events were unfolding that would shape the future for generations in Europe.

Spring came quite a bit later to Wallenberg in neutral Stockholm than it had come to Eichmann near Berlin, five hundred miles farther south, and so did the call to Budapest. Walpurgis Night, 30 April, is traditionally the start of spring in Sweden – supposedly the end of seven cold, dark months, but all too often merely a continuation of seemingly endless winter. But in 1944 a warm spring arrived on schedule and Wallenberg and his friends – a charmed circle of privileged young people in a haven of neutrality – celebrated it that night.

The next day Wallenberg and his friend Magnus von Platen lunched al fresco with two pretty girls in Stockholm's Djurgörden Park.

Jeanette von Heidenstam, Wallenberg's girl friend at the time – later to become a celebrated Swedish television personality – recalls the relaxed mood of that day, the brass band playing Viennese waltzes, the students strolling by in their white caps, and blue and white anemones smothering the grass in the park. 'It was a joyful day, everything just perfect – or so it seems to me looking back – a day of pure delight in an atmosphere of joy and youth, without a fear for the future.

'We had a marvellous lunch, and then we lay in the grass, among the flowers, and talked and talked, and laughed a lot. I can't remember what we talked about. All I can remember is that sense of bliss at the release from winter, and of delight in each other's company.'

Jeanette von Heidenstam also remembers vividly the last day of that magical May, when she received her first proposal of marriage. It was from Wallenberg. He took her to Drottningholm, on the outskirts of Stockholm, where there is a superb theatre, rather like a miniature Versailles, set in a park. 'We walked hand in hand for a while, then sat by the lake drinking coffee among the little white tables, and suddenly Raoul took my hand and said, "I would very much like you to marry me."

'I was confused. I didn't know what to say. I didn't exactly refuse him, but said something about being very young. I was only eighteen to his thirty-one, and I didn't yet know what I wanted in life, except that I had ambitions to be an actress or something of the kind and was not at all ready for marriage. I liked him very much and felt tremendously flattered by his proposal, but somehow he didn't overwhelm me, otherwise I might have said Yes. He never asked me again. Some time later he phoned me to say he was going to Budapest on a mission for the government. He didn't say what kind of mission it was, though I remember him saying it might be very dangerous. He left shortly after that and I never saw him again.'

It was only a few days after Wallenberg proposed to Jeanette that he was unexpectedly given the chance he had perhaps been waiting for – the chance to do something more purposeful and worthy of his talents than dealing in delicatessen imports and exports. Would he be interested, he was asked, in going to Budapest to organize and run a humanitarian department at the Swedish legation? It was felt that this was a job that might best be done by someone who was not a professional diplomat, although he would be given full diplomatic status to carry out his mission.

The task of the new department would be to extend the protection of the Swedish crown to as many as possible of Hungary's Jews, who were now in danger of falling victim to the same Nazi savagery that had engulfed their co-religionists elsewhere in Nazi-occupied Europe.

That neutral Sweden should feel compelled to act, however belatedly, on behalf of the Jews of Europe was a radical departure; that it should choose such an apparently unlikely agent for that purpose was exceptional. But from the moment Wallenberg was offered the job – though he was to question, argue, and haggle over the conditions under which he would take it on – he was committed to it and all thoughts of marriage were abandoned.

The man had met the mission and they were to prove perfectly matched, much more so than the mandarins of the Swedish Foreign Office could have imagined.

# Chapter 1

On 12 March 1944 all the SS officers of Eichmann's Department IV-B-4 were assembled at Mauthausen. There was no time to lose, Eichmann told them. Operation Margarethe, the German occupation of Hungary, was to be launched in seven days. It would be quick and, if at all possible, bloodless. The Eichmann Kommando would go in with the army and begin work immediately. Eichmann outlined a provisional programme for his subordinates. Hungary would be cleared province by province, from east to west, leaving Budapest to the last, and the whole operation would be completed in record time. 'Now the turn of Hungary has come. It will be a deportation surpassing every preceding operation in magnitude.' But he cautioned: 'For the time being I just want to finish off the prominent Jews; but at the same time I want to make sure that the political and economic life of Hungary is not interfered with, because the Wehrmacht depends on the stability of these institutions.'

On 18 March Dieter Wisliceny and Hermann Krumey, Eichmann's principal lieutenants, left Mauthausen at the head of a convoy of 30 vehicles to link up with the German invasion force. Eichmann stayed behind to celebrate his thirty-eighth birthday, 19 March, at home and then followed on at the head of a 120-vehicle convoy. This unit was integrated with the Wehrmacht's columns for their show-of-force parade through Budapest.

Then Eichmann went to the five-star Hotel Majestic, which had been commandeered by the SS. For all his dedicated professionalism and devotion to duty, Eichmann was a man who liked his creature comforts. In addition to hard work, there would be the Hapsburg-style luxury of Budapest's Majestic and its superb dining-room to look forward to. He would have his horses and his dogs. And there would be wine and women – the best that Europe had to offer.

The path which brought Adolf Eichmann to Budapest had begun when he joined the Austrian Nazi Party on 1 April 1932, at the age of twenty-six. The following year he quit his job as a sales representative for the Vacuum Oil Company of Vienna and joined the Austrian SS as a full-time member. His first big opportunity came after Hitler forcibly united his Austrian homeland with the Third Reich in early 1938. Eichmann came to the attention of Dr Hans Globke, one of the authors of the Nuremberg Laws, the series of statutes by which the Nazis gave legal substance to the brutally direct paragraph of their party programme that read: 'Only a member of the Race can be a German subject. Only a person of Germanic blood can be a member of the Race, regardless of religion. Consequently, no Jew can be a member of the Race.'

In 1938 the Nuremberg Laws were also to be effected in Austria, and to expedite this process a 'Central Office for Jewish Emigration' was established in Vienna. Eichmann – who by diligent study had turned himself into an 'expert' on Jewish affairs – was appointed head of this bureau. A few months later he was promoted to the rank of SS Hauptsturmführer, or captain.

It was in this capacity that he set about the task of ridding Austria of its Jewish population – not, as in later years and in other countries, by extermination, but by enforced emigration. The Jews of Austria had already been thoroughly demoralized by a reign of terror. Now, from his office in the commandeered Rothschild family mansion in Prinz Eugen Street, Eichmann offered them a way out. Working through the leadership of the Jewish community, whom he bewildered and frightened with a mixture of crude threats and honeyed words, combined with a disconcerting display of knowledge about Jewish religious and cultural matters, he secured their co-operation in his ingenious emigration programme.

9

What it came down to was that well-to-do Jews were stripped of all their assets but left with enough to pay their way out of the country. It was up to them to find visas for themselves and their families, genuine or forged. But Eichmann could 'help' them with the problem of foreign currency, without which they would not be admitted to foreign countries. He arranged for the Reichsbank to make this currency available to them at exorbitantly high rates of exchange. Only the rich Jews could pay these amounts, and the enormous profits made on the exchange were used to buy foreign currency for their poorer brethren. Thus, the ingenious Eichmann used the rich Jews to finance the departure of the poor Jews without it costing the Reich a pfennig.

Eichmann also ordered the Jewish community leaders to create an emigration fund to help the poor Jews get out and sent Jewish fund-raisers abroad to collect for it. They came back with almost $10 million, a very substantial sum in those days, and before long almost one hundred thousand Jews had left Austria 'voluntarily'. Impressed, SS Chief Reinhard Heydrich came to Vienna to congratulate him personally. Other important officials came from Berlin to study his methods and went away as impressed as Heydrich. Eichmann's *modus operandi* was to become a model for use elsewhere. His star was never to shine more brightly than during those days in Vienna.

Eichmann's next assignment was in Prague, after the Nazis took over Czechoslovakia in March 1939, and there he had similar success in terrorizing the Jews and expelling them in large numbers. He was also given overall charge of a similar bureau in Berlin, but there he was not so successful. This was partly because, right at the seat of Nazi power, there were hordes of rival officials and partly because the leaders of the Berlin Jewish community seemed less co-operative* than their counterparts in Prague and Vienna.

With the outbreak of World War II, on Hitler's invasion of Poland, the enforced emigration programme came to an abrupt end. From now on the fate of the Jews was to be physical destruction,

---

* 'You old shitbag,' Eichmann shouted at one community leader in a moment of frustration when the cool, correct mask slipped momentarily, 'you've been out of the concentration camp too long.'

though this would make no difference to Eichmann's enthusiasm for his work. By their conquest of Poland the Germans eventually 'acquired' another three and a half million Jews, whose disposal Eichmann assumed would become his responsibility. When German military units began killing off large numbers of Polish Jews in a series of unconnected, localized atrocities, Eichmann felt, as did Heydrich, that this approach was inefficient and unprofessional. The time had not yet come, however, for the Final Solution and, meanwhile, there was another job to be done.

The triumphant Nazi leadership had decreed that the parts of Poland that bordered on the Reich were to be incorporated into it. Consequently, there would be a vast population exchange; the ethnic Germans of Poland were to be brought into the border regions, while the Jews living there, as well as most of the local Poles and all the Gipsies, would be moved eastwards. Eichmann was put in charge of this operation and soon hundreds of thousands of Poles, Jews, and Gipsies were moving eastwards under appalling conditions while the Volksdeutsche were transported in considerably more comfort from central Poland and the Baltic states to occupy the homes and farms Eichmann had emptied for them.

The Jews were concentrated into ghettos in central Poland to await their fate, but Hans Frank, the Reichsprotektor of this region (known as the General Government), did not want the SS meddling in his territory. He had no feelings of warmth for either Poles or Jews, but felt only contempt and dislike for Himmler and Heydrich; nor could he tolerate having their subordinate Eichmann interfering in his fiefdom. It took a long time, but Frank was persistent enough, clever enough, and close enough to Hitler to keep Heydrich and Eichmann at arm's length and finally to get them off his back altogether. Thus was Eichmann cheated of the opportunity to dispatch the three and a half million Jews of Poland to the death camps when the gas chambers and crematoria were ready to receive them. That task was carried out by others.

But there were compensations for Eichmann. The Germans rapidly overran much of Europe until, taking into account satellites and allies, another three and a half million Jews came under their control. When the time was ripe, Eichmann was confident, his Department IV-B-4 would deliver them to their fate.

Meanwhile, the Nazis had also invaded the Soviet Union, and on the heels of the advancing Wehrmacht went a new instrument of warfare, the special units known as Einsatzgruppen, each of battalion strength, whose duty was to kill unarmed civilians – Jews and Soviet commissars – whom they found in the newly occupied areas. 'The Jews of the East are the mainstay of Bolshevism and, therefore, according to the Führer's wish, must be exterminated,' the four Einsatzgruppen commanders were told.

Eichmann was not one of them. His special talents lay in the field of organization, administration, and logistics and, indeed, it is possible that he had no particular stomach for the actual killing. However, he did go to inspect the Einsatzgruppen at their grisly work, as they machine-gunned naked men, women, and children by the hundreds on the edge of burial pits. He did not make a habit of such visits, though, for he found the mass shooting a messy business. Years later, during his pre-trial interrogation in Jerusalem, he was to recall with real or feigned distaste: 'I can still see a woman with a child. She was shot and then the baby in her arms. His brains splattered all around, also over my leather overcoat.'

The mass-shooting methods of the Einsatzgruppen had many drawbacks. Hardened and indoctrinated though they were, the troopers involved in this ghastly work had to take more and more alcohol to keep going, and some had even been known to go mad and turn their guns on their officers. 'Look at the eyes of these men,' SS General Erich von dem Bach–Zelewsky told visiting SS Reichsführer Himmler during one action. 'Observe how shattered they are. These men's nerves are ruined for the rest of their lives.' Above all, this method was inefficient, untidy, and rather too public. 'A more elegant method' would have to be found, and again Eichmann was brought in.

He went to the Lublin district of Poland, where experiments were being carried out with gas. Jews were crammed into a sealed bus whose exhaust system emptied the carbon monoxide gas into the vehicle. The bus was driven for several minutes until enough gas had been pumped in, then stopped alongside a ditch. When the doors were opened, the dead and dying were shovelled out into the ditch. Effective, but not good enough. Rudolf Hoess, the commandant of Auschwitz, was also busy with experiments to find the best means of mass slaughter. Himmler sent Eichmann to liaise with Hoess, an old friend. Eichmann mentioned the mobile slaughterhouse he had seen at work in Poland, but they agreed it would be inadequate for the vast hordes Auschwitz would later have to cope with. Before Eichmann went back to his headquarters in Berlin, he said he would try to find a suitable gas.

At the end of November 1941 just such a gas was discovered, though not by Eichmann. The almost instantly lethal Zyklon B had been tried out with great effect on Russian prisoners of war. In addition to being quick-working, one of the great advantages of the gas was that it could be stored in dry, solid form in cans, the pellets turning to gas on exposure to the air. Zyklon B was soon being manufactured in great quantities.

More or less coincidentally with the discovery of Zyklon B's properties, SS Reichsführer Heydrich summoned Eichmann, other SS and Gestapo men, and a number of senior officials of various ministries to a top-secret conference in the smart Berlin suburb of Wannsee. Meeting at Germany's Interpol headquarters on 20 January 1942, they were told by Heydrich that Hitler had given the go-ahead for the Final Solution to the Jewish problem. Responsibility for carrying out this programme of mass extermination, regardless of geographical boundaries, lay with Heydrich himself.

Somewhat optimistically, Heydrich presented an estimate showing that the overall operation would involve 11 million Jews, including those of Britain and of neutral Ireland, Sweden, Switzerland, Spain, and Turkey – not to mention those in the unconquered parts of the Soviet Union. Europe was 'to be combed from east to west' for Jews, and in the execution of this vast operation Eichmann was to play an absolutely key role, answerable only to Heydrich himself. It was another of the peaks of his career, one of those times of great elation that he experienced whenever his formidable organizational skills were to be put to the test.

In the lively debate on ways and means to bring about the Final Solution, Eichmann played a prominent role. The delegates were especially interested in the fate of the part-Jews, or *Mischlinge*. What proportion of Jewish blood should properly qualify a person for extermination? The experts tried to devise means of calculating this with some precision. Eichmann was one of the hard-liners who thought it all foolishness: all *Mischlinge* should be dispatched as though they were full-blooded Jews, he argued. Eichmann was obviously not aware of the rumour, current only in the highest Nazi circles, that Heydrich himself had one Jewish grandmother. In any event, the matter was finally deferred for consideration at a later date.

The conference broke up in a good mood after drinks and dinner. Heydrich, Gestapo chief Müller, and Eichmann stayed behind for a fireside chat at which Heydrich confirmed that all organizational, technical, and material requirements for the Final Solution were to be Eichmann's responsibility. Soon afterwards, Eichmann launched concentration and deportation actions throughout occupied and satellite Europe – though not in Poland, which had almost as many Jews as all the other countries put together. Despite Heydrich's claim to complete responsibility, regardless of geography, Reichsprotektor Frank remained determined to keep him and his minions out of his bailiwick. Heydrich's assassination in Prague, in June 1942, inadvertently set the seal on Frank's victory in his private war with the SS and finally confirmed Eichmann's exclusion from dealing with the Polish Jews.

He bore his disappointment as best he could, and despite his regret at Heydrich's death ('I never knew a cooler dog,' he said admiringly), he was no doubt gratified that after the demise of his boss he became responsible directly to Himmler himself for his work on the Final Solution. He was like the head of some grotesque pan-European travel agency, dealing in one-way package tours to oblivion. From his office in Gestapo headquarters on Berlin's Kurfürstendamm, Eichmann kept an overview of the work of the Kommando leaders he dispatched to the four corners of the Continent. From time to time he dashed off on an inspection visit to one of the capitals concerned and wherever and whenever he went, the pace of concentration and deportation quickened.

Despite his zeal and undoubted efficiency, the total of Eichmann's deportations between the Wannsee Conference and March 1944 – in the region of three-quarters of a million – was not impressive compared with the targets the conference had set. Terrible though the figure seems, it was only a fraction of a total Eichmann was later to boast of to a friend: 'I will jump into my grave laughing because the fact that I have the deaths of five million Jews on my conscience gives me extraordinary satisfaction.' Eichmann's victims numbered as follows:

• Belgium – 25,000. 'It was a very meagre affair,' Eichmann told a confidant after the war. The reason was partly the significant resistance of the Belgian population, which enabled many Jews to escape the dragnet, and partly the slackness of the German military authorities in registering Jews.

• Bulgaria – 12,000. An increasingly reluctant ally of the Nazis and with a strong liberal tradition, Bulgaria, stubbornly resisting the mass deportation of its Jews, proved to be another disappointment for Eichmann.

• Czechoslovakia – 120,000. The Nazi grip was almost total, especially in the savage repression which followed Heydrich's murder in Prague.

• France – 65,000. Some 200,000 French Jews escaped the net. Some of the reasons for this were: the refusal of Vichy leader Marshal Henri Pétain to sign a deportation decree; the refusal of the authorities in the Italian zone of occupation to take part in the Final Solution; the rescue activities of the French *maquis*; and the growing disgust, even of French anti–Semites, with Nazi extermination methods.

• The Greater Reich: Germany – 180,000; Austria – 60,000. On his home ground Eichmann encountered no significant resistance to the deportation of the remnants of the two Jewish communities.

• Greece – 60,000. Most of the Jews were already concentrated in the port city of Salonika, where there had been a community for some 2500 years, and thus were easy to round up and deport.

• Holland – 120,000. The German hold on the Netherlands was total; virtually all Dutch Jews were deported.

• Italy – 10,000. Germany's principal ally was uncooperative where the Jews were concerned, declining to let them be deported either from Italian soil or from those parts of France, Yugoslavia and Greece which Italy occupied. Things 'improved' only after the Nazis occupied northern Italy, following the Allied invasion of Italy and the fall of Mussolini.

• Poland. In the German zone, two big ghettos, Litzmannstadt (the German name of Lódź during World War II) and Bialystok, were not under the control of Hans Frank, Eichmann's *bête noire*. But even here Eichmann was frustrated. With great effort, he deported no more than 10,000 Jews from Bialystok to Auschwitz because the local administration protested that they were needed for war-work. At Litzmannstadt, Eichmann ran up against even more powerful opposition from local officials who were making a vast profit out of the slave labour of the ghetto. Eventually, it was agreed that the ghetto would be 'gradually reduced.'

• Rumania – 75,000. Of the large Jewish community, about half, 400,000, survived the war. Despite its earlier barbarities, even the rabidly anti-Semitic régime of Marshal Ion Antonescu, Hitler's ally, balked at the Final Solution, in which tens of thousands of Jews were driven across the border and shot.

• Scandinavia: Denmark – 425; Norway – 700. The Jewish communities in these two countries were small and, in both, the non-Jewish population helped their Jewish compatriots to get away to neutral Sweden.

• Yugoslavia – 10,000. For 'technical' reasons, most of the Jews of Serbia and Croatia (the two main zones of a dismembered Yugoslavia) were shot or gassed on the spot rather than deported. However, many thousands managed to escape to the zone held by Tito and to join his partisans, and thousands more were given sanctuary by Hitler's Italian allies.

If Eichmann fell far short of the quotas, he also fell short of his own exacting standards. As he told his friend Hoess during one of their boozy evening chats, he felt obliged to destroy every Jew he could lay his hands on. 'Any compromise, even the slightest, will have to be paid for bitterly at a later date,' said Eichmann.

Many top Nazis had 'favourite' Jews whom they helped to escape or for whom they secured better-than-average treatment. Many others allowed themselves to be bribed, or entered without qualms into official negotiations to sell Jews their freedom. Not so Eichmann. He was determined that there should be no exception for any reason, whether of sentiment, personal gain, or high policy. As Heinrich Karl Gruber, a German Protestant clergyman, recalled at Eichmann's trial in Jerusalem, whenever he went to plead with him for an individual Jew, the answer was always negative. 'He was like a piece of ice or marble,' said Gruber. 'Nothing ever touched his heart.' Or his common sense, it would seem. Once one of his assistants urged that an exception be made for a Jew named Abraham Weiss. Weiss had invented an electric light that was invisible from the air and thus of great value during night-time bombing raids; such a fertile mind might be employed to produce more useful gadgets for the Reich; Weiss would be useful to the Nazi war effort. But Eichmann ruled that 'as the patent has already been transferred to the Reich Patent Office, there is no further interest in the affair.'

Although disposing of the lives of hundreds of thousands, the omnipotent Eichmann's eye was 'on the sparrow.' Thus when he heard that a French Jew named Max Gollub was about to obtain a South American passport, he ordered a special action to have Gollub picked up individually and sent to Auschwitz on the next transport.

Nothing better illustrates this meticulous attention to detail and determination to allow no individual to escape than the case of Jenni Cozzi, the Latvian-born Jewish widow of a senior Italian officer, who was caught in the net when the Nazis overran her native country. In Rome, comrades of her late husband urged the Italian Foreign Ministry to secure her release. The Italian Foreign Ministry referred the matter to the German Foreign Ministry, which passed the request on to Eichmann's headquarters. They were rebuffed. The Italians tried again; it was, after all, a debt of honour to the memory of a distinguished officer to save his widow, herself an Italian citizen. Again, Eichmann refused. The request was 'unjustifiable,' he told his Foreign Ministry, asking them to urge the Italian ambassador to abandon his efforts on behalf of 'the Jewess Cozzi.' Still the Italians persisted and eventually Fascist Party headquarters in Rome wrote to Nazi Party headquarters in Berlin on behalf of the signora. Again Eichmann said No and the Italian officer's widow never did emerge from the Riga concentration camp. As Eichmann once explained to a colleague, 'Any exception will create a precedent which would impede the de-Judaization measures.'

Whether this single-minded and relentless pursuit of every last Jew arose from a personal hatred of the Jewish people, from a total acceptance of Nazi ideology, from a pathological obsession with efficiency for its own sake, or from all three is difficult to say. Some years later, while in hiding in Argentina, Eichmann would tell the Dutch Nazi journalist Willem Sassen: 'Personally, I never had a bad experience with a Jew ... The enemy was not persecuted individually. It was a matter of a political solution, and for this I worked one hundred percent.' But like his boast of having sent 5 million Jews to their deaths, this may merely have been said for effect.

What seems certain, though, is that Eichmann's dedication was painfully conscientious. What seems likely, therefore, is that he felt at least some sense of failure at the inability of his department to meet its target figures throughout Europe. Whether his superiors judged his efforts as harshly is unknown. It may be significant that Eichmann never did get a promotion beyond the rank of Obersturmbannführer – lieutenant-colonel – which he achieved in October 1941, and was not decorated until towards the end of 1944, when Himmler, with some show of irritation, pinned a medal on him. On the other hand, when the 'big job' came up – the destruction of Hungarian Jewry – Eichmann was entrusted with it, so it must be assumed that Himmler still had great confidence in him.

However that might be, Eichmann may well have felt the need to prove himself again, to both himself and his superiors, which would go a long way towards accounting for the maniacal zeal with which he met the challenge posed by the eight hundred thousand Jews of Hungary. His efforts to destroy them all would later be described by Winston Churchill as 'probably the greatest and most horrible crime ever committed in the whole history of the world – done by scientific machinery by nominally civilized men in the name of a great state and one of the leading races of Europe.'*

But even at the zenith of his achievements, Eichmann was ultimately to be frustrated – and largely by the extraordinary efforts of the 'Righteous Gentile,' Raoul Wallenberg.

* Notwithstanding this ringing denunciation, Churchill and the other Allied leaders, citing strategic reasons, rejected repeated Jewish pleas to bomb the railway line to Auschwitz – and the camp itself. The best way to save the Jews, they held, was to end the war quickly.

# *Chapter 2*

Raoul Wallenberg's father died eight months after his marriage to the beautiful and spirited Maj Wising and three months before the birth of their son. The child had been conceived before the first symptoms of cancer appeared. The illness ran its course with lightning speed, and Raoul Gustav Wallenberg died, in great pain, a week after his bride's twenty-first birthday. He was twenty-three and had been an officer in the Swedish Navy, as were many men of the sprawling Wallenberg clan. Other Wallenbergs had been, and still are, bankers, diplomats, and bishops of the Lutheran Church. Wallenberg was, and still is, a highly regarded name in Sweden.

Maj Wising Wallenberg, daughter of Sweden's first professor of neurology, Per Wising, was devastated by her bereavement and sustained only by the thought of the child in her womb. A few days after her husband's death, in May 1912, she wrote to his parents, Ambassador and Mrs Gustav Wallenberg, at the Swedish embassy in Japan: 'This horrible emptiness and sense of loss grows greater and greater. How is it ever going to end? I should have understood long ago that so great a happiness as I had been given could not last. Now I have to live on the happy memories that he gave me. Oh, Mother, how will it be with our little one? May God grant that my baby is well-formed and healthy . . .'

On 5 August 1912 Professor Wising wrote to Ambassador Wallenberg: 'Our dear Maj was delivered yesterday morning of a boy, as she wished, whom she wants to call Raoul Gustav, a dear name. She is very well, although in the final months she was very tired and had moments of the deepest despair.'

Four days later Mrs Wising (Maj's mother) wrote to the ambassador and his wife: 'It is a beautiful, warm day, and Maj is lying in her bed at my side on the verandah and little Raoul is at her side, sleeping in his basket. She is very happy with her little son, but sorrow and loss overwhelm her now and then. It is very difficult to console her, but her own admirable self-control and the fear of causing harm to the little one helps her to get over these moments.'

By 28 August Maj was herself writing again to her in-laws: 'I can't describe how happy I feel with this child, a living memory of my happy marriage.' Little more than three months later Maj wrote to Tokyo again – this time to tell the numbing news of her father's sudden death from pneumonia, a week earlier: 'I had no strength to write to you before. This blow is too hard, and it was all I could manage to keep myself composed so that my baby should not suffer.'

As Wallenberg's half-sister, Nina Lagergren, was to put it a lifetime later: 'All of a sudden, in that once-happy house, there were two widows and this baby boy.' The two bereaved women focused all their love on the half-orphaned child who, says Nina Lagergren, 'gave and received so much love that he grew up to be an unusually generous, loving, and compassionate person.'

Six years after her husband's death, Maj Wallenberg remarried. Her second husband, Fredrik von Dardel, was as retiring as she was outgoing. He was a quiet, bookish young civil servant in the Health Ministry and rose to the post of administrator of Sweden's largest hospital, the Karolinska. They had two children, Guy (who was to become one of Sweden's leading nuclear physicists) and Nina. 'We never thought of Raoul as being of a different father,' says Nina. 'He was completely of us and we of him, and my father adored him as much as the two of us.'

Nonetheless, Raoul *was* a Wallenberg, and his paternal grandfather, Ambassador Gustav Wallenberg, insisted on supervising his upbringing and education. He was determined that the boy should grow up with an enlightened, cosmopolitan outlook. After Raoul had graduated from high school and completed his compulsory nine months' military service, Gustav sent him to France for a year to perfect his French. He was already proficient in English, German, and Russian.

After that Raoul went to the United States to study architecture. Although his grandfather wanted him eventually to follow one of the strands of family tradition and go into banking, Raoul had always been fascinated by building and architecture. As a small boy in Stockholm he haunted the major building sites and talked eagerly to the architects, builders, and engineers he found there. Grandfather Wallenberg agreed that Raoul could study architecture first, if he would then learn the ways of commerce and banking.

In 1931 Wallenberg went to Ann Arbor to take the University of Michigan's architecture course. He was an outstanding student, completing the course, which normally took four and a half years, in three and a half and winning a medal that was awarded to one student out of each class of eleven hundred. Thirty-five years later Dr Jean Paul Slusser recalled at Ann Arbor: 'He was one of the brightest and best students I think I had in my thirty-year experience as a professor of drawing and painting.' Classmate Sol King remembered him as 'a very talented yet modest person who showed great insight in finding simple solutions to complex problems. Neither his conduct nor his manner of dress gave anyone who knew him the slightest clue to his high station in life as a member of one of Sweden's most distinguished families.'

In his English examination papers of the period Wallenberg revealed that although an idealist, he was by no means starry-eyed. Writing on the subject of European union, he observed: 'Those who base their hope in union on an idealized conception of man are bound to be disappointed.' Writing on 'The Open Mind,' he commented: 'The open mindedness of humanity, even in our generation, is a myth. Maybe the individual is open-minded on one question, but on this question he generally belongs to the minority. In most other things he generally is extremely reactionary.'

During the summer vacation of 1933 Wallenberg worked in the Swedish pavilion at the Chicago World's Fair, earning three dollars a day. Hitchhiking back to Ann Arbor, he was picked up by 'a gentleman in a fine car,' as he told his mother in a letter. 'We were going along at about 70 miles an hour, when all of a sudden we saw a train crossing the highway about 150 yards ahead.' The driver braked violently, went into a skid, and badly damaged his car, but he and Wallenberg emerged unhurt. After his benefactor had left in the tow truck, Wallenberg, laden down by two suitcases, tried to thumb another lift. It was some time before a car with four men in it picked him up.

'They didn't look at all nice,' Wallenberg told his mother, 'but by this time I was desperate so I got in with them. They began asking me about money and how much would it be worth to take me all the way to Ann Arbor. I told them I didn't have any.' After a while the car drove off the highway and along a side road into a wood. 'I was told to get out of the car. One of them had a revolver, so I obeyed. They asked for money and I gave them what I had.' The robbers dumped Wallenberg into a ditch, with his suitcases on top of him, he half expecting a bullet as a good-bye. It never came. When he had pulled himself out, Wallenberg made his way to a railway track, where he eventually flagged down a suburban train. 'I will not give up hitchhiking because of this experience,' he told his mother. 'Instead, I will take less money with me and be more cautious.'

The following summer Wallenberg and a college friend drove to Mexico in a battered old Ford. He stayed for a few weeks with an aunt and uncle who lived on the outskirts of Mexico City. His cousin Birgitte Wallenberg, then eight years old, recalls his visit: 'Mother adored him; he was her pet. I adored him, too. He was wonderful with me, playing with me and trying to teach me chess. He was so unlike most grown-ups; he actually took notice of me, a lonely only child. I remember that his specialty was imitating animal sounds. He was a marvellous mimic and could do twenty-five to thirty different animals. He was good at foreign accents, too, and used to keep us all in stitches. It was always fun being with Raoul.'

On his return to Stockholm with his diploma from Ann Arbor, Wallenberg entered a public competition for the design of a swimming-pool and recreation area in the gardens of one of the

Swedish capital's palaces. Scores of established architects submitted entries. Wallenberg came in second. But he had promised his loving but authoritarian grandfather to study commerce and banking, and Gustav kept him to his word.

His next stop was Cape Town, South Africa, where he spent six months working for a Swedish firm owned by two acquaintances of his grandfather's. He travelled all over the country selling building materials, timber, and chemicals. The partners wrote glowing testimonials when he left. Albert Florén found him 'a splendid organizer and his ability to carry on negotiations has been made use of to the full. Of seemingly boundless energy and vitality, he has great imaginative powers and . . . a clear and original mind.' The other partner, Carl Frykberg, wrote in similar terms and also of Raoul's 'tremendous energy and remarkable gift of quickly and thoroughly acquainting himself with whatever he sets his mind to.'

In 1936 Gustav Wallenberg was Swedish ambassador in Istanbul. There, he became friendly with Erwin Freund, a Jewish banker from British-ruled Palestine. Gustav discussed Raoul's future with Freund, who suggested that the youngster should come and work for his Holland Bank branch in Haifa. So Raoul moved from Cape Town to Palestine, via Istanbul, where he visited his grandfather.

He was nearing twenty-four and beginning to fret at his grandfather's well-meant attempts to direct his life. In a letter from Haifa, dated 6 June 1936, he tried diplomatically to get this view across. He was tired of working as an unpaid trainee, he said, and now wanted a real job with a proper salary. He thought the period spent in Cape Town had been 'a complete waste of time,' despite the glowing references. 'A reference is worth something only if the man who writes it is willing to pay you,' he said.

He admitted he had felt his grandfather's plans for his future were too rigid and was glad to see from the old man's last letter that he was willing to be flexible. 'Under the circumstances, I am willing to co-operate and follow your wishes more than I had previously been willing to,' he wrote. Then, tiptoeing respectfully around his main point, he went on: 'Possibly, I am not cut out for banking . . . Architecture is another thing. I showed at university that I have the

23

talent for that profession . . . A banker should have something of the judge in his makeup and a cold, calm, calculating outlook. Freund and Jakob* are very typical of that type, and I feel I am so unlike them. I think I have the character for positive action, rather than to sit at a desk and say No to people.'

To soften the impact of his dissent, Raoul added: 'I can never forget the love and care you have lavished on me . . . If I were a worthy grandson, I suppose I would thank you and follow your instructions without question . . . But I do not repent of my comments and suggestions, because I do not think any good would come from hiding my real feelings.'

Later that month Gustav replied: 'Your disappointment at not yet having a real job is not justified; what you have done up to now has been only to give you experience. I think that our plan has not failed, because what you have experienced has surely been of some use.' Raoul was wrong, he said, to think his references were useless. 'If your modesty makes you think you do not merit the praise, I ask you nevertheless not to belittle it.'

In August 1936, in a letter to a friend, Gustav wrote of his grandson: 'First and foremost I wanted to make a man of him, to give him a chance to see the world and, through mixing with foreigners, give him what most Swedes lack – an international outlook.' Gustav seemed satisfied that he had succeeded. 'Raoul *is* a man,' he said. 'He has seen much of the world and has come into contact with people of all kinds.'

Among the people with whom Raoul had come into contact – and the experience seems to have made a lasting impression on him – were a number of young Jews who had fled from Hitler's Germany to Palestine. He had met them at the 'kosher' boarding-house in Haifa, where he had taken a room. It was his first experience of the results of Nazi persecution and it affected him deeply – not just because of his humanitarian outlook but also, perhaps, because he was aware that he himself had a dash of Jewish blood.

* Jakob Wallenberg was Raoul's father's first cousin and was a director of the family-owned Enskilda Bank.

His great-great-grandfather on his mother's side, a Jew named Benedicks, had come to Sweden towards the end of the eighteenth century, one of the first Jews to settle there. Benedicks converted to the Lutheran faith, married a Christian girl, prospered rapidly, and within a year was jeweller to the court of King Gustav IV Adolf. He subsequently became financial adviser to a later king, Charles XIV John, Napoleon's Marshal Bernadotte. Benedicks's son was one of the pioneers of the Swedish steel industry. Other descendants showed great artistic talent, and they became known as a highly cultured family – one member, a singer, studied under Liszt.

Raoul was aware of his one-sixteenth Jewish blood, and proud of it. Professor Ingemar Hedenius recalls* a conversation with Raoul dating back to 1930, when they were together in an army hospital during military service: 'We had many long and intimate conversations. He was full of ideas and plans for the future. Although I was a good deal older – you could choose when to do your service – I was enormously impressed by him. He was proud of his partial Jewish ancestry and, as I recall, must have exaggerated it somewhat. I remember him saying, "A person like me, who is both a Wallenberg and half-Jewish, can never be defeated."'

Professor Hedenius found Wallenberg 'intensely likeable – both original and prudent. He seemed courageous, intense, and vital, and though he had a high opinion of his own abilities he did not express this in a boastful or unpleasant way.'

Raoul became aware of the Jewish blood in his mother's side of the family much sooner than his younger siblings. Nina Lagergren says that when they were children they had no idea of their fractional Jewish descent, 'not, I'm sure, because Mother wished to hide it, but because the Jewish ancestor was so far back and none of his descendants had been brought up in the ways of the Jewish people. So we didn't become conscious of this until the mid-thirties, when one of my maternal cousins went to Germany to marry a nobleman. I was only a child at the time, but it seems that the Nazis investigated

---

* Recorded in 1980; Professor Hedenius is one of Sweden's leading academic philosophers.

her background and this caused a lot of talk in the family.'*

In the autumn of 1936, not long after Wallenberg's return from Haifa, his grandfather fell ill. It was the end of his plans to interest influential acquaintances in the idea of founding an international bank, in which Raoul would play an important part. In early 1937 Gustav Wallenberg died and Raoul, freed from the loving tyranny of the old man, found himself wondering what to do next. Architecture, his first love, seemed closed to him. His American diploma did not permit him to practise in Sweden; to do so he would have to qualify all over again and at twenty-five he felt too old to go back to college. Also, the worldwide depression had hit Sweden hard and there was little building going on. His cousins Jakob and Marcus Wallenberg, no doubt aware that he did not feel cut out for banking, did not offer him a post in the family bank or any of its associated undertakings. Maj von Dardel began to worry that, for all his promise and good connections, Raoul would not find a suitable career.

After a while, Wallenberg went into business with a German-Jewish refugee who had patented a new kind of zip fastener. The venture did not flourish. Raoul went to see his cousin Jakob, who had a tract of land near Stockholm that he wanted to develop. Jakob suggested that Raoul should draw up the plans for this project. But in 1939 war broke out and, though Sweden was neutral, development came to a virtual halt.

Finally, through the family banking and business network, Raoul was put in touch with another Jewish refugee, Koloman Lauer, who was director of a flourishing import-export business, dealing in speciality foodstuffs. Lauer needed a reliable Gentile employee who could travel freely in Europe, including the Nazi-occupied countries. Raoul, with his knowledge of languages, his energy and initiative, his negotiating skills, and his attractive personality, seemed ideal for the job. Within eight months he became a junior partner and director of the company, the Central European Trading Company, and had developed a personal friendship with Lauer.

The countries that Wallenberg visited on business for the firm

---

* The cousin was obviously deemed to qualify as an Aryan, for the marriage was permitted.

included Nazi-occupied France, Germany – where he quickly acquired the knack, to be useful later, of dealing with the Nazi bureaucracy – and Hungary, ally of Germany. Lauer's in-laws were living in Budapest, and whenever he went there, Wallenberg would look them up on Lauer's behalf to see that all was well with them. Despite the anti-Semitic laws that curtailed their civil liberties, Hungary was still an island of comparative safety for Jews on the implacably hostile Continent. There was even a considerable traffic in illegal Jewish immigration from other countries in the Nazi sphere of influence. The Jews of Hungary were justifiably uneasy and frightened, but not in any immediate danger of their lives. It was a state of affairs that would soon take a dramatic change for the worse.

Between his business trips around Europe, Wallenberg lived a well-ordered bachelor life in some comfort and style. He had an apartment in the fashionable Lärkstad district of Stockholm and had a wide circle of friends and acquaintances of similar background to himself. Gustav von Platen (subsequently editor of the daily paper *Svenska Dagbladet*) recalls this period: 'He was a very charming host, with the most fabulous wine cellar. He had inherited his grandfather's claret, much of which was on the brink of becoming too old, so it had to be drunk. Some bottles were fantastic.'

Von Platen remembers Wallenberg 'not as a particularly dashing type of person – more of a dreamer,' and this is the recollection of everyone who knew him at the time. Nina Lagergren confirms this: 'He was definitely not the square-jawed hero type, more an anti-hero, I should say. He detested competitive sports and team games, though he kept himself physically fit, and while he was not a military type he was considered a first-class officer in the Home Guard [Sweden's reserve citizens' army]. He had a great gift, too, for irony and self-mockery, behind which he used to hide his true feelings.'

Although of humane and liberal outlook, Wallenberg – like the rest of his crowd – was not a radical. He felt no need to overturn Sweden's existing social order, merely to improve it here and there. As a boy he had sung in the church choir but he was not a believing Christian. 'In the formal sense,' says Nina, 'he had no religion, though in a wider sense I would say he was a deeply religious person.'

Clearly, Wallenberg was dissatisfied with his work, though he did it irreproachably well. Above all, he was appalled by what the Nazis were doing in occupied Europe (though the worst had not yet been revealed) and frustrated at his inability, as a neutral, to do anything about it, apart from helping out in relief work for refugees from Denmark, Norway, and Finland who had found asylum in Sweden.

To the more perceptive of Wallenberg's friends this frustration and disappointment showed. One among them, the economist Bertil af Klercker, thought 'he seemed a little depressed at that time. I had the feeling he wanted to do something more worthwhile with his life.' Occasionally, Wallenberg would open up to one or other of the girls who flitted in and out of his life. Viveca Lindfors, who later became a screen and stage actress of some international fame, remembers one night when he took her to his office after they had been out dancing: 'He started to talk very intensely about the Jews and Germany and about the horrors he had apparently seen. I have this very strong picture of him in that old-fashioned, elegant office, talking to me about it. I was very young and I think I was rather frightened by the intensity with which he spoke and the subject he spoke about. I remember thinking, He's just telling me all these things because he wants to get sympathy so that I will end up in his arms. That's horrible to think of now, but that's how I saw it then. I didn't really believe anything he told me – probably because I didn't want to be made aware of what was going on. In a way, that is a very Swedish thing; when things become too intense and painful we have a tendency to push them away. When I think about Raoul nowadays, I sometimes have this fantasy that we're dancing together and I confess to him how stupid I was that night.'

# *Chapter 3*

In the grim winter of 1942 Raoul Wallenberg spent an evening in the company of his half-sister at a private film show put on by the British embassy in Stockholm. The attraction was *Pimpernel Smith*, an updated version of Baroness Orczy's classic novel *The Scarlet Pimpernel*. In it, the British star Leslie Howard* played an apparently effete and absent-minded university professor who nevertheless out-wits the Nazis and rescues dozens of prospective victims from their clutches.

Wallenberg identified strongly with Howard's quiet, pipe-smoking Professor Smith, whom he physically resembled. 'On the way home he told me that was just the kind of thing he would like to do,' Nina Lagergren recalls. By an astonishing twist of fate, Wallenberg was to get his chance.

It came in the spring of 1944, after the Allied leaders could no longer ignore the evidence of what Hitler's Final Solution really meant, and what was likely to happen to the 750,000 Jews of Hungary unless something were done to stop it. The first authentic eyewitness account of what was happening at Auschwitz, the biggest extermination camp, reached the West, via two Jews who had escaped. In the space of weeks the Hungarian regent, Horthy, was

* Howard, considered by his fans to be the quintessential Englishman, was by odd coincidence actually a Hungarian Jew, born László Stainer.

bombarded with appeals and warnings from, among others, Pope Pius XII, King Gustav V of Sweden, US president Franklin D. Roosevelt, US secretary of state Cordell Hull, and International Red Cross president Karl Burckhardt. While the appeals were directed to the aristocratic Horthy's sense of honour and Christian decency, the warnings threatened retribution to come, both immediately and after the war, should he assist or allow the Nazis to apply their Final Solution to the Jews of Hungary.

Earlier that year, President Roosevelt had belatedly set up, by executive order, the War Refugee Board (WRB), which had the task of saving Jews and other potential victims of Nazi persecution. After the partial Nazi occupation of Hungary on 19 March, Hungary became the WRB's top priority. A WRB report published after the war tells how the board's officials approached their task 'On the theory that the presence of foreigners in official or unofficial capacities would have a deterrent effect, the board late in March 1944 addressed a request to the International Red Cross (IRC) to send effective representation to Hungary in order to protect the well-being of groups there facing persecution.'

The IRC rejected this request 'on the grounds that such a mission might be considered as inconsistent with its traditional functions,' the WRB reported. The best the IRC would agree to do at that point was to relay to the WRB the substance of reports received from the Hungarian Red Cross.

On 24 March the WRB sent a copy of President Roosevelt's statement to the apostolic delegate in Washington and asked him to urge the Holy See to take action. As a result, the papal nuncio in Budapest was instructed to make vigorous representations, and the pope's appeal to Horthy followed. The WRB then turned its attentions to the neutral nations of Europe.

A cable from Cordell Hull in Washington to Herschel V. Johnson, the US minister in Stockholm, said:

Please represent to the Swedish Government that, according to persistent and seemingly authentic reports, systematic mass-extermination of Jews in Hungary has begun. The lives of 800,000 human beings in Hungary may well depend on the restraint that may result from the presence in that country of the largest possible number of foreign observers. To this end, please urge appropriate authorities in the interest of most elementary humanity to take immediate steps to increase to the largest possible extent the numbers of Swedish diplomatic and consular personnel in Hungary and to distribute them as widely as possible throughout the country. It is hoped, of course, that all such diplomatic and consular representatives will use all means available to them to persuade individuals and officials to desist from further barbarisms. Please inform Department forthwith of extent to which Swedish Government is cooperating in this matter.

Switzerland, Spain, Portugal, and Turkey were also asked to expand their diplomatic and consular staffs in Hungary, but the Americans got dusty answers from all but the Swedes. The others declined to act, arguing that since the US government (unknown to the WRB) had already urged them not to recognize the new puppet government in Budapest, how could they now be expected to increase their representation?

The Swedes were more co-operative for a number of reasons. They may have felt guilty that in the early stages of the war, when country after country was falling before the Nazi onslaught, they had allowed the German armed forces transit rights across their territory to Norway and Finland. Now that it was clear the Germans were going to lose the war, the Swedes were less fearful of offending them. They were also conscious that they had a high reputation in humanitarian matters to be upheld. By the spring of 1944 they knew enough about Nazi atrocities – towards the Jews in particular – to be willing to stand up and be counted.

The WRB representative in Stockholm, Ivar C. Olsen, had got together an *ad hoc* committee of prominent Swedish Jews to advise him on the best means of helping their fellows in Hungary. Among this group were the World Jewish Congress representative in Stockholm, Norbert Masur; the Swedish chief rabbi, Dr Marcus Ehrenpreis; and Wallenberg's partner, Koloman Lauer, co-opted as an expert on Hungary. The committee had before it a detailed plan, drawn up by Masur, which called for the recruitment of a suitable non-Jew to go to Budapest on a rescue mission. Obviously, such a person could not represent an official US organization in a state with which the United States was at war, so he should go under

Swedish government auspices. He should have a diplomatic passport and plenty of money – half a million Swedish crowns to start with – and should be empowered to issue Swedish passports with a view to getting as many Jews as possible to Sweden.

Olsen liked the idea, though there is evidence that not all the members of his committee were enthusiastic about the last part of it. In a subsequent letter to his executive director, John W. Pehle, in Washington, D.C., Olsen wrote: 'The following is for your information only, but it is only too true that the Swedish Jews don't want any more Jews in Sweden. They are very comfortably situated here, have no anti-Semitic problems, and are very much afraid that an influx of Jews will not only be a burden to them but will create a Jewish problem in Sweden. Consequently, you will find them very interested in Jewish rescue problems, so long as they do not involve bringing them into Sweden.'*

The committee's first choice for the mission to Budapest was Count Folke Bernadotte,† a relative of the king and president of the Swedish Red Cross. The Swedish government approved him but for reasons that remain obscure – perhaps a German veto – the Hungarian government declined to accept him. The search resumed, and this time Lauer put forward the name of his young business associate, Wallenberg. Rabbi Ehrenpreis was sceptical. He thought that Wallenberg was a lightweight, too young and inexperienced for such a mission. Lauer persisted: his junior partner was the right man. Added to his quick wits, energy, courage, and compassionate nature, he had the advantage of a famous name.

Olsen wanted to know more about Wallenberg before making up his mind. On 9 June Lauer arranged a meeting between them; they met at seven in the evening and talked right through until five the next morning. By that time Olsen's mind was made up: he had found the man.

---

* This may seem a harsh judgement, but it was given unsolicited confirmation in February 1980 by Paul Frankl, a prominent Swedish Jew, who told me that a 'Mayflower complex' was common at the time among his co-religionists.

† By a grim coincidence, he was murdered by Jewish gunmen in Jerusalem in 1948, when he was UN mediator in Palestine.

The next step was to gain the endorsement of Minister Johnson. He and Wallenberg met a few days later and, like Olsen, Johnson was impressed. Then the nomination was turned over to the Swedish government. They had agreed in principle to send a special envoy to Budapest with diplomatic cover, and Wallenberg was quite acceptable. On 13 June Wallenberg was summoned to a meeting at the Foreign Office, but the matter was not to be concluded quickly.

Despite the diplomatic tradition in his family, Wallenberg had learned to despise bureaucracy and conventional diplomatic methods. He was determined not to allow himself to be hamstrung by protocol or tied up by red tape. The Foreign Office mandarins to whom he made his feelings known were shocked; 130 years of neutrality had bred a particularly cautious and protocol-bound outlook among them. Although Wallenberg was keen to go, he felt it had to be under the right conditions. Fourteen days of intensive negotiations followed on a nine-point memorandum drawn up by Wallenberg.

It stipulated that: (1) he should have a free hand to use any methods he saw fit, including bribery; (2) if the need arose for personal consultations with the Foreign Office, he should be free to return to Stockholm without going through the lengthy procedure of getting permission; (3) if his financial resources proved insufficient, a propaganda campaign would be launched in Sweden to raise more money; (4) he should have adequate status to do the job, so he should be appointed first secretary at the legation with a salary of 2000 crowns a month; (5) he should have the right to contact any persons he wished in Budapest, including avowed enemies of the régime; (6) he should be empowered to deal directly with the prime minister or any other member of the Hungarian government without going through the ambassador; (7) he should be able to send dispatches direct to Stockholm via diplomatic courier, again without using normal channels; (8) he might officially seek an interview with the regent, Horthy, to ask for his intercession on behalf of the Jews; and (9) he should be authorized to give asylum in buildings belonging to the legation, to persons holding Swedish protective passes.

Wallenberg's demands were so unusual that the matter was referred all the way up to the prime minister, who consulted the king before passing down the word, through the foreign minister, that Wallenberg's conditions were to be accepted. By the end of June Wallenberg had been appointed. This time the Swedes had decided that if his visa were refused by the Hungarians they would retaliate by refusing to accept the new Hungarian chargé d'affaires. There was no such difficulty.

Maintaining the official fiction that Wallenberg's appointment was an exclusively Swedish affair in which he and Olsen had played no part, Minister Johnson reported it to the US State Department, adding: 'Olsen and I are of the opinion that the War Refugee Board should be considering ways and means of implementing this action of the Swedish Government, particularly with respect to financial support.'

In a further telegram to the State Department a few days later, Minister Johnson said:

We should emphasize that the Swedish Foreign Office, in making this assignment, feels it has cooperated fully in lending all possible facilities for the furtherance of the American program. It is not likely, however, that it will provide the newly appointed attaché with a concrete program, but instead will give him rather general instructions which will not be sufficiently specific to enable him to deal promptly and effectively with situations as they develop in Hungary.

The newly designated attaché, Raoul Wallenberg, feels however that he is in effect carrying out a humanitarian mission on behalf of the War Refugee Board. Consequently, he would like full instructions as to the line of activities he is authorized to carry out and assurances of adequate financial support for these activities, so that he will be in a position to develop fully all local possibilities.

Johnson added that he and Olsen were 'very favorably impressed' by Wallenberg and urged strongly that 'appropriate instructions be forwarded as soon as possible.'

In a reply dated 7 July, by which time Wallenberg had already left for Budapest, Secretary of State Hull outlined at some length the 'general approach' Wallenberg might follow.

Since money and favorable post-war consideration may motivate action impeding, relaxing, or slowing down tempo of persecution and facilitate escapes and concealments, it should be ascertained in what quarters such inducements may be effective.

In other words, bribery; Wallenberg had already thought of that.

Hull continued:

If circumstances warrant, funds will be made available at neutral bank for post-war use or in part in local currency now ... whenever a concrete proposal based on financial arrangements of substantial character or favorable post-war consideration is broached, the matter should be referred to the board for clearance, which will require evidence of effectiveness and good faith ... In order to care for less substantial transactions a fund of 50,000 dollars will be placed at Olsen's disposal which may be used at his discretion in addition to the fund already available to him for discretionary use.

The Hull telegram goes on to suggest that the problem should be tackled on various levels – high official, low official, unofficial, central, and local – and lists a number of organizations and individuals who might prove useful in this context. Wallenberg should take with him a copy of Roosevelt's statement, warning against continued persecutions, a similar statement by the US Foreign Relations Committee, and also a ringing denunciation just made by the Roman Catholic Cardinal Spellman of New York.

'These,' said Hull, 'he might on proper occasions call to the attention of appropriate persons, expressing the view, having just come from outside German-controlled territory, that there is no question of American determination to see to it that those who share the guilt will be punished, but that helpful conduct now may result in more favorable considerations than actions heretofore might warrant.'

Hull's message stipulated that Wallenberg 'cannot of course act as the board's representative, nor purport to act in its name.' However, he was free to communicate with Olsen in Stockholm 'and lay before him specific proposals to help the Jews of Hungary.'

With all the loose ends tied up, and King Gustav's personal approval obtained for his appointment, Wallenberg prepared to leave for Budapest. He spent two full days at the Foreign Office going through recent dispatches from the Swedish legation. What he read must have chilled his blood and filled him with a sense of compelling urgency. As he told Lauer: 'I cannot stay in Sweden beyond the beginning of July. Every day costs human lives. I will get myself ready to travel as soon as I can.'

The reports coming out of Budapest at this time were summarized in a telegram dated 1 July from Minister Johnson to Secretary Hull.

Information just received from Budapest concerning treatment of Jews is so terrible that it is hard to believe and there are no words to qualify its description. Of the total number of Jews in Hungary originally, not more than 400,000 now remain and these are mostly in Budapest. The others, of whom there were well over 600,000 (this is a conservative estimate),* have either been deported to Germany to uncertain destinations or killed. According to the evidence, these people are now being killed en masse by the Germans and large numbers are being taken to a place across the Hungarian frontier in Poland, where there is an establishment at which gas is used for killing people.

This was obviously a reference to Auschwitz, and the Johnson cable went on to give details – all too well known now, but then new and horrifying beyond belief – of how the mass gassing was being carried out.

Johnson also reported on Wallenberg's forthcoming mission.

The Hungarian Jews, in spite of all their difficulties, have collected to the equivalent of 2 million Swedish crowns to be used in aiding the Jews and this has been turned over to the Swedish legation in Budapest. Wallenberg ... was highly praised by Boheman,† who said that if our War Refugee Board could formulate some form of directive for him, which the Foreign Office will be glad to transmit, it would be of great help.

There is no doubt in my mind as to the sincerity of Wallenberg's purpose because I have talked to him myself. I was told by Wallenberg that he wanted to be able to help effectively and save lives and that he was not interested in going to Budapest merely to write reports to be sent to the Foreign Office. He himself is half-Jewish, incidentally.‡

---

* It was an over-estimate.
† Erik Boheman was secretary-general of the Swedish Foreign Office.
‡ Once again, Wallenberg was exaggerating his Jewish blood.

On 6 July 1944 Wallenberg left for Budapest via Berlin. He made the first leg of the journey by air and was met at Berlin's Tempelhof Airport by Nina, by now the wife of Gunnar Lagergren, head of the Foreign Interests Section of the Swedish legation in the German capital.* Nina recalls that Raoul was carrying his clothes and other personal belongings in a rucksack and wearing a long leather coat and an 'Anthony Eden' hat.

'As we drove to my home I told him the minister had booked his onward journey to Budapest by train for the day after next. Raoul was angry about this, saying there was no time to waste and he must go the very next day, on the first available train.

'On the way home he told me about his mission and said he had in his rucksack a list of prominent Jews, Social Democrats, and other oppositionists in Budapest whom he was to contact. I had no idea at the time that his mission would be as dangerous as it turned out to be. I assumed he would carry it out according to the usual diplomatic methods, although knowing him as I did I should have known better. But I was seven months pregnant with my first child at the time, so I suppose I wasn't concentrating much on anything else.'

Wallenberg and Nina reached her temporary home – the gatehouse of a castle on the Wannsee, a lake near Potsdam – just as night was falling. He, Nina, and Gunnar Lagergren talked late into the night. They had not been long in bed before the British bombers came over, as they did every night at that period, and the trio went to a nearby air-raid shelter.

Next morning, after a largely sleepless night, Wallenberg left for the station and his train to Budapest. It was packed with German troops returning from leave, and as he had not booked a seat Wallenberg had to spend the entire journey in the corridor sitting on his rucksack. In his pocket he carried a small revolver – 'not because I intended ever to use it,' as he told a legation colleague later, 'but to give myself courage.'

* Subsequently Marshal of the Realm, chief executive officer of the Swedish royal court.

# Chapter 4

The passenger train that brought Raoul Wallenberg into Budapest on 9 July 1944 quite probably crossed paths *en route* with the
train of twenty-nine sealed cattle cars transporting the last batch
of Hungary's provincial Jews to Auschwitz. With the departure of
this train the previous day, Eichmann and his associates had
completed what he proudly called 'a deportation surpassing every
preceding deportation in magnitude.' In a dispatch to Berlin,
Edmund Veesenmayer, Hitler's proconsul in Budapest, reported
with characteristic precision that 437,402 Jewish men, women,
and children had been shipped out aboard 148 trains between 14
May and 8 July. Now, apart from several thousand able-bodied
Jewish males serving in the labour battalions of the Hungarian
Army, there remained only 230,000 terrified Jews trapped in the
capital.

Emboldened by his success in the provinces – made possible in
part through the dedicated enthusiasm of his Hungarian partners –
Eichmann had prepared an audacious plan to round up the entire
Jewish population of Budapest in a stunning twenty-four-hour blitz,
at some time between the middle and the end of July. That would
surely impress Müller and Himmler sufficiently to win him promotion at last, and perhaps even a personal commendation from Hitler.
'Technical details will only take a few more days in Budapest,' he
had said in a report to Berlin. If carried out, this grand scheme

would have made Wallenberg's mission futile. There would have been no Jews left by the time he could find his bearings.

But the Hungarian regent, Horthy – who had received many appeals, was belaboured by the world's press, and increasingly threatened by the advancing Red Army – plucked up his courage, addressed himself to his best interests, and instructed Prime Minister Döme Sztojay that there were to be no more deportations. Eichmann fell into a fury when he heard of this 'treachery.' 'In all my long experience,' he stormed, 'such a thing has never happened to me . . . It cannot be tolerated.'

But for the time being it had to be tolerated. Horthy had cannily ordered back to the provinces the 1600 Hungarian gendarmes who had been brought into the capital to help round up the Jews; without them Eichmann did not have nearly enough manpower at his disposal to deal with almost a quarter of a million deportees.

Eichmann appealed to Berlin through Veesenmayer. The reply was delayed – no doubt because of the 20 July bomb plot on Hitler's life. When it did come, from SS Reichsführer Himmler, it was a crushing disappointment for Eichmann: Nazi Germany accepted the suspension of deportations. By this time Himmler had a game of his own to play, and the name of the game was mending fences with the advancing Anglo-Saxons in the west before Germany should be over-run by the advancing Bolsheviks in the east. He saw himself as the man to negotiate a separate peace with the Western Allies, and one way to improve his image was to relieve the pressure on the Jews.

An outraged Eichmann was left no alternative but to console himself in contemplation of the great work he had accomplished so far and in anticipation of a change in circumstances which would eventually allow him to finish the job.

He had begun that task within hours of the arrival of his Kommando in Budapest on 19 March. The morning after checking in, Eichmann had sent three of his assistants, Hermann Krumey, Dieter Wisliceny, and Otto Hunsche, to make contact with the Hungarian Jewish leaders. Fifteen frightened representatives of the Jewish community were told by Krumey that from then on 'all the affairs of Hungarian Jewry are transferred to the competence of the SS.' Jews were forbidden to leave Budapest or change domicile without permission; an eight-man Central Jewish Council must be set up immediately to receive the instructions of the Gestapo; for the same purpose a round-the-clock telephone service was to be established. To prevent panic, the Jewish press should carry articles calling for calm. Rabbis should carry the same message by word of mouth. Himmler had warned Eichmann to watch out for signs of another Warsaw-type uprising: the Jews must not be panicked into acts of desperation.

Krumey was reassuring. The Jews had nothing to worry about, he said. There would be some economic restrictions, but no more than the exigencies of war required. Religious, social, and cultural life would be allowed to continue as before. The SS would keep the peace. Having been given other reassurances in this vein, the Jewish leaders left the meeting slightly less apprehensive than when they arrived.

Once the Central Jewish Council had been set up, as ordered, Eichmann addressed them in person. His hour-long address was a curious mixture of threats and honeyed words combined with the usual unnerving display of knowledge of Jewish affairs.

The Jews should notify him if anyone tried to harm them, said Eichmann, and he would punish those responsible, even if they were German soldiers. Those who tried to plunder Jewish wealth would also be severely dealt with. But the Jews should not try to mislead him or they would regret it. He had been handling Jewish affairs for ten years, so nobody could fool him. He knew Hebrew well, for example, perhaps better than they did themselves. His main object was to raise the output of the war factories, and Jewish labour was required for this. If they worked hard no harm would come to them. For the moment he wanted four hundred volunteers. If he did not get them he would take them by force. But, either way, they would be treated properly and paid the same as other workers. From now on, all Jews would have to wear a yellow star. However, said Eichmann, this and all the other measures he would announce soon would only last until the end of the war. Once that was over the Jews would find the Germans the good-natured fellows they were before.

Whatever cautious optimism the Jewish leaders felt after this encounter was promptly shattered. Within days, orders were promulgated by which Jews were forbidden to leave their homes and had to give up their telephones, radios, and cars. Children had to surrender their bicycles. Bank accounts were frozen and food rations reduced. Jews were expelled from the civil service and the professions. Their shops, offices, and factories had to be turned over to Aryan management. The Jews were soon totally bewildered, utterly demoralized. Then the concentration process began in the provinces. The Jews were herded into local ghettos and makeshift concentration camps, the last stage before deportation to the work and death camps in Poland and Germany. The round-up was to be carried out, district by district, by the cock-plumed Hungarian Gendarmerie, with Eichmann's men acting in supervisory and advisory roles. Even they were astonished at the cruelty of the gendarmes. With conscious or unconscious irony the concentration of the provincial Jews began on the first day of Passover, the holy day that commemorates the Israelites' flight from Egyptian bondage.

The horrors of the concentration and deportation of Hungary's Jews have been copiously documented. But no account of mass suffering is quite so poignant as the diary of Eva Heyman, the thirteen-year-old child of a comfortable, middle-class Jewish family from Varad, close to the Hungarian-Rumanian border.

*31 March*   Today an order was issued that from now on Jews have to wear a yellow star-shaped patch ... When Grandma heard this she started acting up again and we called the doctor. He gave her an injection. She is asleep now ... Agi [Eva's mother] wanted to telephone to the doctor but couldn't. Then Grandpa told her that the telephones had been taken away from the Jews and said that he would go and get the doctor. Until now Agi used to speak to Budapest every evening and now ... I can't even talk to Aniko and Marica any more. They also take shops away from the Jews ... I don't know who will feed the children if the grown-ups aren't allowed to work ...

*1 April*   ... God, today is April Fool's Day. On whom should I play tricks? Who thinks about that at all now? Dear Diary, soon I'll be going to Aniko's house and I'm taking along ... my canary in the cage. I'm afraid that Mandi will die if I leave her at home, because everybody's mind is on other things now and I'm worried about Mandi. She's such a darling bird. Whenever I come near her cage she notices me right away and starts singing.

\*

*7 April*   Today they came for my bicycle. I almost caused a big drama . . .
Now that it's all over I'm so ashamed about how I behaved in front of the
policemen. I threw myself on the ground, held on to the back wheel of my
bicycle, and shouted all sorts of things at the policemen: 'Shame on you for
taking away a bicycle from a girl! That's robbery . . .' One of the policemen
was very annoyed with me and said: 'All we need is for a Jewgirl to put on
such a comedy when her bicycle is being taken away. No Jewkid is entitled
to keep a bicycle anymore.' . . . I think the other policeman felt sorry for me.
'You should be ashamed of yourself, colleague,' he said. 'Is your heart made
of stone? How can you speak that way to such a beautiful girl?' Then he
stroked my hair and promised to take good care of my bicycle. He gave me a
receipt and told me not to cry because when the war was over I would get
my bicycle back.

*20 April*   Every day they keep issuing new laws against the Jews. Today, for
example, they took all our appliances away from us: the sewing machine, the
radio, the telephone, the vacuum cleaner, the electric fryer, and my camera
. . . Agi said we should be happy they're taking things and not people. She's
right about that. I may even have a Zeiss-Ikon camera to work with until
I'm old enough to be a news photographer, but a mother or a grandfather
can never be replaced. Poor Grandpa, now he can't even go to his pharmacy
anymore. He looks at Agi in such an odd, sad way and keeps caressing her
all the time, as though he is saying good-bye to her. Agi even said to him:
'Don't cling to me as though we are saying good-bye, my sweet Papa,
because my heart is breaking.' Agi wants to go on having a father for ever. I
can understand, because I also want all of us to stay alive.

*1 May*   Dear Diary, from now on I'm imagining everything as if it really is a
dream. We started packing those things and exactly in the quantity that Agi
read in the notice. I know it isn't a dream, but I can't believe a thing. We're
also allowed to take along bedding and right now we don't know exactly
when they'll come to take us, so we can't pack the bedding. I'm busy all day
making coffee for Uncle Béla; Grandma drinks cognac. Nobody says a word.
Dear Diary, I've never been so afraid.

*5 May*   Dear Diary, now you aren't at home anymore, but in the ghetto.
Three days we waited for them to come and get us . . . Dear Diary, I'm still
too little a girl to write down what I felt while we waited to be taken into the
ghetto. Between one order and the next, Agi would cry out that we deserve
what we get because we are like animals, patiently waiting to be slaughtered
. . . The two policemen who came for us weren't unfriendly; they just took

42

Agi's and Grandma's wedding rings away from them. Agi was shaking all over and couldn't get the wedding ring off her finger. In the end Grandma took the ring off her finger. Then they checked our luggage and they wouldn't allow us to take Grandpa's valise because it is genuine pigskin. They didn't allow anything made out of leather to be taken along. They said: 'There's a war on and the soldiers need the leather . . .' One of the policemen saw a little gold chain around my neck, the one I got for my birthday, the one holding your key, Dear Diary. 'Don't you know yet,' the policeman said, 'that you aren't allowed to keep anything made of gold? This isn't private Jewish property anymore, but national property!' Whenever something was being taken from us, Agi would always pretend not to notice at all, because she had an obsession about not letting the policemen think it bothered us that our things were being taken, but this time she begged the policeman to let me keep the little gold chain. She started sobbing and said: 'Mr Inspector, please go and ask your colleagues and they will tell you that I have never begged for anything, but please let the child keep just this little gold chain. You see, she keeps the key to her diary on it.' 'Please,' the policeman said, 'that is impossible! In the ghetto you will be checked again. I, so help me God, don't need this chain or any other object that is being taken from you. I don't need any of it. But I don't want any difficulties. I am a married man. My wife is going to have a baby.' I gave him the chain . . .

Dear Diary, the most terrible thing happened when we got to the gate. There, I saw Grandpa cry for the first time in my life. From the gate arch you can see the garden, and the garden never looked so beautiful . . . I will never forget how Grandpa stood there looking at the garden, shaking from the crying. There were also tears in Uncle Béla's eyes. And only now I noticed how Grandma had turned into such an old woman . . . She walked out of the gate as though she was drunk or sleepwalking . . .

When it got dark we lay down on the mattress. I cuddled up with Marica and the two of us – believe it or not, Dear Diary – were happy. Strange as it seems, everybody . . . was here together, everybody in the world whom we loved . . . We chose Marica's mother, Aunt Klari Keckskemeti, to be in charge of the inhabitants of our room. Everybody has to obey her. In the dark room she gave a speech and even though I was almost asleep I understood that we all have to take care that everything is kept clean, because that is very important, and that we all have to think of one another . . .

*

*10 May*   Dear Diary, we're here five days, but word of honour it seems like five years. I don't even know where to begin writing, because so many awful things have happened since I last wrote in you. First, the fence was finished and nobody can go out or come in ... From today on, Dear Diary, we're not in a ghetto but in a ghetto–camp, and on every house they've pasted a notice which tells exactly what we're not allowed to do ... Actually, everything is forbidden, but the most awful thing of all is that the punishment for everything is death. There is no difference between things; no standing in the corner, no spankings, no taking away food, no writing down the declensions of irregular verbs a hundred times the way it used to be in school. Not at all – the lightest and the heaviest punishment is death. It doesn't actually say that this punishment also applies to children, but I think it does apply to us, too ...

Every time I think: This is the end, things couldn't possibly be worse, and then I find out that it's always possible for everything to get worse and even much, much worse. Until now, we had food, and now there won't be anything to eat. At least we were able to walk around inside the ghetto, and now we won't be able to leave the house ...

*14 May*   We can't look out of the window, because even for that we can be killed. But we're still allowed to hear and so I and Marica heard the ice-cream vendor ringing his bell on the other side of the fence. I like ice-cream and I must say I like the ice-cream they sell in cones on the street much more than the ice-cream they sell in confectionery shops, even though in the confectionery shops it's much more expensive! Of course, I don't know, because I can't see if the one ringing on the other side of the fence is the same ice-cream man who used to come to us, but in all of Varad there were just two ice-cream pedlars. Maybe it really was him and now he is sad because his customers are locked up behind the fence ...

*17 May*   I did write in you, didn't I, Dear Diary, some time ago that every misfortune can be followed by something worse? You see how right I am? The interrogation has begun in the Dreher beer factory ... The gendarmes don't believe that the Jews don't have anything left of their valuables. They say that they probably hid them or buried them in the ground somewhere or deposited them for safe-keeping with the Aryans. For example, we deposited Grandma's jewellery for safe-keeping with Juszti, that's true. Now they come to the ghetto houses and pick up people, almost all of them rich ones, and take them to the Dreher beer factory. There they beat them until they tell where they hid their possessions. I know that they beat them terribly because Agi said that you can hear the cries in the hospital. Now everybody in the house is afraid that they will be taken to be beaten at Dreher.

*18 May*   Last night, Dear Diary . . . I couldn't sleep and I overheard what the adults said . . . They said that the people aren't only beaten at Dreher but also get electric shocks. Agi cried as she told this, and if she hadn't told it I would have thought that it was all just some awful story out of a nightmare. Agi said that from Dreher people are brought to the hospital bleeding at the mouth and ears and some of them also with teeth missing and the soles of their feet swollen so they can't stand. Dear Diary, Agi also told other things, like what the gendarmes do to the women, because women are also taken there, things that it would be better if I didn't write them down in you, things that I am incapable of putting into words . . . I even heard . . . that in the ghetto here there are many people who commit suicide. In the ghetto pharmacy there is enough poison, and Grandpa gives poison to the older people who ask for it. Grandpa also said it would be better if he took cyanide and also gave some to Grandma . . .

*22 May*   . . . Today they announced every head of family will be taken in (to Dreher) so Grandpa also has to go. Terrific screaming comes from the direction of Dreher. All day long an electric gramophone keeps playing the same song – 'There's Just One Girl in the World.' Day and night the noise of this song fills the ghetto. When the record stops for a moment we can hear the yelling . . . Agi keeps comforting me by saying that the Russians are doing so well in the war that it can't be that we will be taken to Poland, because by the time we get there we will fall right into the arms of the Russians. Agi thinks we're going to be taken somewhere in Hungary, to the Plains area, where we will be put to work in the fields. It will soon be harvest-time and all the farmers have gone into the army. Oh, I wish only that Agi should be right . . .

*29 May*   And so, Dear Diary, now the end of everything has really come. The ghetto has been divided up into blocks and we're all going to be taken away from here . . .

*30 May*   . . . That gendarme in front of the house, the one Uncle Béla calls a friendly gendarme because he never yells at us and doesn't even speak familiarly to the women, came into the garden and told us that he will have to leave the gendarmerie because what he saw in Redey Park [the railway station] isn't a fit sight for human beings. They stuffed eighty people into each wagon and all they gave them was one pail of water for that many people. But what is even more awful is that they bolt the wagons. In this terrible heat we will suffocate in there . . . Dear Diary, I don't want to die; I want to live, even if it means I'll be the only person here allowed to stay . . . I would wait for the end of the war in some cellar, or even on the roof, or in some secret cranny. I would even let the cross-eyed gendarme, the one who took our flour away from us, kiss me just so long as they didn't kill me, only that they should let me live. Now I see that friendly gendarme has let Mariska come in. I can't write anymore, Dear Diary, the tears run from my eyes. I'm hurrying over to Mariska.*

As described by Eva Heyman, conditions in the Varad ghetto seem to have been a good deal better than in some others. Dr Martin Földi described a more typical state of affairs at the town of Uzhorod: 'The ghetto was established at a brick factory. It could have housed perhaps two thousand people with difficulty. We were fourteen thousand. The sanitation conditions were indescribable. There were no latrines. We improvised something in the open that was awful and had a depressing and demoralizing effect. A German Gestapo officer told me: "You live here like swine."'

When the Jewish Council in Budapest protested to Eichmann about what they had heard of conditions in the provincial ghettos he replied that they were no worse than those experienced by German soldiers on manoeuvres. 'You are starting again with the propaganda stories,' he warned. Eichmann and Lászlo Endre, an under-secretary of state at the Hungarian Interior Ministry, went on an inspection tour of the camps. They liked what they saw. On their return to Budapest, Endre said: 'I found everything in order. The ghettos in the country are virtually like sanatoria. At last the Jews are getting some fresh air; they have exchanged their former mode of life for a healthier one.'

By this time the Eichmann Kommando had established permanent office and living quarters in the commandeered Hotel Majestic on Schwab Hill, an elegant district of Buda filled with

* Eva's diary was kept by Mariska, referred to in the last entry, who was a Gentile woman in the service of Eva's family for many years. Subsequently the diary found its way into the Yad Vashem archives. Eva was entrained for Auschwitz on 2 June 1944. She arrived four days later and survived until 17 October, when she was among Jews dispatched to the gas chamber by the notorious Dr Josef Mengele – who escaped to South America after the war.

the summer homes of the wealthy. The downtown branch, where Hungarian liaison chief Lieutenant-Colonel Lászlo Ferenczy was installed with his gendarmes and plainclothesmen, was in the back wing of the Pest County Hall on the eastern bank of the Danube. It was disguised, with grim irony, as International Warehouse and Transport Ltd but known more directly by its occupants as the Hungarian Jew-Liquidating Command. When the deportations began, Eichmann threw a small celebration at the Majestic, inviting Ferenczy, Endre, and another under-secretary at the Interior Ministry, Lászlo Baky. They drank champagne, flown in from Paris.

The deportations proceeded at a ferocious pace. Often as many as five trains a day left for Auschwitz, each carrying up to four thousand men, women, and children, packed like sardines seventy, eighty, or even a hundred to a wagon. Into each wagon went one pail of water and one empty pail for slops. The journey to Auschwitz took three or four days. When Jewish leaders protested about conditions on these transports, Otto Hunsche, one of Eichmann's assistants, snapped: 'Stop bothering me with horror stories . . . There are no more than fifty to sixty dying *en route* in any single transport.' Endre was more threatening: 'The Jews have only been overtaken by the fate they deserve. If members of the Jewish Council stubbornly insist on their allegations they will be dealt with as ordinary rumour-mongers.'

On arrival at Auschwitz, deportees, picked at random, were required to send a picture postcard, bearing the dateline Waldsee – supposedly a summer resort in Austria but entirely fictitious – and a message, such as 'All well. I am working here.' These were intended to dispel panic among those yet to come. The Nazis still feared another Warsaw uprising.

The Jews were now arriving at Auschwitz in such numbers that, despite the extra gas chambers and ovens recently installed, Hoess rushed to Budapest to tell Eichmann he just could not cope. Eichmann reluctantly agreed to a reduced schedule of three trains a day, but even this was a testament to his extraordinary persistence and influence. With the German Army hard-pressed by the Russians, every piece of rolling stock was desperately needed for military purposes. Eichmann's transport officer, Franz Novak,* kept meeting obstacles. Eichmann appealed direct to Himmler, who in turn referred the problem to Hitler's general headquarters for a ruling. The answer was that the army could claim priority on transport vehicles 'only when it is advancing.' Since it was now retreating, Eichmann got his trains. This meant that German troops, pulling back across the plains of eastern Hungary, had to leave their heavy weapons behind. At the most desperate stage of the war, with the Reich itself now threatened, it was considered more important to use the available rolling stock to transport Jewish civilians – some to the war factories, where they were quickly worked to death, others straight to the gas chambers.

When the full realization of what was happening to their fellows in the provinces became clear to them, the Jewish executive committee in Budapest issued a clandestine leaflet appealing to 'the Christian people of Hungary, with whom they have for a thousand years lived side by side in this motherland, sharing good fortune and ill alike.' It described in detail the horrors of the transports, expressed the Jews' faith in the 'sense of justice of the Hungarian nation,' and concluded 'should we, however, raise our supplication in vain – beseeching the Hungarian nation for our bare lives only – we ask them only to forbear from the horrors and cruelties preceding and accompanying the deportations and to put an end to our sufferings at home, allowing our bodies at least to rest in the soil of our native country.'

By chance that despairing appeal more or less coincided with Horthy's decision to suspend deportations and with Wallenberg's arrival.

In mid-1944 neutral diplomatic missions in Budapest included those of Portugal, Spain, Sweden, Switzerland, Turkey, and one or two Latin American states. In addition there was a papal nuncio and representatives of the International Red Cross. After the Nazis forced Horthy to install the Sztójay puppet government in March, the Swedes and others had downgraded their mission from embassy to legation as a sign of non-recognition. The Hungarian ambassador

* While Eichmann was to become known to the Western press as 'the forwarding agent of death,' Novak earned the title 'the Stationmaster.'

48

in Stockholm was obliged to return home, although the Swedish envoy, Carl Ivar Danielsson, remained in Budapest with the title of minister.

Under the pressure of growing world concern about the fate of the Hungarian Jews, sparked off by revelations from escaping prisoners about what was happening at Auschwitz, these neutral missions had already begun to make some uncoordinated moves towards protecting limited numbers of Jews in the capital, although for those in the provinces they had been unable to do anything. Even before Wallenberg's arrival, for example, the Swedish legation had begun to issue an agreed quota of 650 protective passes to Jews who could show that they had family or business links with Sweden. The Swiss, who as representatives of British interests had set up a Palestine Office at their legation, had possession of a few hundred emigration certificates for British-controlled Palestine. These were being issued by the Palestine Office and the recipients' names were entered into a collective passport against the day when it might be possible for them to leave.

Such documents were of doubtful validity and could scarcely have proved effective had Eichmann been able to launch his blitz on the capital's Jews, but they were a beginning, and Wallenberg quickly set about building on that foundation. On his arrival at the legation he had been warmly welcomed by Minister Danielsson, who had initiated King Gustav's appeal to Horthy. Although an old-school diplomat, brought up in the traditions of ambassadorial correctitude, he approved wholeheartedly of Wallenberg's mission and even of the unconventional methods he knew his new colleague had been sanctioned to employ. So did a younger diplomat, Per Anger, who had known Wallenberg in Sweden. Many years later, when he was Swedish ambassador to Canada, Anger recalled reaction to Wallenberg in the Swedish mission: 'To start with, he shocked some of us professional diplomats by his unconventional methods, but we very soon found he had the right approach.'

Wallenberg's approach was based on a few salient points which he had been quick to recognize had bargaining value. First, the Hungarian puppet régime desperately desired respectability and international recognition as the legitimate government of the country. Second,

Sweden represented both Hungarian and German interests in a number of important countries at a time when the tide of war had turned so decisively against the Nazis and their allies. Third, individual Hungarians in high places were increasingly susceptible to threats of post-war retribution and promises of Swedish good offices according to their present behaviour. In addition Wallenberg was quite prepared to descend to outright bribery and blackmail where these might prove effective, and had plenty of funds for such purposes.

Wallenberg was fully aware, too, of the importance of appearances in dealing with German and Hungarian officialdom and the first thing he did, after setting up his Department C at the legation, was to design an impressive-looking Swedish passport to replace the somewhat mundane certificates so far issued. Here his architect's training in design and draughtsmanship came into play, and the Wallenberg passport was a stroke of genius. He had it printed in yellow and blue, embellished with the triple crown of the Royal Swedish government, and dotted with seals, stamps, signatures, and counter-signatures. Though it had absolutely no validity in international law, it inspired respect, serving notice to the Germans and Hungarians that the holder was not an abandoned outcast but under the protection of the leading neutral power of Europe. These passports also gave a big boost to the morale of those Jews who received them. 'They made us somehow feel like human beings again after being reduced to mere things by all the measures and propaganda against us,' recalled Edit Ernster, one of the earlier recipients (she emigrated to Sweden after the war). As Wallenberg wrote in his first report to Stockholm: 'The Jews are in despair. One way or another we must give them hope.'

At first, the Hungarian Foreign Ministry gave Wallenberg permission to issue only 1500 of these passports. By skilful stick-and-carrot negotiation he progressively got this quota increased to 2500 and finally to 4500. In fact, he eventually issued more than three times that number, bribing and blackmailing Hungarian officials to turn a blind eye. When things became really desperate in the final days, when he could get no more of his 'official' passports printed, his office was to issue a much simplified version, a mere cyclostyled form, bearing Wallenberg's signature. In the chaotic conditions then prevailing, often even that worked.

Noting the effectiveness of the Wallenberg passports, other neutral missions began to follow suit, Consul Charles Lutz, head of the foreign interests department at the Swiss legation, issued at first hundreds, then thousands of passports – more, even, than Wallenberg. The so-called 'glass house,' the section that dealt with Jewish affairs at the Swiss legation, was besieged daily by hundreds of Jews clamouring for these *Schutzpasse*. So, of course, was Wallenberg's office, which by this time had a staff of 250 Jews, working around the clock in shifts. Through Wallenberg's skilful intercession with the Hungarian authorities, all his staff were exempted from wearing the yellow star and from service with the Hungarian Army's labour battalions.

The small Latin American missions caught the infection and, eventually, the mission of Franco Spain. The Spanish mission actually issued protective passports to a handful of Jewish families whose ancestors had fled from the Spanish Inquisition four and a half centuries earlier, but who had preserved their Spanish language and cultural traditions. Quite independently, and at the prime instigation of Cardinal Angelo Roncalli (then apostolic delegate in Turkey; he later became Pope John XXIII), the papal nunciature began issuing thousands of baptismal certificates and safe-conduct passes. The emphasis of official Roman Catholic policy in Hungary was thus turned from one of seeking protection only for converted Jews to one which embraced all of Jewish descent.

Meanwhile, Wallenberg was now setting up hospitals, nurseries, and soup kitchens throughout the city, buying food, medicine, and clothing with the unlimited funds available to him through the American–Jewish Joint Distribution Committee and the War Refugee Board. The International Red Cross belatedly followed suit. Wallenberg also initiated co-ordination of all neutral relief and rescue efforts by organizing a joint committee of heads of mission with the papal nuncio, Angelo Rotta, at their head. Wallenberg's staff increased to four hundred, and while they still worked around the clock in shifts, Wallenberg allowed himself no more than four hours' sleep a night. He was showing a zeal, energy, and administrative and organizational skills that, put to a different purpose, even Eichmann might have envied.

His efforts were certainly being noticed in Stockholm. On 10 August Ivar Olsen, the War Refugee Board representative, wrote to John Pehle, his superior in Washington: 'I get the impression indirectly that the Swedish Foreign Office is somewhat uneasy about Wallenberg's activities in Budapest and perhaps feel that he has jumped in with too big a splash. They would prefer, of course, to approach the Jewish problem in the finest traditions of European diplomacy, which wouldn't help too much. On the other hand, there is much to be said for moving around quietly on this type of work. In any case, I feel that Wallenberg is working like hell and doing some good, which is the measure.'

On the general situation in the Hungarian capital, Olsen reported that he had talked the day before with 'a chap from Hungary' from whom he had learned that 'the Jews are so terrified that they are now simply hiding in their homes. He believed that if the Jews weren't so terrified the best thing they could do would be to take off their yellow stars *en masse*, which would cause so much confusion, particularly because of the air raids around Budapest, that many of them could escape out into the country where they could be hidden. He said that about 80 percent of the Hungarian metropolitan population are quite unmoved by the Jewish persecutions and simply shrug their shoulders. The others are too frightened to help.'

Four days later, having just had lunch with 'the First Secretary of the Swedish Legation in Budapest, who is here for a short while,'* Olsen wrote to Pehle again: 'He is a fine chap and had many interesting comments to make. He said Wallenberg is working very hard and doing everything possible . . .

'He is very sceptical as to the possibility of bringing to Sweden the two-thousand-odd Jews who up to now have been issued Swedish papers. He stated that both the Hungarians and the Germans had agreed to provide transit visas . . . but later the Germans said there must be a *quid pro quo*, which was that the rest of the Hungarian

* Presumably Per Anger.

Jews of working age *must be delivered to the German labour camps*.' (Olsen's emphasis)

Olsen's luncheon guest gave a graphic description of what being 'delivered to the camps' entailed. 'He said that even he did not believe some of the atrocities until he himself was an eyewitness. He went over to a brick factory where they had over ten thousand Jews herded together into an area so small that they were forced to stand up closely packed together for five days, old people and young children alike, without any sanitary facilities.

'He saw them himself standing there, and also being loaded into box cars, eighty (he said eighty were counted out very carefully) into each car, after which the doors were nailed shut. He said many died, just standing in the brick factory.'

The Swedish diplomat was obviously referring to an incident he had seen before Horthy suspended the deportations. He went on to give Olsen a description of more current incidents, such as 'young girls of fourteen and fifteen being stolen in the streets, taken into other areas where they had "war whore" tattooed on their arms. Some of them – young Jewesses of good family – had been observed as far away as Hamburg.'

Olsen continued: 'He lamented very much the total lack of courage among the Hungarian Jews, since they could do so much to help themselves, even when they knew it was only a matter of a short time before they would be killed.'

Despite such horrors going on in the streets of Budapest, these were none the less days of comparative calm. The deportations were still officially suspended and Horthy was resisting German demands that they be resumed. The real confrontation between Wallenberg and Eichmann and the worst ordeal of Budapest Jewry were yet to come.

# *Chapter 5*

One of the first people with whom Wallenberg had made contact on his arrival in Budapest was Dr Samu Stern, the hapless president of the Central Jewish Council, which Eichmann had insisted be set up to make manipulation of the Jews easier. After the liberation, the elderly and ailing Stern was to write down his agonized memories of that time.

In his accounts the names of Eichmann and Wallenberg occur time and again. He describes Eichmann as 'a born, inveterate criminal to whom other beings' pain was lust. In moments of sincerity he called himself a bloodhound.' In contrast, he saw Wallenberg as 'unselfish, full of endless élan and the will to work, like all truly great men – his example induced the other neutral legations to emulate him and join in the struggle.'

Stern begins his account with the arrival of Krumey, Wisliceny, and Hunsche at the Jewish Community Centre in Sip Street the day after Operation Margarethe. They 'laid stress upon making their visit more emphatic through machine guns, ready to fire.' Of Krumey's, and later Eichmann's, attempts to calm the terrified Jews, Stern wrote, 'They have always shunned sensation, disliked creating fear and panic, worked noiselessly, coolly, and in deepest secrecy, so that the listless, ignorant victims should be without an inkling of what was ahead of them.'*

* Stern himself seems to have been taken in by these methods for a while.

He recalls the repeated and increasingly preposterous material demands made upon the Jews by Eichmann and his officers, who were always accompanied by SS troopers pointing sub-machine guns. 'One holiday . . . an officer, screaming at the top of his voice, ordered us to send three hundred mattresses and six hundred blankets to the Hotel Royal within ninety minutes. When we retorted that we were unable to do so he shouted like a madman that as ten minutes sufficed to execute ten thousand Jews, ninety minutes must suffice to comply with his wish . . .

'The demands came in every day and were of the most differing kinds – from champagne glasses to typewriters, from brooms to dishcloths and pails . . . On one occasion we were asked to furnish paintings by Watteau and no other artist; an apartment was being arranged for a high-ranking officer.'

In a similar post-war memoir, Dr Ernö Petö, another prominent member of the Jewish Council, recalled the vivid impression made by Wallenberg's arrival on the scene. After their first meeting, Petö wrote: 'I spoke to my family about the visit of this young-looking Wallenberg. My son then told me that when as a student he had spent a summer in a student hostel at Thonon-les-Bains in France, he had been together with a Swede by the name of Wallen-berg, whose grandfather was at that time the minister to Istanbul. He immediately took out a group photograph and I determined that the Wallenberg in the picture was the representative of the Swedish king.'

When Petö's son and Wallenberg met in Petö's office a little later they embraced as old friends. 'The contact between them became permanent,' wrote Petö senior. 'He was often our guest and his relationship with me also became closer . . . I can remember him only with the greatest admiration and praise.'†

Petö and Wallenberg often discussed how best the Swedish king's goodwill could be put to the help of the Hungarian Jews. An opportunity arose during the second half of July 1944, when Wallen-berg told Petö that a Swedish legation courier would be leaving for

† When Petö wrote this memoir in Brazil in 1955, he believed Wallenberg had died in 1945.

Stockholm the next day and would be able to carry a message for the king from the Jewish Council.

According to Petö's account, 'There was no time to spare, so I called Károly Wilhelm [another member of the Jewish Council] to my apartment the same evening and together we wrote the letter to the King of Sweden in which we thanked him for what he had done so far and described what would be needed to save the about two hundred thousand Jews still alive.

'We asked him to propose to the Germans and to the Hungarian government that the Swedish government was willing to remove the Jews of Budapest and for this reason they should place ships at his disposal at the Rumanian Black Sea, etc. In a separate memorandum prepared by my son . . . we reviewed the difficult situation in which Jewry was compelled to live, in fear of further deportations . . . We were ready at dawn.'

The Jewish leaders, and apparently Wallenberg, too, set great store by these documents – signed by Stern, Petö, and Wilhelm – reaching King Gustav. Consequently, they were alarmed when they learned that the courier had failed to reach Stockholm on schedule, a couple of days after leaving. While he was *en route*, the 20 July bomb plot against Hitler's life had occurred. In the massive security operation that followed, all Germany's borders were sealed. The courier was stuck inside the Reich. 'We heard nothing of him for days,' wrote Petö. 'Wallenberg himself became nervous.' Stern recalled: 'It would have been fatal for us if he had been caught and the letter found in his keeping. We only breathed freely again when Wallenberg informed us of the courier's safe arrival.'

Just how precarious was the situation of the Budapest Jews, despite Horthy's order stopping the deportations, is well illustrated by what came to be known as the Kistarcsa affair. On 14 July, defying the ban on further deportations, Eichmann sent an SS detachment to the Kistarcsa internment camp, where fifteen hundred prominent Jews were being held. This detachment overpowered and disarmed the Hungarian guards – who apparently made only a show of resistance – before loading the Jews onto a train which Franz Novak, Eichmann's transportation specialist, had secretly obtained.

The train headed immediately for the border and Auschwitz. But word of what had happened quickly reached the Jewish Council. Dr Petö had the secret telephone number of Admiral Horthy's son, Miklós, through whom he told the regent of what Eichmann had done. Horthy acted immediately, telephoning the Interior Ministry with instructions that the train must be stopped and returned to Kistarcsa 'even if you have to use force.' The order was obeyed and the deportation train was turned back just before it reached the frontier.

Eichmann was livid when he heard of Horthy's 'audacity,' as he called it, and enraged at the Jewish Council, whom he felt had no business to interfere with his plans. Council member Fülöp Freudiger recalled later: 'It is typical of the German mentality that, incredible as it seems, Eichmann made violent reproaches because of this to a member of the Central Council, accusing this person [Freudiger himself] of intervening with the Hungarian government. He quite seriously took the attitude that it was the duty of the Central Council to further the deportations with all their might.'

Eichmann was determined to avenge the Kistarcsa setback. '[He] felt the prestige of the SS was at stake and the defeat made him rave,' Stern recalled. 'He ordered every member of the Jewish Council to report to SS headquarters on Schwab Hill on 17 July, at 8 a.m. We did not have the slightest idea why we were there. At first we were kept waiting for hours in a room which we were not allowed to leave. The telephone was disconnected and we could not make contact with anybody.

'At last an officer [Hunsche] let us enter. He was acting as a substitute for Eichmann and conferred with us in an absolutely useless manner and without end on how the panicky atmosphere among Jewry could be disposed of. The deliberations went on the entire afternoon and we were dismissed after twelve hours at 8 p.m.'

While the eight-man council were thus kept incommunicado at the Hotel Majestic, a 150-man SS detachment, led by Eichmann himself, again raided the Kistarcsa camp and again overpowered and disarmed the Hungarian guards. This time they took the extra precaution of cutting the camp's telephone wires. The 1500 Jews who had previously been rescued by Horthy's command were put back on the waiting train and again sent, this time at express speed, to the border and Auschwitz. There was no chance of interference. 'Before we could try they had already crossed the frontier,' wrote Stern.

Emboldened by this *coup*, Eichmann began insisting again that all the Jews of Budapest must be deported. Horthy again said he would not permit this. Eichmann flew to Berlin for fresh instructions and was told to see if a show of force would weaken Horthy's resolve. When Eichmann returned, the number of SS men in and around the capital began to increase noticeably. Soon they were 9500 strong. 'Now certain of their preponderance,' Stern wrote, 'the SS troops, in full armour, held a great parade through the streets of Budapest.'

Having staked out his position by these dramatic means, Eichmann began to prepare for a lightning round-up and deportation action in late August. He now felt he had enough forces of his own at his disposal to carry out such an operation without any help from the Hungarians. To make sure there was no further interference by the Jewish Council, Eichmann had Stern, Petö, and Wilhelm arrested.

On 17 August the seventy-year-old Stern, ill with pneumonia, was dragged out of his sick-bed by the Gestapo and put into an open car for the drive to Schwab Hill. Petö, in the same car, had some incriminating documents on him, including a letter from Wallenberg. 'I threw my notes from the car,' he recalled in his post-war memoir. 'I had a letter of Wallenberg's which I wanted to tear up before throwing it to the wind. Hearing the crumpling of paper, the detective turned round and took the half-torn letter from my hands.

'During my interrogation I saw the letter, pasted together again, in the hands of the Gestapo ... The Gestapo investigator, who seemed a bit drunk, was obviously incensed by the Wallenberg letter and mistreated me severely ...' (Petö's memoir, unfortunately, does not disclose the letter's contents.)

Horthy, however, was informed of Eichmann's action, and intervened on behalf of the Jewish leaders. Within twenty-four hours the Gestapo released them, though not before giving them a brutal working over.

Stern and Petö were among Horthy's favoured Jews, and his

relations with them aptly illustrate his – and his son's – ambivalent attitude towards the Jewish people. For some years, Stern had been a member of Horthy's Privy Council, while Petö's son-in-law had been private secretary to the regent's son. Both Stern and Petö had regular private meetings with either the regent or his son in Buda Castle, entering by a back staircase. As already seen, Petö also had the son's secret phone number. Petö felt that the younger man was quite sympathetic, although afraid of being denounced by palace spies for his continuing contacts with Jewish leaders. His room was frequently searched for hidden microphones.

Another prominent Jew, the Zionist activist Ottó Komoly, had secret meetings with the younger Horthy at about this time. In his diary, recovered after his death at the hands of the Hungarian Nazis, he gives a revealing account of the attitude of the regent and his son to their Jewish fellow-countrymen. 'By birth and upbringing I am an anti-Semite,' the young Horthy told Komoly. 'It could not have been different with us in view of the way they spoke about Jews in our parents' home. For example, it would be inconceivable for me to marry a Jewish woman or for my children to have Jewish blood.

'But then I got involved in economic life.* I saw what happened there . . . Our civil servants have no feeling for the economic interests of the country. As far as they are concerned, the country could go bankrupt. This is why there is a need for the Jews who, while looking after their own interests, have advanced the interests of the country . . . As a sportsman, I know that peak results can only be obtained through competition. The Hungarians need the competition the Jews represent. The extent of Jewish emigration must be regulated in accordance with the interests of the nation . . .'

Some other prominent Hungarians were displaying great ambivalence about the Jews at this time, most notably Lászlo Ferenczy, liaison officer between the Hungarian Gendarmerie and the SS – 'an opportunist rotten to the marrow,' as Stern called him. According to Stern's post-war account, Ferenczy entered into a plot with the

---

* It was the practice of the Hungarian gentry to disdain business and the professions, hence the preponderance of Jews in these spheres.

Jewish Council to foil Eichmann's plan for a deportation raid scheduled for 26 August.

'We played the comedy of being entirely convinced of his good intent and humane feelings,' Stern wrote. 'We went as far as to declare to his face that he was the only possible man to rescue Budapest Jewry from certain annihilation . . . He would acquire glory and never-fading acclaim, for he would wash the stain from the nation's name.'

The plan (according to Stern, cooked up by himself and Ferenczy) was to have enough gendarmes brought quietly into Budapest from the country to outnumber the SS, backing up these gendarmes with police and reliable military units. Ostensibly, these forces would be brought in to help with the deportations; actually, their purpose would be to prevent them. Ferenczy insisted that he must get clearance for the plan from Horthy himself and – seemingly unaware of the irony of the request – asked Stern if he could arrange a meeting for him with the regent. On learning the details, Horthy agreed to play his part in the plan by pretending not to object to the impending deportations.

Then, as Stern later explained it: 'When the preparations reached the desired point, one or two days before the date set for the deportation, the regent would inform the Germans that all deportations were prohibited and that he was committed to enforce this measure by force of arms if necessary.' Stern thought that while it might come to an unavoidable clash, it was much more likely that the Germans would back down rather than risk an open and irreparable breach with an ally, however uncertain, at such a crucial point in the war. It certainly was crucial for Germany: their Rumanian allies were at the point of making a separate peace with the advancing Russians; Normandy and Brittany were in Anglo-American hands; Paris was on the point of falling; and the south of France had been invaded.

The neutral missions in Budapest, having got wind of the impending deportations, were also busy at this point. Wallenberg, as Stern noted, 'put all of his energies into a siege of the ministerial offices.' On 22 August, at Wallenberg's initiative, there was a meeting of neutral representatives chaired by Monsignor Angelo Rotta, the papal nuncio, at which a strong note was drafted for delivery to

Prime Minister Sztójay. The neutral nations, they said, were well aware that a mass deportation was being planned. Ostensibly, this was for labour service in Germany, but 'we all know what that means,' the note added in an unusually undiplomatic turn of phrase.

Acting in response to these pressures, and knowing that he had enough forces on hand to neutralize Eichmann's SS, Horthy forbade the deportations. To underline this, Ferenczy warned Eichmann that the nineteen thousand Hungarian soldiers, police, and gendarmes now in the capital would, if necessary, use force to stop him.

'Furious with rage,' recalled Stern, 'Eichmann realized he had been deceived, yet he dared not order the use of arms and so turned to Berlin for instructions.' The reply – direct from Himmler himself and received during the night of 24 August – was not to proceed. A couple of days later, Horthy dismissed Sztójay and appointed the moderate General Géza Latakos in his place as premier, giving him secret instructions to draw up a three-point programme: to restore Hungarian sovereignty as far as possible under the partial German occupation; to stop the persecutions against the Jews; and to prepare the ground for an armistice, to be carried out at the appropriate time.

With the fall of Sztójay and his replacement by Latakos, it seemed that for the Jews of Budapest the worst might be over. But the removal of Sztójay – to be followed by the temporary banishment of Eichmann – was only a respite, the end of one phase in the martyrdom of Hungarian Jewry.

Three members of the Jewish Council, Fülöp Freudiger, Sándor Diamant, and Gyula Link, who escaped to Rumania in mid-August – thereby laying themselves open to the accusation that they had deserted their fellows – wrote a joint account of that period. They singled out a number of Hungarian Fascists for special condemnation. Among them was Péter Hain, chief of the Hungarian Gestapo, which was 'dedicated to surpass its model in brutality and baseness.' László Endre and László Baky, who worked closely with Eichmann, were 'radical anti-Semites, convinced that all the evil in this world is due to the activity of the Jews.' Of Endre, the joint account says, 'Even his friends considered him a pathological case, who acknowledged no laws for his own person and gave way to his passions without any considerations whatsoever.'

The account also describes how, following Operation Margarethe, anti-Semitic propaganda began to flood the press and radio to soften up the Gentile population for condoning the deportations that were to come. 'For weeks they propagated nothing but the worst kind of Jew-baiting. It almost seemed as if Hungary had only one problem – the Jewish one . . . All anti-Jewish literature was hailed as a brilliant intellectual achievement and 'The Protocols of the Elders of Zion'* was presented to the population daily as spiritual nourishment.'

Meanwhile, the Jews of Budapest were 'occupied literally for weeks with the filling out of questionnaires, declarations of every kind, or they had to stand in line in front of government offices, police stations, etc., in order either to obtain the necessary forms or to return them . . . They never knew whether they could return to their homes, whether a member of their family had been deported or interned, or whether their houses, if not already requisitioned, were not destroyed by bombs.'

Every Allied bombing raid gave rise 'to the most ridiculous stories with only one theme – that the Jews had signalled to the bombers or given the enemy information by wireless.' One such story, current at the time, was that British and American pilots were dropping dolls filled with explosives for Hungarian children to pick up. Somehow the Jews were supposed to be co-operating in this, for dolls of the same kind were reportedly found in the cellar of a Jewish house. How the Jews managed to get the dolls up to the bombers, so they could then be packed with explosives and dropped back onto the city, was not explained.

'The Jews felt helpless and outlawed . . . When they walked in the streets they kept close to the walls of the houses, as they never knew when they would be arrested on the false charge of having pinned the yellow star on wrongly, or even of intentionally hiding it. This became a kind of game among the younger police members. Those

* A discredited document, probably forged by the tsarist secret police of Russia at the end of the nineteenth century, purporting to show how the Jews were plotting to take over the world.

who were arrested were taken to the internment camp, from which there was neither release nor escape.'

Suddenly, and at random, certain streets would be sealed off and all the Jews thus rounded up would be sent off to forced labour. Since, at Eichmann's instructions, the Jewish Council had already organized a labour service among able-bodied Jewish males to provide workers on demand, they asked the Obersturmbannführer why he did not make use of it. Eichmann simply answered that the street arrests were 'part of the procedure.' As the joint account points out, 'It would have been impossible to state more clearly that it was meant to terrorize the Jews.'

Eichmann had certainly managed to mystify the authors of this account by his pretensions to expert knowledge of Jewish affairs. 'He was born in Palestine, where his German parents had settled,' they wrote, 'and spent a great part of his youth there. It therefore does not appear paradoxical that Eichmann, who hated Jews violently and was possessed with the idea of exterminating them, spoke the Hebrew language well, and was very proud of this.' Other prominent Jews who came into contact with Eichmann were less easily taken in. They knew he was born in Germany and concluded that his knowledge of Hebrew was limited to a few liturgical phrases any first-year theology student might know. As for his knowledge of Yiddish, that language was basically a Middle High German patois, easy for a German to comprehend.

Of Eichmann's two principal lieutenants, the joint account notes that Wisliceny liked to call himself Baron (which he was not), while its authors thought Krumey 'the most humane of the senior SS officers.'

Although during this phase the Jews of Budapest mainly escaped deportation, Jewish Council headquarters were constantly receiving reports from the provinces – usually brought in by sympathetic Gentiles – of the brutalities being perpetrated there. The joint account tells of one small town where the Jews, on their way to the deportation trains, were 'driven through the mud-filled streets' and 'children of more than one year were forced to walk at the same speed as the adults, driven on by blows of the whip.'

At another town, a number of Jewish men lay down on the

railway tracks and refused to get in the waiting train. 'All of them were shot dead on the spot.'

In a town called Tata, 'a young mother who ten minutes before had given birth to twins ... was picked up by the hands and feet and thrown into the van; the new-born babies were pitched in after her.'

In a town called Kassa, the eighty-four-year-old mother of a prominent Jewish citizen was taken from the operating table after having her foot amputated and put into a railway car. 'Her son, who was present, tried to shoot himself. The weapon was knocked out of his hand, so that he only managed to shoot away half of his face. Covered with blood and unconscious, he was also put into the wagon.'

It was during this period that negotiations which were to be the subject of great post-war controversy took place between the SS and Rudolf Kasztner, one of the Jewish leadership though not a member of the Central Jewish Council. These negotiations, in which the Nazis offered to trade a million Jewish lives for ten thousand trucks and other non-lethal war material, were opened by an apparently reluctant Eichmann on Himmler's orders. In retrospect, it seems clear that Eichmann's preference was to send all of Hungary's Jews to the gas chambers, even if it meant denying the hard-pressed Reich the chance of obtaining badly needed material. Had he really intended to do business, he could easily have stopped or slowed down the deportations. On the contrary, he conducted them with frenzied haste, as we have seen, so that, daily, there were fewer lives over which to haggle with Kasztner and his aide, Joel Brand.

Despite this, Kasztner – and world Jewish leaders abroad who were privy to these secret negotiations and hoped to persuade the Anglo-Americans to agree to a deal – clung desperately to the hope that a substantial number of Jews might thus be rescued. The negotiations dragged on month after month.

Himmler, who it seems really did want to strike a deal, eventually put Kurt Becher, another SS Obersturmbannführer, in charge of the negotiations, relegating Eichmann to a supporting role. But, as the Jewish Council leaders noted, Eichmann was at odds with

Becher. 'Becher was against the deportations because he had to obtain the goods by all means and clearly realized that without living Jews as exchange objects no goods or materials would be forthcoming.' Eichmann, on the other hand, 'took the attitude that continued deportations would stimulate the Jews abroad to greater efforts to satisfy his demands, even if the number of Jews in Hungary decreased more and more.' What emerges is that he merely hoped there would soon be no Jews left to haggle over, and the whole business could be dropped.

In the event, the United States and Britain refused in principle to bargain with the Nazis or to consider supplying them with material to help their war effort against the Russians. Even if the Allies had been more flexible, the 'trucks for lives' negotiations seem in retrospect to have been bound to founder on the rock of Eichmann's opposition. Kasztner's only accomplishment was to organize the passage of 1700 prominent Jews – including members of his own family – who eventually reached Switzerland, via Belsen, having paid the Nazis $2000 a head.*

One prominent Hungarian Jew who never had any illusions that the Kasztner negotiations would succeed was Miklós (now Moshe) Krausz,† the Jewish Agency representative in Budapest. As a radical Zionist, his interest was not just in rescuing Jews but in getting them to Palestine, then under British rule, as citizens of a future Jewish

---

* In 1956 Kasztner was murdered in Tel Aviv by unknown assailants, who felt he had betrayed his trust by enabling a wealthy handful to buy their freedom, leaving the rest of the Jews to their fate.

† Curiously, Krausz was the only one among scores of witnesses and sources consulted in the preparation of this book who tried to diminish Wallenberg's role in the rescue of the Budapest Jews. In Jerusalem in the summer of 1979, he told me that Wallenberg was sent to Budapest largely at his (Krausz's) instigation, and that when he arrived he was 'rather naïve' and had to be shown by Krausz how to go about his task. Krausz stated categorically that Wallenberg never went out in person to rescue people from the 'Death Marches' (see Chapter 7), that he had not enjoyed good relations with Per Anger, and that it was not true that Wallenberg had ever been in Haifa. He thought Wallenberg had become something of a legend only because his family had 'paid journalists to write about him.'

state. The Swiss legation in Budapest was representing British interests and Krausz knew they had at their disposal several hundred immigration certificates for Jews waiting to go to Palestine.

He convinced the Swiss that it might be possible to negotiate an agreement for Jews holding these certificates to travel by rail to the Rumanian Black Sea port of Constanza, and then by sea to Istanbul, and on to Palestine. The Swiss approved the idea and began negotiating with the Hungarian and German authorities. To carry out the administrative work involved in preparing such a transport, the Swiss gave Krausz office and living space in one of their legation buildings. The Germans and Hungarians were cautiously receptive to the plan, the Germans if only because they believed that by letting a couple of thousand Jews escape they might be able to get on with the task of deporting the rest to the extermination camp without arousing a world outcry.

About the middle of July 1944 Horthy announced his government's agreement in principle to the scheme, provided the Rumanian and Turkish governments agreed to co-operate. Krausz was told to go ahead and prepare a transport of approximately 2200 people. This transport was to travel under a collective Swiss passport, under the flag of the Red Cross, and be accompanied by officials of the Red Cross and the Swiss legation. News of the impending transport spread like wildfire among the Jews of Budapest and thousands of them besieged the Swiss legation's 'Palestine Office' in Vadász Street, clamouring for places on the train.

But the transport never did leave. Krausz's best efforts, and those of the enthusiastic Swiss consul-general, Charles Lutz, were thwarted by the endless prevarications of the Nazis, who, among other reasons, did not want to upset their friend and ally, the Palestinian leader Haj Amin al-Husseini, the Grand Mufti of Jerusalem, by allowing Jewish immigrants to enter the Holy Land.

# *Chapter 6*

The new-found resolve that Horthy demonstrated in sacking Sztójay, and along with him the two most virulent anti-Jewish officials of his régime, Endre and Baky, was strongly influenced by the withdrawal of neighbouring Rumania from the war and by the combined pressure of the neutral missions in Budapest. These had been galvanized into action by the tireless Wallenberg, who bombarded the Sztójay government with requests, demands, and protests.

At Horthy's instructions the new Latakos government sent a note to the head of the German legation, Edmund Veesenmayer, demanding that the management of Jewish affairs be restored to the Hungarian authorities and that Jewish possessions stored in German warehouses be handed over. Horthy even called Veesenmayer to Buda Castle and reiterated these demands personally, adding the new demand that Eichmann and his Sondereinsatzkommando be withdrawn. This unprecedented display of independence in a satellite caught the Nazis in an uncharacteristic moment of self-doubt. The collapse of their Rumanian allies, the advances of the Russians in the east and the Anglo-Americans in the west, and the trauma following the 20 July bomb plot against Hitler all combined to deprive them temporarily of their customary brutal self-confidence.

Veesenmayer referred Horthy's demands to Berlin. SS Reichsführer Himmler replied on 25 August that after the loss of the Rumanian oilfields it was not worthwhile to risk a crisis with Horthy and his new government on account of the remaining Hungarian Jews. This might jeopardize the now indispensable oil production of Hungary's Zala region.

On 30 August the Germans reached a new agreement with the Latakos government. Eichmann and his Kommando would leave. It was undoubtedly the greatest setback and humiliation Eichmann had suffered in his entire career. Dumbfounded, he flew to Berlin, where he appealed in vain to Himmler. He turned next to Hitler's cabinet office. They were immersed in graver matters than the Hungarian Jewish question and did not hear him out. Himmler, determined not to let his efforts at personal fence-mending be wrecked by Eichmann's insistence, tossed a compensatory morsel to his embittered subordinate – the Iron Cross, Second Class. It was the first decoration Eichmann had received in his eleven years of loyal service with the SS.

With most of his officers now on enforced leave, Eichmann himself went off with his Iron Cross to nurse his grievance. He was the guest of his similarly unemployed friend, László Endre, at the latter's castle near the Austro-Hungarian border.

The departure of Eichmann did not, however, mean that all threat was suddenly over for the Jews of Budapest. Horthy and Latakos knew they had gone about as far as they could go in reasserting Hungary's sovereign rights over its own citizens and that the Germans would not tolerate the removal of restrictions on the Jews, especially with the Russians beginning to advance into the eastern Hungarian Plain.

Horthy's agreement with Veesenmayer therefore provided for the concentration of all able-bodied Jews, male and female, in camps in the Hungarian provinces, where they would be put to work for the Hungarian–German war effort.

Children, old people, and those unfit for labour would be concentrated in two other camps, while the sick would be sent to 'hospitals.' To the Jews of Budapest and their would-be protectors among the neutrals it looked better than the cattle trains to Auschwitz, but not much better. Mass extermination could be achieved by slower methods than gassing; overcrowding, undernourishment, back-breaking labour, insanitary conditions, and generally brutal treatment could be expected to take a heavy toll in such camps. Furthermore, the concentration of Jews in this way would make it easy for them to be suddenly sent off to the death camps if and whenever the Nazis decided to reassert their control over Hungary.

The Hungarians, however, had managed to get inserted into the agreement a proviso that conditions in the provincial concentration camps were to be 'consistent with European standards,' to be verified by the Red Cross. It was at this point that the International Red Cross belatedly began to vindicate itself after a long period of foot-dragging. The IRC delegation in Budapest, at last augmented by headquarters in Geneva, accepted the task of inspecting the proposed camp sites and, as Samu Stern was to record later, 'courageously siding with us ... failed, in the course of one and a half months, to find a single site in all of western Hungary which was suitable for "accommodation consistent with European standards."' As a result – and as a consequence of repeated Allied and neutral protests – the Hungarian government was apparently glad to drop the plan altogether.

On 29 September Wallenberg reported to Stockholm: 'The agreement reached between the Hungarians and the Germans that all Jews were to be evacuated from Budapest to the countryside outside the capital has hitherto been completely sabotaged by the Hungarian authorities and has not yet resulted in a single Jew leaving Budapest.' But he warned that as a consequence the Germans were threatening to take things into their own hands and were again concentrating SS units in Budapest.

'It has not been possible to ascertain whether it is again their intention to send these Jews out of the country, but it may be assumed that they will be unable to put their plans into effect without resorting to violent measures against the government.'

Thus, cautiously optimistic that the worst was over, Wallenberg was beginning to run his operation down and thinking about returning home. 'Certain members of the staff have been dismissed in accordance with the decision to bring the work of the department gradually to an end,' he reported. 'The number of employees is now about one hundred. About forty of these will have to return their identity cards to the legation within the next ten days. They will be allowed, however, to retain the cards issued by the Hungarian Home

Office. These exempt them from wearing the Star of David and from labour service.'

Wallenberg was also able to report that holders of Swedish protective passports who had been drafted for labour service were being released from the labour companies the following day and that 'the general release of internees can to a great extent be attributed to the work of this department.' Wallenberg added cryptically but revealingly, 'The official on whose order these people are being released has been worked upon with great diligence.'

The same day, 29 September, Wallenberg wrote to Koloman Lauer: 'I am going to do everything possible to get home soon, but you must understand that such a big organization cannot be wound up easily. The moment the [Russian] occupation is accomplished this organization will automatically cease to function. Until then, though, the work of our organization will remain necessary. It would be very hard just to stop it. I will try to get home a few days before the Russians arrive.'

Things continued to improve. On 12 October, with the air full of rumours that Horthy was about to sue for a separate peace with the Allies, Wallenberg reported to Stockholm: 'The release of internees has now been completed. Now only Jews who are considered to be criminals remain interned by the Hungarians.' Jews were being sent to dig fortifications on the eastern approaches to Budapest, but 'in so far as it is possible to judge, the treatment of these Jews is not inhuman,' and 'an effort to obtain the release from labour service of those Jews who possess Swedish protective passports has met with some success.

'The Russian advance,' Wallenberg continued, 'has increased the hope of the Jews that their unfortunate plight will soon be ended. Many have of their own accord already ceased wearing the Star of David. Their fears that the Germans might at the last moment carry out a pogrom still remain, however, despite the fact that there are no positive signs that any such happening will occur.'

The same day Wallenberg sent a personal note to Ivar Olsen, obviously in an 'end of term' mood.

*When I now look back on the three months I have spent here I can only say that it has been a most interesting experience, and I believe not without results. When*

*I arrived the situation of the Jews was very bad indeed. The development of military events and a natural psychological reaction among the Hungarian people have changed many things. We at the Swedish legation have perhaps only been an instrument to convert this outside influence into action in the various government offices. I have taken quite a strong line in this respect, although of course I have had to keep within the limits assigned to me as a neutral.*

*It has been my object all the time to try to help all Jews. This, however, could only be achieved by helping a whole group of Jews to get rid of their stars. I have worked on the hypothesis that those who were no longer under the obligation to wear the star would help their fellow-sufferers. Also I have carried out a great deal of enlightenment work among the key men in charge of Jewish questions here. I am quite sure that our activity – and that means in the last instance yours – is responsible for the freeing at this time of the interned Jews. These numbered many hundreds . . .*

*Mr Olsen, believe me, your donation in behalf of the Hungarian Jews has done an enormous amount of good. I think that they will have every reason to thank you for having initiated and supported the Swedish Jewish action the way you have in such a splendid manner.*

If Wallenberg's mission had ended there and then, as he obviously believed it was about to do, he could have returned home well satisfied that he had performed an extremely worthwhile humanitarian task. But dramatic events were about to unfold that would make everything so far accomplished seem of minor importance.

Horthy had sent a special emissary to Moscow to relay his decision to sue for a separate peace. Incredibly, he thought he could do this without the Germans finding out. Warned of the mission to Moscow by their palace spies in Buda Castle, the Nazis began quietly to prepare to forestall Hungary's defection from the Axis camp by an operation code-named Panzerfaust. Without taking the most elementary precautions first, such as bringing in large troop formations to secure the capital, Horthy sent a proclamation to the radio station on 15 October telling his people that, for them, the war was over.

László Szamosi, a resourceful young Jewish activist then living in Budapest and moving about the city with forged identity papers, recalls the memorable Sunday morning of the Horthy broadcast: 'This was the moment that we Jews had been awaiting so eagerly during the terrible months when we expected to be deported at any time,' he wrote in a memoir many years later. 'At first it seemed incredible that this meant our deliverance, our freedom. Hardly could we comprehend that we could now go out into the street and cast off our yellow stars, that we could go and look for our relatives. The ecstasy of the people living in our star-marked house was beyond description.'

But Szamosi had that morning made a personal reconnaissance of the city and was not so sure himself that deliverance was at hand. 'I had seen well-equipped motorized German units heading out of the city, but not a single Hungarian soldier, not even at the bridgeheads, which until now had been guarded by Hungarian and German soldiers.'

After the radio proclamation, following which the Jews in the house where he was living took down the big yellow star which marked it, Szamosi went out for another look round. 'Observing not without anxiety that there was not the slightest sign of the Hungarian Army taking over the city, and not seeing any corroboration of the broadcast proclamation, my heart filled with fear. This proclamation was repeated several times on the air, but at the same time the radio started warning about an impending air raid, still using the German passwords and playing German music in the intervals.

'Suddenly a new voice could be heard on the air, which started announcing ceaselessly the names of well-known Arrow Cross men.* It now became clear that the Arrow Cross mob, armed by the Germans, was seizing power. The Germans were streaming back into the city. They reoccupied the radio station with a few rifle shots and, with that, the Arrow Cross Government came into being and all our hopes were cruelly dashed.'

* Members of the Hungarian Fascist Party, the most extremist of all the right-wing groups.

# Chapter 7

This time the Nazis were taking no chances of their plans again being thwarted by Horthy. They prepared the putsch by kidnapping the regent's son and taking him off to Germany. The kidnap operation, carried out by Waffen SS Colonel Otto Skorzeny,* was achieved by luring young Horthy out of the regent's palace for what was supposed to be a meeting with representatives of. Tito, the leader of the Yugoslav partisans. As young Horthy drove from the palace with a bodyguard of three Hungarian Army sergeants, his car was ambushed, the bodyguard shot, and he was dragged away, wounded, to a waiting vehicle. When the regent heard that the Nazis were holding his son hostage, he caved in, abandoned his country to the Arrow Cross, and allowed himself to be taken away to Germany, a virtual prisoner.

The Germans now installed Arrow Cross leader Ferenc Szálasi as both prime minister and head of state, under the title Leader of the Nation. The next day Eichmann returned to Budapest in triumph. 'You see, I am back,' he told a small group of Jewish leaders who were immediately summoned to his headquarters. 'Our arm is still long enough to reach you.'

During his enforced vacation, Eichmann had conceived a brutally

---

* Skorzeny was the leader of the daring raid that had snatched Benito Mussolini from Allied captivity in 1943.

simple way of resuming the Jewish deportations, this time without having to fight the German Army for every locomotive and cattle car. 'The Jews of Budapest will now be deported – this time on foot,' he announced to his staff. 'We need our vehicles for other purposes. Now we are going to work, briskly and efficiently. All right?'

'During the first night of the putsch,' Wallenberg reported to his Foreign Ministry, 'numerous arrests and many pogroms took place and between a hundred and two hundred people are believed to have been killed. Moreover, a number of Jewish houses were emptied of their occupants by members of the Arrow Cross . . . Some hundreds have disappeared.' Wallenberg said the putsch had had 'a catastrophic effect' on his department. 'The whole of the personnel as well as the motor car . . . disappeared, and furthermore a number of keys to various locked rooms, cupboards, etc., could not be found. During the whole of the first day, the undersigned had to ride around the bandit-infested streets on a lady's bicycle trying to gather together the threads. The second day was spent in moving by car such people as were in danger to safe hiding-places . . .' Wallenberg located and liberated all but ten of his staff.

When Wallenberg's dispatch reached Stockholm, Minister Johnson cabled the State Department the gist of it, adding: 'It appears that Wallenberg is throwing his full energy into his task and doing remarkably well considering enormous difficulties. Olsen thinks official recognition by WRB of Wallenberg's efforts, which would be forwarded through the Foreign Office, well justified. Swedish government continuing to make strong representations to Hungarian government regarding treatment of Jews.'

The acting secretary of state, Edward Stettinius, cabled back conveying the US government's 'sincere appreciation of the humanitarian activities of the Swedish government and of the courage and ingenuity displayed by Mr Wallenberg.'

On 18 October the Arrow Cross interior minister, Gábor Vajna, went on the radio to announce his government's policy towards the solution of the Jewish problem in general – 'this solution, even if it shall be ruthless, shall be such as the Jews deserve by their previous and present conduct' – and in particular towards those who had been enjoying the limited protection of foreign countries and the churches.

'I recognize no Jews belonging to the Roman Catholic or Lutheran churches,' said Vajna. 'I recognize no letter of safe conduct of any kind, or foreign passport which a Jew of Hungarian nationality may have received from whatever source or person . . . Let not a single person of Jewish race believe, then, that with the help of aliens he can circumvent the lawful measures of the Hungarian State.'

Wallenberg did not wait to convene a meeting with the other neutral missions. This was a case for immediate action, rather than a protest note. He decided to work through the new foreign minister, Baron Gábor Kemény. Kemény's idea of the way a minister of foreign affair should dress when in public or when receiving ambassadors was to wear riding boots and a pistol at his belt. It did not seem likely that he would be swayed by humanitarian arguments. However, there were three factors that Wallenberg felt could be exploited: the desire of the new régime, apparently as strong as its predecessor's, for international recognition; the personal rivalry between Kemény and Vajna; and Kemény's wife.

Wallenberg had already met the baroness at one of the many parties and diplomatic receptions that he found time to attend with the object of making as many influential and potentially helpful contacts as possible. In the beautiful and spirited Elisabeth Kemény he was to find an exceptionally valuable ally. Born of aristocratic Austrian stock and raised in the disputed Italian Tyrol, she had come to Budapest in 1942 as the bride of the dashing Baron Kemény. She was now pregnant with their first child.

At an arranged meeting in the apartment of a mutual friend in Pest, Wallenberg came quickly but politely to the point. The neutral missions were most concerned about the new government's non-recognition of their protective passports. Her husband wanted the recognition of their governments, but this would never happen if the Szálasi Régime reneged on its predecessor's agreement over the passes. The baroness would surely appreciate that. She should also consider the likely fate of the Arrow Cross leaders, now that the Red Army was hammering at the gates of Budapest. When the city fell, they would all be hanged as war criminals . . . with the possible exception, of course, of those for whom a good word might be said. The baroness would surely wish the baron to do everything possible to avoid such a fate.*

On a purely departmental point, Wallenberg argued, the question of foreign passports was a matter for the Foreign Ministry, not the Interior Ministry, and therefore beyond the competence of her husband's rival, Vajna. In short, Wallenberg felt sure that the baroness would want to do everything possible to help her husband, herself, and their unborn child by prevailing on the baron to get the Interior Minister's decree countermanded. Elisabeth Kemény, her conscience already troubled by what she had seen and heard of the treatment of the Jews, promised to take the matter up with her husband.

Soon afterwards, Baron Kemény raised the issue with the Leader of the Nation. Szálasi was at first unsympathetic. The Jews must be got rid of, once and for all. He had assured the Germans that this time there would be no backsliding. Kemény countered quickly. He, too, wanted a quick solution to the problem, but it seemed to him that if they gave a little ground now, the new government might quickly achieve not one but two prime objectives: they could win the goodwill of the Swedes, the Swiss, and the other neutrals by re-validating their documents, then they could demand in all good conscience that these nations should remove persons under their protection from Hungary by a stipulated date, leaving them free to get on with disposing of the rest of the Jews.

By letting at most some sixteen thousand Jews escape to neutral countries and Palestine – always providing that transport could be found for them and transit arrangements made – they would be in a position to get rid, once and for all, of ten times that number. Put that way, the idea appealed to Szálasi; it might commend itself to the Germans, too.

When the baroness informed Wallenberg that she had been successful in her mission, it was only to find that he had a further demand.

* Baron Kemény was in fact arrested by Allied troops in northern Italy soon after the war and handed over to the Hungarians. He was tried for war crimes by a 'people's court' and executed.

76

It would not be sufficient for Kemény merely to notify the diplomatic corps of this reversal in policy. He must make the announcement publicly, as the interior minister had made his – on the radio – so that the local authorities, the Arrow Cross branches, and the general public should be in no doubt about the validity of the protective passes. Furthermore, the announcement should stress that protected houses were not to be entered without authorization or their occupants molested. Yet again, Wallenberg's arguments were powerful enough to convince the baroness that she must urge them on her husband.

At first, Kemény was unwilling. He did not want a showdown with the already disgruntled Vajna. But the baroness insisted; Vajna had made him look foolish – he must return the compliment or lose face. 'Your friend Wallenberg is causing me a lot of trouble,' he grumbled. 'Always he wants something more. Knowing him is like suffering the Chinese water torture.' Again the baroness insisted, even threatening – so she recalled many years later – to leave him. The still-infatuated Kemény could not refuse her, and the next day he went to the radio station with orders from his wife not to leave the studio without making his broadcast.

According to rumours still current in Budapest long after the war, the real reason why Baroness Kemény was willing to co-operate with Wallenberg was that she was herself of part-Jewish descent. She denies it. 'I have no Jewish blood,' she told a visitor to her apartment in an affluent Munich suburb in 1980. 'I was born into an old Catholic family. No, I began feeling concern for the Jews one day when I looked out of my window and saw a group of old people, staggering down the street under armed guard. They were barely able to walk and small children were wandering untended among them. I called down to the guards, "Who are these people and where are you taking them?" and they answered, "Jews, and we're taking them to work." I knew this must be a lie. They were too old and weak to work. I guessed they were on their way to the slaughter and I felt I must do something. And then Wallenberg came along and it's no wonder that we got on so well from the start. We were allies in a fight for humanity.'

Another rumour current in post-war Budapest was that she and

77

Wallenberg were lovers. 'Ridiculous!' says the baroness. 'I was very pregnant at the time I knew him and although he was very charming he was not nearly as good-looking as my husband.'

On 1 November Kemény summoned Wallenberg and the Swiss consul, Lutz, to the Foreign Ministry. Having restored the validity of the 4500 Swedish and 7000 Swiss passports officially issued (he knew there were more, but they were of no consequence to him), the Hungarian government now required the governments of those two countries to repatriate their 'nationals' as quickly as possible and by the end of the month at the latest. If they were not gone by then, the protected Jews would be treated the same as the rest. Kemény hoped that by the time of their departure both Sweden and Switzerland would have accorded recognition to the Szálasi government. Would the Swedes and the Swiss now kindly make all appropriate arrangements for the transportation of these people? He would be speaking to the Germans about transit arrangements.

Wallenberg and Lutz, both of whom could see the dangers involved, replied that they would consult their governments. Once their officially protected Jews were gone, they realized, they would have no further function and no basis on which to act on behalf of the thousands more whose passports exceeded the agreed quotas. Wallenberg, at least, also was determined to see what he could do for the scores of thousands of unprotected Jews. Then, even if transport could be arranged to take 'his' Jews across Germany to Sweden, what guarantee could there be that they would not meet with some unfortunate 'accident' en route? No, the only thing to do was to accept in principle and play a stalling game. They had until the end of the month, and with the Russians advancing steadily that might be long enough. On 2 November, in fact, an advanced Soviet unit actually penetrated the south-eastern outskirts of the city.

While all this had been going on, protected and unprotected Jews alike were being terrorized by bands of Arrow Cross thugs, some of them only teenagers, who roamed the city beating, robbing, and killing; there was little or no interference from the police. But this activity, though terrible enough, was sporadic and uncoordinated. On 20 October 1944 Eichmann went to work in a more systematic way, with a mass round-up of Jewish men between the ages of sixteen and sixty, ostensibly to provide workers for the Hungarian Army labour service. The sick, the halt, the lame, and the crippled, as well as the fit and the healthy, were routed from their star-marked houses. They were given one hour to get ready and equip themselves with food for a three-day march. In a few cases those with foreign passports managed to get themselves exempted, especially those with the impressive 'Wallenberg passports.' Some Jews managed to buy their way out of the dragnet with bribes. Altogether some fifty thousand recruits were marched off to a racecourse and a sportsground, where they were formed up into companies before being marched to various locations on the outskirts of Budapest to perform back-breaking work – digging trenches and throwing up earthwork defences in the path of the Russian advance. Hundreds died of exhaustion, exposure, and ill-treatment.

With much of the male population gone, it now became the turn of the women and older children. Despite determined attempts by Wallenberg and other members of the diplomatic corps to prevent it, Eichmann's promised programme of deportations on foot began on 8 November. So began the first of the 'death marches' along a 120-mile route from Budapest to the Austrian border at Hegyeshalom, under conditions so dreadful that even hardened Nazis were to protest. It was during these marches, which went on almost until the end of November, that Wallenberg's reputation among the despairing Jews became legendary.

Miriam Herzog, now a well-preserved grandmother living comfortably in a Tel Aviv suburb, has a vivid recollection of the march, and of how Wallenberg saved her and a hundred others from one transport. Her account, though more articulate than most, is typical.

'The conditions were frightful. We walked thirty to forty kilometres a day in freezing rain, driven on all the time by the Hungarian gendarmes. We were all women and girls. I was seventeen at the time. The gendarmes were brutal, beating those who could not keep up, leaving others to die in the ditches. It was terrible for the older women. Sometimes at night we didn't have any shelter, let alone anything to eat or drink. One night we stopped in a square in the middle of a village. We just lay down on the ground to rest. There was a frost in the night and in the morning many of the older women were dead. It was so cold, it was as though we were frozen into the ground. The thirst was even worse than the hunger. I recall that somewhere along the road a villager came out with water for us. The gendarmes tried to stop him, but he just fixed them with a stare. "I'd like to see you try to make me," he said – and went on giving us water. The gendarmes were so amazed, they did nothing about it.

'There were some good people in Hungary but the gendarmes were absolute animals. I hate them even worse than the Germans. At one point along the road we met a convoy of German soldiers going the other way, towards the front. Ordinary Wehrmacht men, not SS. When they saw how the Hungarian gendarmes were treating us, they appeared to be horrified. "You'll be all right when you get to Germany," they told us. "We don't treat women like this, there." I suppose they didn't know about the extermination camps.'

When the marchers reached the frontier, trains were waiting to take them to the camps. Miriam managed to slip away to a barn where hundreds of women claiming Swedish protection were being held.

'I didn't have a Swedish passport, but I thought it was worth a try and I had this tremendous will to survive, even though I was so weak from dysentery and wretched from the dirt and the lice that infested me, that all I could do was find a space on the floor and lie down. I don't know how much later it was – maybe days – but suddenly I heard a great commotion among the women. "It's Wallenberg," they said. I didn't know this name, but somebody told me he was a Swedish diplomat who had saved many Jews already. I didn't think he could really help me, and anyway I was now too weak to move, so I lay there on the floor as dozens of women clustered around him crying "Save us, save us." I remember being struck by how handsome he looked – and how clean – in his leather coat and fur hat, just like a being from another world, and I thought, Why does he bother with such wretched creatures as we? As the women clustered around him he said to them: "Please, you must forgive me, but I cannot help all of you. I can only provide certificates for a hundred of you." Then he said something which really surprised me. He said: "I feel I have a mission to save the Jewish nation and so I must rescue the young ones first." I had never heard of the idea of a Jewish nation before. Jewish people, of course, but not a Jewish nation. Later I was to think about this quite a lot. Anyway, he looked around the room and began putting names down on a list, and when he saw me lying on the floor he came over to me. He asked my name and added it to the list. After a day or two, the hundred of us whose names had been taken were moved out and put into a cattle truck on a train bound for Budapest. We were warned to keep quiet *en route*, because if we were discovered we might all be sent back to Auschwitz. I don't know how Wallenberg managed it; I suppose he must have bribed the railway officials and guards. Because the railway lines had been bombed the journey back to Budapest took three days, instead of three or four hours, and we were in a terrible state when we arrived. There were a lot more dangers and hardships ahead of us, but we were alive – and it was thanks entirely to Wallenberg.'

Wallenberg, his colleague Per Anger, and others travelled tirelessly up and down the road between Budapest and Hegyeshalom during those terrible November days, taking vanloads of food, medicine, and warm clothing with them, Wallenberg clutching his 'book of life' listing the names of Jews to whom passports had been issued, and carrying fresh passports to be filled in and issued on the spot. This period is recalled in Per Anger's memoirs, published in 1979 after his retirement as Sweden's ambassador to Ottawa.

On one of the first days of December 1944, Wallenberg and I went for a drive along the road on which the Jews were being marched away. We passed these groups of unfortunate people, who were more dead than alive. Grey-faced they tottered while the soldiers were urging them along with their rifle butts. The road was edged with corpses. Our car was loaded with food, which we distributed in spite of the prohibition against doing so; but we did not have enough for everybody. At Hegyeshalom we saw how those who had arrived were handed over to a German SS command headed by Eichmann, who counted them one by one as if they had been cattle. 'Four hundred and eighty-nine – right' ('*Vierhundertneunundachtzig – stimmt, gut!*'). The Hungarian officer was given a receipt stating that everything was in order.

Before this handing over, we succeeded in rescuing about a hundred Jews. Some of them had Swedish protection passports, others we got out by sheer bluff. Wallenberg did not give up and made repeated trips, during which he succeeded, again bringing a number of Jews back to Budapest.

With the co-operation of the International Red Cross, lorries for the distribution of food were organized. At Wallenberg's initiative, controls were placed on the main roads leading out of Budapest and at the border station in order to prevent the deportation of Jews holding protection passports. It was estimated that in this way about 1500 Jews were rescued and brought back to Budapest.*

Zvi Eres, one of the founders of a now-flourishing kibbutz in southern Israel, remembers how as a fourteen-year-old he, his mother, an aunt, and a girl cousin were saved by Wallenberg.

'As we approached Hegyeshalom at the end of the march, we saw two men standing by the side of the road. One of them, wearing a long leather coat and a fur hat, told us he was from the Swedish legation and asked if we had Swedish passports. If we hadn't, he said, perhaps they had been taken away from us or torn up by the Arrow Cross men. We were on our last legs, but alert enough to take the hint and we said, yes, that was exactly what had happened, though in fact none of us had ever had a Swedish *Schutzpass*. He put our names down on a list and we walked on. At the station later we again saw Wallenberg and some of his assistants, among them – as I learned only later – some members of the Zionist youth movement, posing as Red Cross officials, and representatives of the papal nuncio. A group of Hungarian officers and Germans in SS uniforms were there, too. Wallenberg was brandishing his list, obviously demanding that everybody on it should be allowed to go. Voices were raised and they were shouting at each other in German. It was too far away for me to hear exactly what was being said, but clearly there was a tremendous argument going on. In the end, to our

* With characteristic modesty, Anger failed to mention that he made some forays to the border without Wallenberg and was personally responsible for a number of rescues. In 1956, when he was attached to the Swedish embassy in Vienna, he again went to the Austro-Hungarian border to help refugees from the Soviet takeover that followed the Budapest uprising of that year. He told the author how he saw a group of people coming across the border, including some Jewish women, one of whom fell into his arms and said: 'Per Anger, this is the second time you have saved me.'

amazement, Wallenberg won his point and between 280 and 300 of us were allowed to go back to Budapest.'

Between dashing up and down the road to Hegyeshalom, Wallenberg found time for more conventional but equally essential kinds of diplomatic activity. On 16 November, as secretary of the Diplomatic Humanitarian Committee, he convened a meeting which agreed to send a stiff joint note to the Hungarian government, protesting at the 'ruthless severity' of the deportations and 'the acts of inhumanity the whole world is witnessing.' Szálasi rejected the protest. Jews who had been 'loaned' to the German government and were 'fit to work' would continue to be deported, he replied. Having drafted this answer for delivery through the Foreign Ministry, he scrawled petulantly at the bottom of the page, 'I do not wish to discuss the subject with anyone again!'

In a report to Stockholm on the marches, Wallenberg had written: 'The sights that we witnessed moved even some of the grim-visaged, bloodthirsty gendarmes. More than one remarked that he would prefer being in the firing line . . . We saw that in many places the corpses of people who had died or been murdered by the Arrow Cross men covered the roadside. Nobody had thought of burying them.' Wallenberg had also received a confidential report from a senior Hungarian police officer saying that he estimated some ten thousand death marchers had already crossed the frontier, with another thirteen thousand *en route*. 'In addition, ten thousand Jews have disappeared on the highway, some having escaped but most having died or been killed by their guards.' At one point, the officer reported, he saw people hanging from trees and he 'had the impression that these people had committed suicide.'

Those women, children, and old men who survived as far as Hegyeshalom were joined there by the younger men of the labour battalions. These men had been sent from Budapest at an earlier date to dig trenches in the path of the Soviet advance. Now they had been marched to the frontier by different routes to be handed over to the Germans for similar work. Diplomats from the Swiss legation who saw a group of two thousand of these labour battalion men reported: 'They arrived at Hegyeshalom barefoot, half naked, in the worst state of demoralization imaginable. On the way they were not fed, but received many beatings. Many of them died of exhaustion *en route*.' As for the women and children, the Swiss reported that 'the endless ordeal of the marches, the almost complete lack of nourishment, the constant dread that in Germany they were to be taken to annihilation in the gas chambers, have brought about such a condition . . . that they no longer possess human shape and lack all human dignity.'

A group of observers from the International Red Cross reported on a night-stop by marchers aboard barges moored on the Danube. 'Many of the people in this dreadful situation committed suicide. Scream after scream pierced the night. People resigned to death threw themselves in the freezing waters of the Danube rather than endure further suffering.' The IRC team mentioned that they had taken 4000 metres of film of conditions on the march on behalf of the papal nuncio.* 'Every frame testifies to the terrible treatment thàt group of the capital's Jewry suffered which, according to the Szálasi decree, were handed over to the Germans as "loan Jews" so that they should work for "Hungary's welfare in exchange for war material."' This phrase, said the Red Cross report, 'only conceals the essence: the Szálasi régime simply handed over the Jews of the capital to be exterminated.'

With even the ultra-cautious IRC putting in reports like this, Himmler thought it time to find out exactly what his zealous subordinate Eichmann was up to. He sent SS General Hans Juettner on an inspection tour. Juettner expressed himself shocked. 'I was told that Eichmann was responsible,' he said later, 'but since he was not in Budapest I spoke to an SS Sturmbannführer whose name I have forgotten [it was Theo Dannecker] and gave him a piece of my mind.' At Hegyeshalom, Juettner met Dieter Wisliceny, who told him Eichmann had instructed him to pay no attention to illness, age, or protection passes: 'The main thing is statistics; every arriving Jew must be mercilessly taken over.'

---

* While preparing a television documentary about Wallenberg the British Broadcasting Corporation attempted unsuccessfully to locate this film. Both the Vatican and IRC headquarters in Geneva said they had no idea what had happened to it.

Himmler, now preparing the ground for his peace feelers to the Allies, summoned Eichmann to Berlin and told him the death marches must stop. 'If up to now you have been busy liquidating Jews,' he explained icily, 'you will from now on, since I order it, take good care of them, like a nursemaid.' When Eichmann protested that this was contrary to his understanding of the Führer's wishes, and that Gestapo chief Müller had approved of the marches, Himmler snapped back, 'I remind you that it was I – and neither Gruppen-führer Müller nor you – who founded the RSHA. I'm the one who gives orders here!' Eichmann backed down and Himmler dismissed him. By way of consolation prize, Himmler later awarded Eichmann another decoration, his second in two months, the Cross of War Merits, First Class, with Swords.

Years later, in Argentina, Eichmann was to reminisce with pride on how he had conceived and executed the death marches; faced with a lack of road or rail transport, a lesser man might have called off the deportation programme. In an obvious reference to his run-in with Himmler, he conceded, 'There were, of course, difficulties on all sides ... But Winkelmann [the Nazi police chief in Budapest] congratulated me on the elegant performance. So did Veesenmayer. So did Endre. We even had a drink on it. For the first time in my life I drank mare's milk alcohol.'

At the beginning of December 1944 Wallenberg reported to Stockholm in a matter-of-fact way that during the death marches 'it was possible to rescue some two thousand persons from deportation through intervention for some reason or another.' He added, almost as a throwaway, that the Swedish mission had also secured the return of fifteen thousand labour service men holding Swedish and other protective passes.

# *Chapter 8*

As the advance guard of Soviet Field Marshal Rodion Malinovsky's army battered its way into the eastern and southern outer suburbs of Budapest against stern Nazi resistance, conditions for the capital's inhabitants became desperate. Day and night, in turn, the heavy bombers of the American and British air forces pounded the city; right around the clock, the field artillery of the Red Army contributed to the destruction.

Rations were drastically reduced. Household fuel became virtually unobtainable. Epidemics spread and hospitals were critically over-crowded with the sick and wounded. Municipal services scarcely functioned. Along the road west to Hegyeshalom the pathetic columns of women, children, and the aged again made their painful way. This time, though, they were not driven on by the blows, curses, and shots of the gendarmerie; this time, for those who survived the march, no gas chambers and crematorium ovens were waiting. This time the marchers were not Jewish deportees but Gentile refugees.

The Jews were trapped in the city, and though life there was a nightmare for everyone, no section of the population suffered as they did. They had now been herded into two ghettos. There were 35,000 Jews – all holders of foreign passes – in the International Ghetto consisting of Swedish, Swiss, and Red Cross 'protected' houses, and about 70,000 unprotected Jews crammed into the enclosed General Ghetto. The overcrowding in both ghettos was appalling, with people fighting for living space on staircases, in cupboards, and on window ledges.

In a general atmosphere of anarchy and lawlessness, bands of Arrow Cross gunmen – some of them delinquents of fifteen and sixteen – roamed the city, looting Jewish property, violating Jewish women, and dragging Jewish men off to be tortured and killed. Protective passes were often no real protection for Jews caught out in the streets by the Arrow Cross, but in a surprising number of cases the 'Wallenberg passes' retained their power to impress. Joni Moser, a member of the Jewish underground in Budapest, recalled some twenty years later how 'the protective passports issued by the Swedes looked like normal passports, with a seal, name, photo, and signature. They were therefore respected. The Swiss passports were of a general nature, without name and signature of the responsible person in the legation. They were rarely effective.'

Wallenberg himself was to report to Stockholm on 8 December: 'Up to now Jews in possession of Swedish safe-conducts have been treated leniently in comparison with those enjoying the protection of other neutral powers. As far as can be ascertained, only ten Jews with Swedish safe-conducts have up to now been shot in and around Budapest.' In the same report Wallenberg also recorded that 'thousands of Jews with Swiss and Vatican passports are removed daily from the [International] Ghetto and transferred to the General Ghetto or deported.'

The role Wallenberg played is movingly revealed in the account of Tommy Lapid, subsequently director-general of the Israeli Broadcasting Authority in Jerusalem. In 1944 he was thirteen years old and one of nine hundred people crowded fifteen or twenty to a room in a Swedish-protected house.

'We were hungry, thirsty, and frightened all the time and we were more afraid of the Arrow Cross than of the British, American, and Russian bombardments put together. Those people had guns and they thought the least they could do for the war effort was to kill a few Jews before the Russians got there, so they were entering these houses, which were undefended, and carrying people away. We were very close to the Danube and we heard them shooting people into the river all night.

'I sometimes think that the greatest achievement of the Nazis was that we just accepted the fact that we were destined to be killed. My father was in Mauthausen concentration camp and perished there. I, an only child, stayed with my mother. I kept asking her for bread. I was so hungry. (Years later, if there was no bread in the house, she would get out of bed at night and go down to a café and ask for two slices of bread – although then a very well-to-do lady in Tel Aviv, she had to have some bread in the house because of those days when she couldn't supply me with any.)

'One morning, a group of these Hungarian Fascists came into the house and said all the able-bodied women must go with them. We knew what this meant. My mother kissed me and I cried and she cried. We knew we were parting for ever and she left me there, an orphan to all intents and purposes. Then, two or three hours later, to my amazement, my mother returned with the other women. It seemed like a mirage, a miracle. My mother was there – she was alive and she was hugging me and kissing me, and she said one word: "Wallenberg."

'I knew who she meant because Wallenberg was a legend among the Jews. In the complete and total hell in which we lived, there was a saviour-angel somewhere, moving around. After she had composed herself, my mother told me that they were being taken to the river when a car arrived and out stepped Wallenberg – and they knew immediately who it was, because there was only one such person in the world. He went up to the Arrow Cross leader and protested that the women were under his protection. They argued with him, but he must have had incredible charisma, some great personal authority, because there was absolutely nothing behind him, nothing to back him up. He stood out there in the street, probably feeling the loneliest man in the world, trying to pretend there was something behind him. They could have shot him there and then in the street and nobody would have known about it. Instead, they relented and let the women go.'

Time and again, as in the testimony of Joni Moser, Wallenberg's extraordinary personal authority and lonely courage comes through.

'I was Wallenberg's errand boy. As I spoke German as well as Hungarian I could pass through barriers and therefore was well equipped to be a messenger. I had been served with a deportation order by the Germans but had escaped, and I used to show the deportation order, embellished with the swastika, to young Arrow Cross men who could not read German. They only saw the swastika and let me pass. I always took care to avoid the Germans but they caught me once, and it was almost the end for me. But just then Wallenberg happened to come by in his grand diplomatic car. He stopped and asked me to step forward for questioning. "Jump in, quick," he said – and before the astonished soldiers realized what had happened we were gone. Wallenberg was fantastic! His conduct, his power of organization, his speed in decision and action! What a strategist! Wallenberg was the initiator of the whole rescue action, remember that.'

Moser recalls the day when Wallenberg learned that eight hundred Jewish labour service men were being marched to Mauthausen. He and Wallenberg drove to the frontier and caught up with the column. Wallenberg asked that those with Swedish protective passports should raise their hands. 'On his order,' Moser says, 'I ran between the ranks and told the men to raise their hands, whether they had a passport or not. He then claimed custody of all who had raised their hands and such was his bearing that none of the Hungarian guards opposed him. The extraordinary thing was the absolutely convincing power of his behaviour.'

Moser feels that Wallenberg was supremely happy during the brief period of his most intense activity. 'It is not given to many men to live such a life, equipped with the spark of initiative, an irresistible personal radiance, and a tireless energy, and with these to be able to save thousands of one's fellow-men.'

Sándor Ardai was sent by the Jewish underground to drive for Wallenberg after his personal driver, Vilmos Langfelder, was arrested by the Arrow Cross on 7 November. Ardai's first impression was that Wallenberg didn't look at all like a hero – 'he seemed rather dreamy and soft.' Ardai's first mission was to drive Wallenberg to Arrow Cross headquarters on 9 November and wait outside 'until he had got Langfelder back.

'As he vanished with long strides into the Arrow Cross headquarters I thought to myself, He'll never do it. How was it possible that the Arrow Cross would release a prisoner just because one man demanded it? But when I saw him come back down the stairs he had Langfelder with him. They jumped into the car and I drove them straight to the legation. Nobody commented on what had happened and I began to understand the extraordinary power that was in Raoul Wallenberg.

'During the month and a half that Langfelder and I took turns to drive him I never heard him speak an unnecessary word, never a superfluous comment or a word of complaint, even though he often had only a few hours' sleep over several days. Only once I saw him upset. It was when an Arrow Cross gang had occupied his office. He asked the government, without success, to have it returned. Then he led a small group of us straight back to the office and threw out the intruders. Once that was done, he sat down at his desk. We felt sure that there would be reprisals, but astonishingly nothing happened.'

Ardai tells how, one day in November, he drove Wallenberg to the Józsefváros Railway Station, where Wallenberg had learned that a trainload of Jews was about to leave for Auschwitz. The young SS officer supervising the transport ordered Wallenberg off the platform. Wallenberg brushed past him.

'Then he climbed up on the roof of the train and began handing in protective passes through the doors which were not yet sealed. He ignored orders from the Germans for him to get down, then the Arrow Cross men began shooting and shouting at him to go away. He ignored them and calmly continued handing out passports to the hands that were reaching out for them. I believe the Arrow Cross men deliberately aimed over his head, as not one shot hit him, which would have been impossible otherwise. I think this is what they did because they were so impressed by his courage.

'After Wallenberg had handed over the last of the passports he ordered all those who had one to leave the train and walk to a caravan of cars parked nearby, all marked in Swedish colours. I don't remember exactly how many, but he saved dozens off that train, and the Germans and Arrow Cross were so dumbfounded they let him get away with it!'

There are many eyewitness accounts of Wallenberg facing down German and Hungarian officers in this way. With the Germans, especially, his technique was to pull rank. 'How dare you attempt to remove these people who are under the protection of the Royal Swedish legation?' he once berated a young Nazi lieutenant in charge of a transport of Jews. 'Don't you realize that your government relies on my Foreign Ministry to protect its interests in many of the most important countries of the world? And this is how you protect our interests! Wait until word of this affair reaches your superiors. I shall complain direct to Berlin. I shall have your head on a platter!'

'But I have my orders,' replied the flustered lieutenant. 'All the Jews on this list are to be transported.'

'Your list cannot possibly include Jews who hold Swedish passports,' snapped Wallenberg. 'And if it does then someone has made a grievous mistake that he will pay for.' Then he produced a list of his own, which he brandished in front of the intimidated young Nazi. In the end, he got 'his' Jews off the train.

There were times when Wallenberg elevated bluff to a fine art, such as the occasion when he got a group of Jewish deportees to win their freedom by producing all kinds of official-looking but irrelevant documents – like driving licences and tax receipts – which he showed to a German officer as evidence of their protected status, banking successfully on the likelihood that the Nazi could not read a word of Hungarian.

Using his well-tried methods of bribery, coercion, and occasionally outright blackmail, Wallenberg was able to build up an impressive private intelligence network that gave him lightning information about deportations, raids on protected houses, and new official anti-Jewish measures. Time after time he was able to turn up – often alone, except for his driver, always unarmed – in time to make a decisive intervention. Once, during the round-up of Jewish men for forced labour, Wallenberg went to a Swedish-protected house which had been forcibly entered by a detachment of Hungarian gendarmes. 'This is Swedish territory,' he told the officer in charge coldly. 'You have no right to be on these premises.' The officer replied that he had orders to take all the able-bodied men. 'Nonsense,' replied

Wallenberg. 'By agreement between the Royal Swedish government and the Royal Hungarian government, these men are specifically exempted from labour service.'

The Hungarian, though obviously discomfited by this calculated reference to not one but two 'royal governments,' nevertheless insisted. 'I have my orders,' he said. 'I must take them.' Wallenberg played his last card: 'If you want to take them you will have to shoot me first.' The officer faltered and gave in. He and his men left empty-handed.

For individual Jews saved by Wallenberg's intervention the danger was by no means over. Miriam Herzog recalls the conditions she encountered in a Swedish protected house after her rescue from the column of death marchers at Hegyeshalom.

'I was really ill, I felt I was dying. I had to lie on the cold stone floor in the cellar of this house, with scores of other women pressing around me. A Jewish doctor came to look at us and, as I found out later, he decided that if I was left on the floor I would probably die.

'He had the house searched for something for me to lie on and, by some miracle, an old deck chair was found. The doctor said I was to have hot tea and sulfa – I was quite incapable of eating – and a boy about my own age was detailed to give me these every couple of hours. Very slowly I recovered and when, on the fifth day, I asked for a piece of soap and washed my hair in cold water, they knew I was going to live.'

Miriam was obviously an unusually spirited girl. Once she felt fit enough to sit up and take notice, she decided she would fend for herself. On the seventh day, she told the boy who had been bringing her tea that she was going to leave the house and find a Christian relative, an aunt by marriage, who lived in Buda on the other side of the river. He was amazed. 'You must be mad! Don't you know what's going on out there? The Arrow Cross are killing every Jew they can lay their hands on. There are Jews hanging from all the lamp-posts – you won't get more than a few hundred metres.'

But Miriam was determined to leave. 'I don't know why,' she says, 'but I was sure it was safer out on the street than packed in that house with hundreds of others, waiting for the Arrow Cross to slaughter us.' So she slipped out, while the door guard was looking the other way.

'I had long blond hair and didn't look Jewish but I had no identification papers and that was very dangerous. Of course, I had removed the yellow star from my coat but it seemed to me that everyone could see the patch where it had been. Once when I was stopped by police and asked for my papers I said my home had been bombed and all our papers destroyed. It worked. I had tremendous *chutzpah* in those days and an absolute will to live. The most difficult thing was getting across the bridge and I can't to this day remember exactly how I talked my way through. But I did and eventually I arrived at my aunt's house.'

Miriam's premonition that it was safer outside the house than inside turned out to be correct. Some time after the liberation she bumped into Motke, the youth who had tried to talk her out of leaving. 'He threw his arms around me and kissed me, saying I had saved his life. When I asked what he meant he explained that after thinking things over he had decided to follow my example and break out. Three days after that the Arrow Cross had burst into the house and killed dozens of people.'

In the midst of all this chaos and frenetic life-saving activity, Wallenberg found time to write to his friend and partner in Stockholm, Koloman Lauer, to let him know about his wife's family. 'Your relatives are employed at the legation and are still quite well,' he reported in a letter dated 8 December. 'About other individuals I cannot give you any information . . . Because such dramatic events have taken place in the past few days I cannot deal with individual cases. I am so overworked that I am no longer able to look after the fate of individuals.' Wallenberg went on to reveal that he was now employing 340 people in his C Section, while more than 700 people were living in the C Section offices as well. 'The work is unbelievably absorbing,' he wrote, but 'the situation in the town is extremely hazardous. The bandits are chasing people in the streets, beating, killing, and torturing them. Even among my own staff I have had 40 cases where people were abducted and tortured.' But in general, Wallenberg said, he was 'in good spirits and eager for the fray.'

On the same day, Wallenberg wrote to his mother.

*Dearest Mother,*

*I don't know how to atone for my silence, and yet again today all you will receive from me are a few hurried lines via the diplomatic pouch.*

*The situation here is hectic, fraught with danger, and I am terribly snowed under with work ... Night and day we hear the thunder of the approaching Russian guns. Since Szálasi came to power diplomatic activity has been very lively. I myself am almost the sole representative of our embassy in all government departments. So far I have been approximately ten times to the Ministry of Foreign Affairs, have seen the deputy premier twice, the minister of the interior twice, the minister of supply once, and the minister of finance once.*

*I was on pretty close terms with the wife of the foreign minister. Regrettably she has now left for Meran [sic].\* There is an acute lack of food supplies in Budapest, but we managed to stockpile a fair amount in advance. I have the feeling that after the [Russian] occupation it will be difficult to get home and I assume that I will reach Stockholm only around Easter. But all that lies in the future. So far, nobody knows what the occupation will be like. In any event, I shall try to get home as soon as possible.*

*I had firmly believed I would spend Christmas with you. Now I am compelled to send you my Christmas greetings and New Year wishes by this means. I hope that the longed-for peace is not too distant ...*

The letter was typed in German by a secretary who could not take dictation in Swedish. At the bottom Wallenberg scrawled in his own language 'Love to Nina and her little one.'

With the arrival of the next diplomatic pouch from Stockholm Wallenberg received a personal letter from War Refugee Board executive director Pehle commending him on 'the difficult and important work' he had been doing. 'You have made a very great personal contribution ... I wish to express our very deep appreciation for ... the vigor and ingenuity which you brought to our common humanitarian undertaking.'

The effect of Wallenberg's activities in this period was perhaps best summarized by Samu Stern after the war: 'He never tired and

---

\* Baroness Kemény was evacuated with other government wives and families – and most of the diplomatic corps – on 29 November. Wallenberg went to see her off at the station, taking a bunch of flowers.

was at work day and night. He saved human lives, travelled, bargained, threatened the interruption of diplomatic relations, was in consultation with the Hungarian government – in short, achieved something that makes him a sort of legendary figure.'

Wallenberg's inventiveness was apparently as boundless as his energy. At a time when the Arrow Cross were attacking protected houses with alarming frequency he thought of a truly original deterrent. Barna Yaron, twenty-two years old and an escapee from a forced labour battalion, was living with his young bride, Judith, in a 'Wallenberg house' in Tatra Street, close to the river.

'Late one night,' he says, 'I received a message asking me to go down to the street where Wallenberg was waiting in his car to see me. Wondering what he might want, I went down. As we sat together in the back of the car he told me he had hit on the idea of starting rumours of a typhus epidemic in the Swedish houses as a ruse to keep the Arrow Cross gangs from daring to enter. But to make it convincing, he said he needed a "genuine" typhus case to report to the city health authorities. Would I be it? I was mystified until he went on to explain that he wanted a volunteer to have an injection that would produce what would look like the symptoms of typhus. Well, I was young and strong in those days, and considered myself something of a daredevil, so I said "What the hell" and agreed, but I can tell you I was really scared. Anyway, we went along to the Jewish clinic for me to get my injection, but it seems that the doctor concerned got cold feet and decided that it really was too dangerous and he might start a real epidemic. So the whole idea was called off, but you can see how Wallenberg's mind was working all the time.'

Wallenberg never forgot the importance of paper-work. He bombarded the Hungarian Foreign Ministry with protest notes every time he had evidence of the violation of a protective pass or the unauthorized entry of a protected house. Since such infringements were happening all the time he was sometimes sending two protests a day to the Foreign Ministry. In the first half of November he sent twenty. They had their effect. Ministry officials, worn down by this relentless paper assault, would plead with police, gendarmerie, and Arrow Cross officials to leave the Swedish-protected Jews alone.

Thanks to Wallenberg, it was even possible for some of the Jews to find something to laugh at in this situation. Edit Ernster recalls this grim humour: 'It seems so strange, this country of super-Aryans – the Swedes – taking us under their wing. Often, when an Orthodox Jew went by, in his hat, beard, and sidelocks, we'd say: "Look, there goes another Swede."'

Overworked as he was, and concerned with the fate of thousands, Wallenberg nevertheless found time for acts of individual kindness. All hospitals were barred to Jews and conditions in the houses were atrociously overcrowded and insanitary. When Wallenberg heard that the wife of Tibor Vándor, a young Jew who was working on his C Section staff in a legation office in Tigris Street, was about to have a baby, he swiftly rounded up a doctor, taking him and the young couple to his flat in Ostrom Street. There, he turned his own bed over to Agnes, the young mother-to-be, and went out into the corridor to sleep. In the small hours of the morning he was awakened by the doctor, who told him that Agnes Vándor had given birth to a healthy baby girl. Wallenberg went in to inspect the new arrival and the Vándors begged him to be her godfather. He consented happily and the child was named Yvonne Maria Eva.

This episode had an extraordinary sequel thirty-five years later, when it was described in the course of a long article on Wallenberg in *The Star*, a Toronto daily. Mrs Yvonne Singer, who read the article, recognized the circumstances of her own birth and was greatly moved. But she phoned the newspaper to say they had made a mistake: her parents were not Jewish. But there was no mistake: it turned out that her mother and father, determined to blot out a legacy that had brought only suffering, had brought her up to believe they were a Christian family. So set were they on this course that when she grew up and fell in love with a Jew they forbade her to marry him. She defied them, converted to Judaism, and married the man of her choice. It was ironical to discover, through the article, that she was Jewish by birth.

To Eichmann, dedicated as he was to the idea that not a single Jew should escape, Wallenberg's increasingly effective interference in his operation became intolerable – so much so that one day towards the end of November he completely lost control and, within the hearing of a Swedish Red Cross representative, shouted, 'I will kill that Jew-dog Wallenberg!'

This remark quickly got back to Carl Ivar Danielsson, the Swedish minister in Budapest and Wallenberg's nominal chief, who lost no time in passing the story on to Stockholm. Within a few days, the Swedish ambassador in Berlin, Arvid Richert, called on the Nazi Foreign Office to protest at this crude threat to the life of a Swedish diplomat. Gerhard von Erdmannsdorff, the German official who received the ambassador, tried to calm Swedish outrage by saying he felt sure the remark – if indeed it had been made at all – could hardly have been meant seriously. However, he said, Eichmann's irritation might perhaps be partly justified: by all accounts, he said, Herr Wallenberg's behaviour was somewhat unconventional, if not downright illegal.

A Foreign Ministry telegram to Veesenmayer in Budapest conveyed the Swedish complaint and it may be assumed that the word was passed to Eichmann that no matter how infuriating he might find Wallenberg's activities, no attempts must be made on his life – at least, none that could possibly be traced back to the Germans; at this stage of the war, Germany could ill afford a serious difference with Sweden.

However, Eichmann *was* apparently responsible for at least one attempt on Wallenberg's life. On an evening early in December 1944 Wallenberg's diplomatic car was rammed by a heavy truck, which then sped off into the night. Though the car was almost a total wreck, Wallenberg and his driver, Langfelder, emerged shaken but unscathed.

According to Lars Berg, also a secretary at the Swedish legation, Wallenberg marched straight into Eichmann's headquarters at the Hotel Majestic and protested. Eichmann deplored the 'accident' but, as Wallenberg left, he smiled and said, 'I will try again.'

Berg and Göte Carlsson, another legation secretary, were fascinated witnesses of a memorable confrontation between Eichmann and Wallenberg shortly before this incident. Wallenberg had decided to invite Eichmann to dinner with his deputy Krumey; he wanted to meet the SS man face to face and try to find out what made him tick. Eichmann, no doubt inspired by a similar curiosity, accepted. On the day in question Wallenberg, having been called out on some urgent business concerning 'his' Jews, completely forgot the invitation he had offered and got home just in time to see an SS car drive up to his apartment block and disgorge Eichmann and Krumey. He had no food to speak of in the house and had given his manservant the night off. As Eichmann and Krumey came up the stairs, Wallenberg hurriedly telephoned Berg and Göte Carlsson, who were living nearby in a house rented from a nobleman who had fled the city. Could they help out? Wallenberg asked, and to his great relief they could. Berg's description of the evening, as recounted in his memoirs, is worth quoting at length.

There was no panic in my house . . . [it] was fully equipped and we had taken over the noble family's staff of servants, including the most exquisite cook. She was used to the unlimited resources of a Hungarian manor-house and to cooking for many people, and in spite of food rationing and the fact that Göte and I were only two, we were never able to change her habits. Usually this extravagance worried us . . . but this particular evening we were very grateful for it. Raoul arrived with his Germans and while Göte and I were doing our best with the cocktail shaker the table was laid with the count's best china and silverware. Thanks to our excellent cook the dinner was a success and I am sure that Eichmann never found out about Wallenberg's forgetfulness.

But if the dinner itself was confined to the pleasures of good food, fine wine, and inconsequential chatter, what followed was a good deal more difficult for Eichmann to stomach. The two Germans and three Swedes moved into the living-room and, after coffee had been poured, Wallenberg put out the lights and pulled back the curtains from the east-facing windows. 'The effect was tremendous,' Carlsson recalled later. 'The horizon was bright red from the fire of thousands of guns as the Russians closed in on Budapest.' Berg describes what happened next:

Wallenberg, who on this occasion had no special wish to negotiate with Eichmann, started a discussion about Nazism and the likely outcome of the war. Fearlessly and brilliantly he picked Nazi doctrine apart, piece by piece, and foretold the total defeat of its adherents. These were rather unusual words, perhaps, for a Swede far from his country and more or less at the mercy of a powerful German opponent. But that was always Wallenberg's way. I think his intention was not so much to put his own views forward as to pass on a warning to Eichmann that he would do well to stop the deportation and extermination of the Hungarian Jews.

Eichmann could scarcely conceal his amazement that anyone should dare to attack him and criticize the Führer, but he soon seemed to realize that he was getting the worst of the argument. His propaganda phrases sounded hollow compared with Raoul's intelligent reasoning. Finally, Eichmann said: 'I admit that you are right, Herr Wallenberg. I have never believed in Nazism, as such, but it has given me power and wealth. I know that this pleasant life of mine will soon be over. My planes will no more bring me women and wine from Paris, or delicacies from the Orient. My horses, my dogs, my luxurious quarters here in Budapest will soon be taken over by the Russians and I myself, as an SS officer, will be shot on the spot.

'For me there will be no escape, but if I obey my orders from Berlin and exercise my power harshly enough I may prolong my respite for some time here in Budapest. I warn you, therefore, Herr Legationssekretar, that I will do my best to stop you, and your Swedish diplomatic passport will not help you if I find it necessary to have you removed. Accidents do happen, even to a neutral diplomat.'

With these words, Eichmann stood up to leave, but not at all displaying any anger. With the imperturbable politeness of a well-educated German, he bade farewell to Raoul and thanked us for a particularly pleasant evening. Perhaps Raoul did not win very much by his direct attack, but it could sometimes be a great pleasure for a Swede to speak his mind to an SS officer.

# *Chapter 9*

Wallenberg enlisted, or bought, the aid and co-operation of many people in his rescue operations and wherever possible co-ordinated his efforts with those of others, such as the active Swiss consul, Charles Lutz, and the Swedish Red Cross representative, Waldemar Langlet. Yet perhaps his most fruitful collaboration was with the infinitely resourceful and audacious László Szamosi, a Jew who accomplished the remarkable feat of becoming *de facto* ambassador of Franco Spain in the final stages of the siege of Budapest.

Szamosi was a wealthy young Budapest real-estate dealer. Before the German intervention in March 1944, he had taken the precaution of selling a valuable downtown building plot for the substantial sum of 100,000 pengös (a good middle-class salary in those days was 1000 pengös a month) and keeping the cash by him in case of sudden need. When the savage restrictions on the Jews were imposed by the Sztójay government, Szamosi bought Christian identification papers for himself, his wife, and their two small children, and the family went on the run, blending with the general population.

For some time, posing as refugees from the provinces overrun by the Red Army, they moved from one lodging to another. Finally, after the Szálasi putsch, Szamosi decided the time had come to stop running. At this time a number of homes were being set up under the nominal patronage of the International Red Cross for the abandoned or orphaned children of Jewish parents who had been rounded up for deportation or already sent to the extermination camps. Szamosi went with his family to one of these homes, where his wife volunteered to help look after the children. 'As for myself,' Szamosi recalls, 'I only wanted to spend a night or two there until I could see how things were shaping up.' But their first evening in the children's home provided an experience which made him decide to stay. He says in his unpublished memoirs that 'A meeting was called by the management, at which there were lengthy discussions about the principles by which the children should be brought up. Although many of the children were infested with lice and suffering from malnutrition, and although the most primitive facilities – such as pots to cook in and dishes to eat from – were lacking, the main point of the discussion was purely hypothetical educational problems.

'I quickly came to the conclusion that my first task should be to attend to the most urgent wants of the children. Then, for all I cared, the management could provide whatever kind of education they saw fit – provided, of course, that the Arrow Cross and the Nazis would allow it.'

By this time, the Jews of Budapest were under permanent curfew and allowed out of their houses for only one hour a day, frightened figures who would scuttle about the streets in frantic search of food and other essentials in the hour allotted to them. Szamosi, thanks to his Christian identification papers, his impeccable Aryan appearance, and a good deal of cool nerve, was able to move about the city freely. The morning after arriving at the children's home, he called on a wholesaler and purchased, at his own expense, dishes, cutlery, soap, paraffin, delousing powder, and other essentials. Then he went to a friendly Gentile who owned a pasta factory and bought 300 kilos of macaroni, which, together with the other goods, he drove back to the children's home in a borrowed van.

'These quick and efficient measures, carried out without any previous conferences, aroused the interest of the children's home,' Szamosi says. 'I finally convinced them that the purpose of this home should be not to provide relative security to the management – whose numbers nearly equalled those of the children – or to discuss pedagogic questions, but to save the lives of as many children as possible.'

Through his work at the children's home in Dob Street, Szamosi quickly became a member of the A Section of the International Red Cross in Budapest, which had overall responsibility for the welfare of parent-less Jewish children. The Swiss official representative of the IRC, Frederic Born, had few staff and few resources and was happy to leave the A Section in the control of undercover Jews, headed by the Zionist leader Ottó Komoly. Komoly had links with another underground Zionist cell which specialized in forging Aryan documents and foreign protection passes. They had tried their hand at the Wallenberg passports, but finding these too difficult to copy convincingly, had concentrated on the Swiss *Schutzpasse*, which they turned out in large numbers.*

Szamosi had a typewriter with the same typeface as the machine that had printed the Swiss passes. He and his wife would find out from the children who were brought to the home the names of their parents who had been taken away for deportation and herded temporarily into a large brickyard on the outskirts of the city. When they knew the names they would type them onto the passes. Armed with his IRC credentials, Szamosi would go to the brickyard and get his new 'protégés' extracted from the transports. It was on one of these missions that he first encountered Wallenberg, doing the same thing. 'He seemed at first rather quiet and reserved, a gentle man, almost effeminate,' Szamosi recalls. 'I soon found out how deceptive this first impression could be.'

When the death marches began in early November 1944 he made another vital contact – Zoltán Farkas, a Gentile former acquaintance who was then legal adviser to the Spanish embassy. Through Farkas, he quickly got an introduction to the chargé d'affaires, Angel Sans-Riz. Appealing to him with all the moral authority of the Red Cross, Szamosi got Sans-Riz to agree that, in addition to the few Spanish-descended Jews already under his country's protection, he would help other Jews by issuing a substantial number of extra protective passes, without inquiring too closely into antecedents. Once again, Szamosi went around collecting parents' names from abandoned

* In their zeal to save lives this group produced 120,000 Swiss passes, which so devalued them that they eventually became virtually worthless.

children and then turned the lists over to the Spanish embassy for the passes to be issued. He wrote: 'I then arranged with Wallenberg that he should join to his Swedish list the Spanish and Swiss lists, which I would hand over to him. Similarly, some safe-conducts were issued by the Papal Nunciature, and I asked Wallenberg to take these to the frontier too. While Wallenberg and his assistants were going to the frontier I persuaded Farkas to get in touch on behalf of the Spanish embassy with the Hungarian officials at the border and send them money to make sure that our lists were honoured. I supported my argument by signing over to Farkas one of my valuable building sites in Buda.'

Whenever Wallenberg sent a group of rescued Jews back from the frontier by train, Szamosi would go out to meet them and help get them safely into Swedish and other protected houses. Since they were generally in a desperate condition after a week on the march and some days packed into cattle cars, and since the streets were constantly being patrolled by Arrow Cross bands, this reception work was no easy matter. Szamosi bribed policemen to help him escort his charges through the streets, brandishing his Red Cross credentials at anyone who made inquiries.

Szamosi had constant battles with the Spanish embassy staff, who complained that the number of protected persons seemed to be far in excess of the number of passes they had issued. They simply refused to deal with the excess. Szamosi solved this and other problems by the simple expedient of getting himself taken on the staff of the seriously undermanned embassy. This was achieved partly through his own contacts with Farkas and Sans-Riz and partly through the good offices of the IRC representative Born, who wrote to the Spanish chargé urging him to give official diplomatic status to both Szamosi and Komoly. Such a thing could perhaps only come about in the chaotic conditions then prevailing in Budapest; soon Szamosi and Komoly were on the embassy staff and the possessors of Spanish diplomatic passports.

In the first week of December things got even better: Sans-Riz and his fellow-Spaniards fled from Budapest, rather than risk capture by the Soviets, leaving Szamosi to all intents and purposes in sole charge of the one foreign mission which recognized the Szálasi régime as legitimate. Szamosi and Komoly thus had all the embassy's stamps, seals, and printed forms at their disposal, plus the offices themselves, a car with diplomatic plates, a stock of Spanish flags, and a considerable store of goodwill with their fellow Fascists of the Arrow Cross and the Hungarian government.

Szamosi lost no time taking full advantage of this superb windfall. To the seven hundred Spanish passes so far issued he added hundreds more. He raised the Spanish flag over the children's home in Dob Street, and also over Komoly's headquarters in Munkács Street, thus claiming extraterritorial status as well as Red Cross protection for both of them. One night when Arrow Cross gunmen burst into the home in Dob Street he indignantly read them a lecture on extraterritoriality before reminding them how close a friend Franco was to Hitler and Szálasi. Mumbling apologies, the intruders left.

In moving about the streets – now armed with three different sets of papers and dressed Arrow Cross style in a fur-trimmed coat with a countryman's hat – Szamosi would display similar audacity, striding arrogantly through Arrow Cross cordons instead of trying to avoid them. 'I was dealing with primitive people and most of the time a resolute voice and overbearing manner would do the trick,' he recalls.

To keep up appearances at the embassy, Szamosi felt he really could do with a genuine Spaniard to act as chargé d'affaires under his instructions. Unable to find a Spaniard in Budapest, he settled for the next best thing, an Italian acquaintance named Giorgio Perlasca, who had been living for some years in an apartment in the embassy building. 'Without much ado,' says Szamosi, 'we "appointed" him, and I must say he made an excellent front man.' On the many protest notes which the neutral missions were to send collectively to the Hungarian authorities from this time on, Perlasca's name would appear as a signatory together with those of genuine heads of mission, such as Monsignor Rotta and Minister Danielsson. In company with Szamosi he would go out on rescue missions to recover Spanish-protected Jews who had been taken by the Arrow Cross, even sometimes marching into the party houses where the Arrow Cross would torture their captives before killing them. While these desperate rescue missions went on, there was still the constant problem of finding food for the children's homes and then getting it to them through the bombing, shelling, and Arrow Cross roadblocks.

Towards the end of December Szamosi, Wallenberg, and the other neutral diplomats engaged in a desperate verbal battle to prevent the fifteen children's homes and their five thousand inmates being moved forcibly into the enclosed General Ghetto, where it would be almost impossible to feed or care for them. On Christmas Eve the diplomatic corps sent a protest note, drafted by Wallenberg, to Szálasi himself. 'Even in war,' they said, 'conscience and the law condemn hostile actions against children. Why, therefore, force these innocent creatures to live in places where the poor mites will see nothing but misery, pain, and desperation? Every civilized nation respects children, and the whole world will be painfully surprised should traditionally Christian and gallant Hungary decide to institute steps against the little ones.'*

But even as Wallenberg's protest note was being delivered, Arrow Cross gunmen were celebrating the birth of Christ by bursting into one of the smaller, unprotected children's homes and slaughtering seven orphans inside. All the efforts of Wallenberg, Szamosi, and the others did not suffice to prevent the most appalling suffering among the children. The management of most of the homes remained intact, but in the final phase of the siege some staff simply fled, leaving the children unattended.

Hans Weyermann, newly arrived IRC representative who replaced Born, reported from one such home: 'Children of two to fourteen years, famished, ragged, emaciated to mere skeletons, frightened to death by the droning of planes and the detonation of bombs, had crept into corners. Their bodies were eaten by filth and scabies, their rags were infested with lice. Huddled up in fear and misery, they made inarticulate sounds. They had not eaten for a long time, and for many days there had been nobody to look after them. Nobody knows where their nurses had gone or when they ran away.'

* This calculated thrust struck home. Szálasi postponed the transfer until New Year's Eve. The children never were moved; by that time things had begun to fall apart altogether.

So desperate was the condition of the children that for many the Russian 'liberation' of the city came too late. Despite the improved food and medical supplies and the continued efforts of the Red Cross – including the tireless László Szamosi – the children from the homes died by the hundreds during January, February, and March 1945.

László Szamosi survived the war and Russian occupation and made his way with his wife and children to British-ruled Palestine, later Israel, where he founded a real-estate business in Haifa. Looking back on those hectic and tragic months in Budapest, he stresses: 'Whatever any of the rest of us may have achieved, it was Wallenberg who was the driving force of the whole rescue operation. It was his idea to co-ordinate the efforts of the Swedish, Swiss, Spanish, Portuguese missions, the Papal Nunciature, and the Red Cross. We all worked in close co-operation under his leadership.'

## *Chapter 10*

Despite his bluster on the night of the dinner party with Wallenberg, Eichmann had no intention of staying behind in Budapest to be killed by the Russians. As the Red Army closed its ring around the Hungarian capital he ordered his Kommando to get ready to move out. But first he had two plans to set in motion. The first, the execution of all the members of the Jewish Council, he intended to supervise personally. The second, the massacre of the entire remaining Jewish population in one lightning action, would have to be delayed until the inhabitants of the International Ghetto could be moved into the General Ghetto. This extermination action would be carried out by Waffen SS troops and the Arrow Cross, if necessary after Eichmann's departure. Early in the evening of 22 December 1944 one of Eichmann's assistants telephoned Jewish Council headquarters inside the fenced-off General Ghetto, where 75,000 people were crammed into 243 houses and 'policed' by a force of 800 Gentiles appointed by the Arrow Cross government. The call was taken by the porter, Jakob Takács. Speaking in German, the SS officer ordered Takács to assemble the Jewish Council members at nine o'clock for a meeting with Eichmann.

At nine o'clock that night three SS staff cars entered the ghetto and pulled up outside the building housing the council's offices. Eichmann and two other officers – probably Krumey and Wisliceny – got out of the middle car, accompanied by a trooper with a sub-machine gun. The two escorting cars were packed with heavily armed troopers. Eichmann marched up to the porter's lodge and knocked peremptorily. 'Well, where are they?' he demanded of Takács.

The porter was puzzled, and frightened. 'The Jewish Council members,' snapped Eichmann, 'where are they?'

Takács protested, 'I was told to get them here for nine o'clock in the morning.' Eichmann flew into a fury. Takács pleaded that his command of German was not too good; he must have misunderstood his instructions on the phone. Hearing the raised voices, Takács's sister emerged from their living quarters to see what was going on. Eichmann drew his service revolver and threatened to shoot both Takács and his sister if the Jewish Council members were not assembled immediately.

The terrified Takács protested that this was not possible. The members had all dispersed to their various houses. It might be possible to find a few, but to round them all up under the prevailing conditions would take all night. Eichmann continued to rage. One of his two colleagues beat Takács repeatedly on the head and shoulders with his pistol butt, leaving him semi-conscious on the floor. Turning to the porter's sister, Eichmann snapped, 'Tell your brother when he comes round that if the entire council is not here at nine in the morning, lined up for inspection, I will keep my word and have both of you shot.'

The next morning, well before nine, the Jewish Council members assembled fearfully. The sight of Takács's heavily bandaged head and his sister's terrified demeanour gave them some idea of what they might expect. But Eichmann never turned up. As the council's diary entry for 23 December records, 'An hour or two, full of anxiety, passed and at last it was learned that the Eichmann detachment had left Budapest most urgently during the night.'

The reason for Eichmann's sudden departure was a swift Soviet thrust late the previous night on the north-western outskirts of the city. Receiving word at the Hotel Majestic after midnight that there was now only one narrow and fast-closing gap through which to escape, Eichmann pulled out in a panic in the small hours of the morning.

So ended Eichmann's personal crusade to ensure the destruction of every last Jew in Hungary. But the Jews of Budapest were by no means out of danger; there was still the Arrow Cross and the German Army.

Compared with Eichmann's methods, those of the Arrow Cross were haphazard and uncoordinated, but they made up in ferocious enthusiasm what they lacked in efficiency. In the final two months of the siege of Budapest they were to murder between ten thousand and fifteen thousand Jews, whom they dragged out of their houses in both ghettos or simply picked up in the streets. Some were hanged from trees and lamp-posts; most were taken to the cellars of the various party houses, where they were horribly tortured before being dragged down to the Danube and shot so that their bodies would be carried away by the river.

The standard Arrow Cross method for such executions was to handcuff the Jews together in threes, strip them naked, line them up facing the river, then shoot the middle of the three in the back of the head. He would drag the other two with him when he fell forward into the river. The Arrow Cross men would then amuse themselves by taking pot-shots at the desperately bobbing heads of the two survivors. This method avoided littering the streets with rotting corpses and also provided some 'sport' for the Arrow Cross killers. The local party headquarters would vie with each other in savagery; one party house was especially notorious for its practice of burning out the eyes of its victims with red-hot nails before taking them for execution.

A particularly active 'Death Brigade' was commanded by a Minorite monk named Father Andras Kun. When he led his band of gunmen through the streets he wore the cowl and cassock of his order, with a rope and a gunbelt at his waist, and sported a death's-head arm-band. He was personally credited with at least five hundred murders. In one night alone, he and his men slaughtered two hundred Jews, invoking the name of the Saviour as they did so. At Father Kun's trial before a People's Court after the liberation, a witness described how, in conducting a mass execution of staff and patients at a Jewish hospital in Buda, Kun had lined up his victims in front of a mass grave and given the firing-squad the order 'In the holy name of Jesus Christ, fire!'

Some of the most notorious Arrow Cross killers were women. A Mrs Vilmos Salzer, described as a woman of 'good' family and superior education, used to wear a grey riding-habit and brown boots as she went about her murderous business clutching a riding crop and a Thompson sub-machine gun. One of her milder forms of entertainment was to burn the most sensitive parts of her female victims' bodies with a candle flame before killing them. She and Father Kun were among many Arrow Cross Death Brigade leaders to be hanged after trial by People's Courts.

One of the Death Brigades' countless victims was the Zionist leader Ottó Komoly, who had worked closely with Wallenberg and Lászlo Szamosi. His International Red Cross and Spanish embassy credentials failed to stop him being dragged away to his death on New Year's Eve. Indeed, under the anarchic and totally lawless conditions which then prevailed it was extremely dangerous even for a genuine Gentile or a bona fide foreign diplomat to be out on the streets. The Death Brigades would frequently disregard legitimate identification papers, and if they felt any doubt about the genuineness of a male suspect's papers, he would be made to display his genitals; for those who were circumcised it meant certain death.

The Death Brigades did not operate entirely without interference. A small band of Aryan-looking young Jews belonging to the underground Hashomer Hatzair organization and equipped with Arrow Cross outfits and forged party cards did manage on a few occasions to liberate groups of Jewish captives. Above all, there was the ubiquitous Wallenberg.

By the end of 1944, with Minister Danielsson's approval, Wallenberg had moved across the river to Pest, the eastern half of the twin city, where the two ghettos were located. Whatever semblance of authority had existed there before had almost completely disintegrated by now. The government had fled, leaving Pest in the uncertain control of the Arrow Cross Party, the police, and the Wehrmacht. Wallenberg began immediately to hunt for sympathetic or bribable contacts among the Arrow Cross and the police, and again his luck and resourcefulness held. At police headquarters he met Pál Szalay, a high-ranking Arrow Cross man who, as a senior police officer, acted as liaison officer between the party and the police. Szalay was quickly to become an invaluable if unlikely ally.*

His motives were almost certainly more than mere self-preservation, for although Wallenberg undoubtedly made the initial contact by use of his well-tried stick-and-carrot technique, it seems that a close relationship of mutual confidence and respect rapidly developed. Szalay admired Wallenberg's courage. There is also reason to believe that, although an ideological anti-Semite, he was genuinely horrified by the atrocities committed by his fellow party-members.

At Szalay's suggestion, Wallenberg took up residence at the abandoned apartment of the authoress Magda Gábor, the flat where he had had his meetings with the Baroness Kemény. Szalay posted two of his most trusted plainclothes policemen there; for the first time, Wallenberg had a round-the-clock bodyguard. At Wallenberg's suggestion, Szalay detailed 100 policemen to the General Ghetto to deter Arrow Cross incursions. When a 'protected' house in Revai Street was attacked on New Year's Day, Wallenberg rushed to the scene with an armed escort provided by Szalay and arrived in time to save the eighty Jewish occupants from certain death.

He was not always in time, though. The same week, another protected house in Legrady Karoly Street was raided and, by the time Wallenberg got to the scene, forty 'Swedish' Jews had been dragged out and murdered. On 8 January, 180 men, women, and children were dragged from another protected house in Jokai Street and slaughtered on the riverbank.

After this atrocity Wallenberg appealed to Szalay to find the men to post permanent and substantial guards on all the houses of the International Ghetto. With the help of money bribes – for Wallenberg still had seemingly inexhaustible amounts of cash on hand – and the promise of Swedish protection after the inevitable fall of Budapest, Szalay managed to round up enough men to do the job adequately. After 8 January there were no more successful attacks on

---

* Szalay was, in fact, the only prominent Arrow Cross man to escape execution after the liberation of Budapest. In recognition of his energetic efforts in co-operation with Wallenberg, a People's Court cleared him of all charges and set him free.

protected houses. Wallenberg felt so indebted to Szalay that – as Szalay was to recall later – he told him, 'After the war I want to take you to Sweden with me to meet the King.'

In the midst of all this, Wallenberg had been fighting another battle. On 2 January Dr Erno Vajna, a brother of the interior minister and 'The Representative of the Arrow Cross Party for Defending Budapest,' had issued an ominous decree. Within three days all the Jews of the International Ghetto were to be transferred on foot to the General Ghetto. Although Wallenberg did not know the reason for this move, he could make a guess. He quickly drafted a protest note to the general officer commanding the German garrison. Wallenberg pointed out that within three days – the date of the proposed transfer – the 75,000 Jews of the General Ghetto would be starving. The individual daily ration was 690 calories a day – by comparison with 1500 calories for the inmates of Hungarian prisons – and 'it is impossible for the Jews to obtain more food by their own efforts as they are not permitted to leave the ghetto.'* For the 35,000 Jews of the International Ghetto, Wallenberg wrote, the position was similar. He added: 'It would be absolutely impossible for them to taken even the minutest quantity of food with them on such a foot march. For humane reasons, this plan must be described as utterly crazy and inhuman.'

The next day Wallenberg followed up his written protest with a personal visit to Wehrmacht headquarters at the Astoria Hotel. There, he demanded, and got, an interview with the town major, whom he pointedly reminded that Sweden was still protecting German interests in many countries. He added that his country could only carry out its obligations as a protective power 'if given the necessary support by the responsible German and Hungarian authorities.' Therefore he demanded an end to the proposed removal of Swedish-protected persons and 'full extraterritorial status and full protection' guaranteed to those sheltering under the Swedish flag.

On 4 January 1945, despite these audacious efforts, the protected

---

* On the limited black market operating inside the General Ghetto, the rate for a loaf of bread was 500 pengös. The official price of rationed bread was 1½ pengös and the black-market price outside the ghetto 10 to 12 pengös.

Jews were told to stand by to move out at an hour's notice. The next day five thousand of them were transferred to the desperately overcrowded and underfed General Ghetto. The situation appeared hopeless, but Wallenberg was not about to admit defeat. He went directly to Erno Vajna to offer a deal: food in return for a cancellation of the transfer. Wallenberg knew that by now the Arrow Cross were also going hungry, and he had larger food stocks hidden away than he had admitted even to some of his closest associates. With this to barter – plus the offer of Swedish protective passes to Vajna and his associates for use when the Russians arrived – Wallenberg was able to strike a bargain.

A letter from Wallenberg to Vajna, dated 6 January, tells its own story: 'I would like to take the opportunity of informing you that I have acquainted His Excellency the Swedish minister with your very friendly remarks concerning Sweden. His Excellency has asked me to voice his deepest gratitude and would like to assure you that the Swedish legation will do everything in its power during these difficult days, as well as in the future, to help the needy and war-afflicted people of Hungary.' Wallenberg had learned well, among all his other lessons, the diplomatic uses of unctuous language.

The letter went on to confirm that 'those stocks of food not required for consumption during the next few days' would be handed over by house wardens to the police. In return the transfers to the General Ghetto would cease and Arrow Cross headquarters would be officially instructed that in the future, Jewish officials in the International Ghetto would be free to move about. Furthermore, 'party authorities are in the future to accord greater respect to those buildings belonging to the legation.'

To prevent the transfer, Wallenberg had taken a gamble on the Russians reaching the International Ghetto before the now seriously depleted food stocks gave out altogether. It was a race against time.

It was about this time that Wallenberg and Per Anger met for the last time. In his memoirs, Anger recalls that Wallenberg came on a short visit to legation headquarters on the western side of the Danube:

I urgently asked him to discontinue his activities and stay with us on the Buda side of the Danube. The Arrow Cross were obviously after him and he took great risks by continuing his rescue activities. However, Wallenberg refused to listen.

While bombs were exploding all around us, we set out on a visit to SS headquarters, where, among other things, I was to request some kind of shelter for the embassy members. We had to stop the car repeatedly because the road was blocked with dead people, horses, burnt-out trucks, and débris from bombed houses. But danger did not stop Wallenberg. I asked him whether he was afraid. 'It is frightening at times,' he said, 'but I have no choice. I have taken upon myself this mission and I would never be able to return to Stockholm without knowing that I've done everything that stands in a man's power to rescue as many Jews as possible.' During the conversation with the SS general [Obergruppenführer Erich von dem Bach-Zelewsky], Wallenberg tried to obtain guarantees that the Jews in the Swedish houses would not be liquidated at the last minute. As usual, Wallenberg presented his errand skilfully and intelligently. The SS general listened sceptically but could hardly hide the fact that he was impressed by Wallenberg's behaviour. I particularly recall that part of the discussion when the German suddenly put the somewhat unexpected question to Wallenberg: '*Sie kennen Gyula Dessewffy sehr gut? Er hat sich übrigens in Ihrem Haus versteckt!*' (You know G. D. very well? As a matter of fact, he is hiding in your house!)* Dessewffy was a Hungarian aristocrat and journalist who had gone underground at the time of the German invasion. He was at that time active in the Hungarian resistance movement and the Germans were frantically looking for him.

In the second week of January 1945 Wallenberg's private intelligence service brought him word that Eichmann's plan for the total massacre of the General Ghetto was soon to be carried out. One of Szalay's men told him that the massacre would be done by a combined task force of five hundred Waffen SS men and an unspecified number of Arrow Cross men led by one Father Vilmos

---

* Wallenberg gave shelter to a number of non-Jewish oposition figures, including the Social Democrats Árpád Szakasits and Anna Kethly. The former became president of Hungary (1948–50), the latter Speaker of the Hungarian Parliament. Dessewffy survived the war and became a liberal member of the first post-war Hungarian Parliament.

Lucska, while a force of two hundred policemen were to ring the ghetto fence to make sure that no fleeing Jews escaped the carnage.

Wallenberg hurried to see Vajna, taking Szalay with him for protection. With the usual threats and promises, Wallenberg demanded that 'this monstrous plan' be cancelled. But it seemed that Vajna no longer cared, even about saving his own skin. He readily admitted that he knew all about the planned operation, and that, in fact, he would be playing 'an administrative part in it.' He would do nothing to stop it.

There was now only one man, General August Schmidthuber, who *could* stop the massacre. The general was the overall commander of the SS troops and one of his detachments would spearhead the killer Kommando. For Wallenberg it was too risky to see Schmidthuber in person: the SS had begun hunting for the Swedish diplomat, and the message he wished to convey to Schmidthuber would brand him as a dangerous witness whom it would be only prudent to kill. Szalay, who volunteered to go as Wallenberg's representative, took to Schmidthuber a message to the effect that, if the massacre took place, Wallenberg would see to it that Schmidthuber was held personally responsible and hanged as a war criminal later.

With the Russian advance guard now no more than a couple of hundred yards from the ghetto and inching forward constantly, the massacre had to be carried out quickly, if at all. There would be no time to find Wallenberg and silence him first. In a fury of indecision, Schmidthuber paced up and down his command headquarters. Finally his nerve broke. He picked up his telephone and ordered that on no account was the ghetto action to take place. Wallenberg had won his last victory.

When the Russians entered the General Ghetto two days later they found 69,000 Jews alive there. In the International Ghetto they were to find 25,000 survivors, and later on, when they captured the Buda side of the twin city, another 25,000 or so Jews emerged from their hiding places in Gentile homes, in monasteries, convents, and church cellars. In all some 120,000 had survived the Final Solution – the only substantial Jewish community left in Europe.

In the view of Per Anger, Wallenberg's closest colleague, Wallenberg must take the credit for the deliverance of the Jews in the

General Ghetto as well as those in the International Ghetto. 'He was the only foreign diplomat to stay behind in Pest, with the sole purpose of protecting these people. And he succeeded beyond all expectations. If you add them all up, 100,000 or more people owed their lives to him.'

# Chapter 11

During those last desperate weeks in Budapest Wallenberg had been thinking about more than saving lives. He had also found time to ponder on the post-war future of Hungary and its decimated Jewish community. As far back as the beginning of November 1944 he had set up a small department of his C Section, under a brilliant young Jewish economist named Rezsö Müller, with a brief to work out a detailed social and economic relief plan to be put into effect after the Nazi defeat.

Wallenberg had even rented additional office space so that Müller's unit could work undisturbed and in privacy. He had told Müller there would be substantial sums of money available to put the plan into effect, through the War Refugee Board and the American-Jewish Joint Distribution Committee. Müller and his small staff went to work enthusiastically and produced a lengthy document, to which Wallenberg put some finishing touches. In an introductory text, he demonstrated again his special brand of practical idealism, plus more than a little political naïveté.

It was, he stressed, 'a plan which will help its participants to help themselves in a co-operative way.' Wallenberg was lavish in his praise of Müller and his planning staff. 'I have come to know my collaborators during the most testing times. I picked them for their qualities of compassion, honesty, and initiative.' Wallenberg explained that in carrying out the plan 'we propose to use the swiftest avenues open to private initiative. We are, of course, willing to accept governmental assistance and to act in harness with the authorities, providing it will not lead to delay in affording assistance to those who need it.'

The main headings of the plan reveal its comprehensive and practical aspects: the search for missing persons and the reuniting of families; emergency food distribution; help with housing and the distribution of household essentials, such as furniture and bedding; medical care; orphans' homes; an information service; the re-establishment of commercial and business life; the creation of employment opportunities. However, Wallenberg displayed an extraordinary lack of political *nous* if he thought the Soviets would allow a free-lance relief operation, funded from the United States, to operate in territory under their control. It was a brand of naïveté, of course, that was shared by many men of goodwill at that time. It was soon to cost Wallenberg his freedom.

Wallenberg was determined to get his plan as soon as possible to the Hungarian Provisional Government that had been established, under the auspices of the Russians, in the eastern city of Debrecen, 120 miles away. He, therefore, again moved his living quarters in the final days of the siege so that he would be in the path of the fastest line of Soviet advance. Wallenberg had a further motive for getting to Debrecen quickly. He wanted to appeal to Marshal Malinovsky, the Soviet commander, for emergency food and medical supplies for the two ghettos. Accordingly, he and his driver, Langfelder, now installed themselves in a Red Cross house in Benczúr Street. On 13 January a platoon of Russian soldiers moved cautiously up the street, checking every house as they advanced. At number 16 they were puzzled to see the blue-and-yellow Swedish flag. To a somewhat bemused Russian sergeant Wallenberg explained – in his fluent Russian – that he was the Swedish chargé d'affaires for the liberated zone of Hungary.

He asked to speak to a Russian officer and in due course a Major Dimitri Demchinkov arrived at the house. They had a long talk and eventually Demchinkov took Wallenberg and Langfelder to the headquarters of General Tchernishev, commander of the Zuglo District. Wallenberg explained there that he wanted to go to Debrecen to see Malinovsky and the Provisional Government. Tchernishev gave him the necessary permit and appointed Major Demchinkov to accompany him with a two-man escort.

Early in the morning of 17 January Wallenberg and Langfelder returned to Benczúr Street, accompanied by Demchinkov and two soldiers on a motorcycle. Wallenberg collected his personal luggage – the faithful knapsack – and a briefcase one of his staff had been guarding. It contained the rest of his funds, totalling 222,000 pengös – an extremely large sum of money in those days.

From Benczúr Street, Wallenberg drove to a Swedish house in Tatra Street to say good-bye to some of his closest collaborators. One of these, Dr Ernö Petö, rode beside him, with Langfelder at the wheel. Demchinkov followed in the sidecar of the Red Army motorcycle. Wallenberg seemed in good spirits. He told Petö the Russians had been looking after him well. Then, pointing out of the back window to his escort, he quipped prophetically: 'I don't know if they're protecting me or watching me. I'm not sure if I'm their guest or their prisoner.'

At number 6 Tatra Street, Wallenberg went upstairs and spoke to his Jewish assistants, while his Soviet escort waited out in the street. Wallenberg explained to Reszö Müller that he was going to Debrecen with his relief plan, then took 100,000 pengös out of his briefcase and handed them over, telling Müller to use the money for immediate expenses. Ödön Gergely, who was also present, recalls Wallenberg's good mood and keenness to get to Debrecen. 'He expected to be back at the most within eight days.'

Dr Petö again accompanied Wallenberg and Langfelder when they left the house in Tatra Street, once again escorted by Demchinkov and his two men. A few blocks away they had a collision with a Red Army truck. According to Petö's account, 'the Russians were furious and dragged Langfelder out of the driver's seat. God knows what might have happened, but just at that moment the motorcycle with the Russian major arrived and he put an end to the altercation.'

Dr Petö adds, 'At the corner of Benczúr Street, I got out, wished Wallenberg all the best on his adventurous trip, and that was the last I saw of him.'

It is the last that anyone has ever seen of Raoul Wallenberg as a free man.

# PART TWO

———

*Gulag*

# *Chapter 12*

For the Jews of Budapest the nightmare was over. For Wallenberg it was just beginning. Soon after arriving at Marshal Malinovsky's headquarters at Debrecen – perhaps even somewhere *en route* – Wallenberg and his driver, Vilmos Langfelder, were handed over to the NKVD, as the KGB were then designated. By the first week of February 1945 they were in separate cells in Moscow's Lubianka Prison, the principal interrogation centre of the Soviet secret police.

It was a while before Wallenberg's friends and associates in Budapest became concerned at his failure to return. Initially, his colleagues at Swedish legation headquarters in Buda did not even know he was gone. The fighting on that side of the river was to continue until the end of February. The Jewish leaders in Pest had expected him to be gone for a week or two, given the distance to Debrecen, the likelihood of bureaucratic delay, and the generally chaotic state of affairs in a country still at war. In any case, though freed from the fear of annihilation by the Nazis and the Arrow Cross, the Jews – like most others in Budapest – still had a struggle for self-preservation in the 'liberated' capital. The Soviet arrival did not bring with it a flood of food and medical supplies and the Red Army behaved loutishly. For everyone, but especially for the de-vitalized Jews, living conditions remained desperately difficult.

In Stockholm, there seemed no cause for alarm. The Swedish

ambassador in Moscow, Staffan Söderblom, had already informed his Foreign Office that Soviet Deputy Foreign Minister Vladimir Dekanosov had notified him by letter on 16 January that Wallenberg was in Russian hands. 'The Russian military authorities have taken measures to protect Raoul Wallenberg and his belongings,' said the note. There was no reason to believe that he would not soon be home.

During February, Wallenberg's mother, Maj von Dardel, called on the Soviet ambassador to Stockholm, Mme Alexandra Kollontai, who told her not to worry: Raoul was safe in Russia and would be back soon. At about the same time Mme Kollontai gave similar information to the wife of the Swedish foreign minister, Christian Günther, adding that it would be better if the Swedish government made no fuss, since this might only delay Wallenberg's return.

In Hungary, on 8 March, the Jews of Budapest and others who had cause to care about his fate were shocked to hear on the Russian-controlled Kossuth Radio that Wallenberg had been murdered *en route* to Debrecen, probably by Hungarian Fascists or 'agents of the Gestapo.' The Swedish Foreign Office immediately cabled Ambassador Söderblom to seek more information from the Russians. Dekanosov promised him that urgent inquiries would be made about the radio report. Meanwhile, Mme Kollontai had been brought back to Moscow for other duties. Söderblom contacted her, too, reminding her of her earlier assurance to Mrs von Dardel.

The Swedish public were beginning to be concerned. They had learned of Wallenberg's exploits in Budapest through a front-page interview in Stockholm's leading morning daily, *Dagens Nyheter*. This reported the stirring account of his rescue operations, as told by a Hungarian Jew who had just arrived in Sweden.

The Americans also began showing official concern. On 4 April Minister Johnson in Stockholm cabled the State Department, urging that his opposite number in Moscow, Averell Harriman, be instructed to help the Swedish legation there in their representations to the Russians, 'as we had a special interest in Wallenberg's mission to Hungary.' On 9 April US secretary of state Edward Stettinius cabled Ambassador Harriman to give 'all possible support' to the Swedes.

US treasury secretary Henry Morgenthau, Jr, added his considerable weight to the official American concern about Wallenberg. A copy of Johnson's cable of 4 April reached his office, via General William O'Dwyer, the new executive director of the War Refugee Board. Morgenthau scrawled across the bottom, 'Let Stettinius know that I am personally interested in this man.'

On 19 April Minister Johnson reported from Stockholm: 'Local newspapers today comment extensively on arrival in Stockholm of the Swedish legation staff from Budapest and particularly the absence of attaché Raoul Wallenberg, who has been missing since January 17. In view of the special interest which the Department and the War Refugee Board had in Wallenberg's mission, as well as our own deep anxiety for his safety, it is suggested that the United States government communicate to the Swedish government its concern in the matter.'

Acting Secretary of State James Grew cabled back two days later instructing Johnson to inform the Swedish government of America's 'great concern and sore distress.' On 30 April the State Department sent a cable to its newly opened mission in Soviet-occupied Hungary, instructing it to ask the Russian military authorities for information about Wallenberg 'and expressing the concern of this Government in his welfare.'

On 12 May George Warren, Stettinius's adviser on refugees and displaced persons, wrote to the WRB's General O'Dwyer asking him to assure Treasury Secretary Morgenthau that the State Department would pursue the Wallenberg inquiry 'as long as any possibilities of information remain to be explored.' What he did not tell O'Dwyer – possibly because it had not yet been drawn to his attention – was that the American offer to help the Swedes had, astonishingly, been rebuffed. Ambassador Söderblom had, in effect, told Ambassador Harriman to mind his own business; the Swedes would handle the Wallenberg affair without American help.

It was to take twenty years for the story of this extraordinary, and perhaps fatal, snub to be made public. Two other blunders of comparable magnitude were perpetrated a year after the rebuff to Harriman: these did not come to light until January 1980 – thirty-five years after Wallenberg's arrest. Together, these miscalculations led to Wallenberg's abandonment to a cruel fate in the Gulag Archipelago, where some believe he may have survived into a bitter old age.

It is clear from the record that Ambassador Söderblom became convinced very early in the game that Wallenberg was dead and that there was therefore no point in annoying the Russians with persistent inquiries about him. As early as 14 April 1945 he was cabling his Foreign Office that Wallenberg had 'probably been killed,' and held out little hope that the matter would ever be 'cleared up.' On 19 April he wrote to his Foreign Office more explicitly on this point: 'What I fear is that the Russians, however much they might like to, cannot clarify what has happened. Firstly there is great disorder in Hungary. Secondly, the troops who were in Budapest in January have now moved to Vienna. Further, one must unfortunately consider it unlikely that Marshal Tolbukhin's headquarters and troops can find time at present to look into a case of this kind.' In a 'strictly confidential' note to Harald Fallenius, under-secretary for administration at the Foreign Office, Söderblom gave his opinion that he thought it 'possible that Wallenberg fell victim to a fatal car crash or was murdered during the journey from Budapest to the east, his disappearance going unnoticed in the general confusion which reigned in the area.'

Foreign Minister Günther was more sceptical. On 21 April he cabled Söderblom a 'definite instruction' to go to Dekanosov and ask for a full investigation. Söderblom had no choice but to comply, though with how much vigour we may guess from a remark in his next message home: 'As I have said before, it is unfortunately possible that it may remain an unsolved riddle.'

On 1 July the Swedish Foreign Office got a message from its embassy in Berne, Switzerland, quoting 'an absolutely reliable source' from Budapest who said he had seen a third party in the Hungarian capital who in turn claimed to have seen Wallenberg alive and well in Pest in April, disguised behind a beard and living incognito. This information was passed on, for what it was worth, to Söderblom in Moscow. On 6 July he cabled Stockholm to say he had received it 'just as I was about to make a *démarche* to the Soviet Foreign Ministry.' As a result, he had held back, thinking that Wallenberg might be hiding from the Russians, having escaped from them. He might pop up in Istanbul or Berne and 'tell sensational stories to the press.'

This, said Söderblom, would put him in 'a very unpleasant position' *vis-à-vis* the Russians, so obviously he should do nothing for the time being. The Foreign Office cabled back six days later to say the report from Berne was very speculative and little more than rumour. He should carry on the Wallenberg inquiries 'by all available means.' But Söderblom apparently preferred to rely on the rumour. 'I take it that as long as you do not hear further from the Swiss source it will not be appropriate for me to take further action in the case,' he cabled on 14 August.

Söderblom's role in the rejection of the American offer of help is partly revealed in the communications so far made public between him and his Foreign Office – but only partly because of the suspicion, widely held by the Swedish press, that a key cable from Söderblom was doctored. We have seen how, on 9 April 1945, Stettinius cabled Harriman in Moscow to give 'all possible support' to the Swedes. On 12 April* Harriman cabled back saying 'the Swedes say they have no reason to think the Russians are not doing what they can and they do not feel that an approach to the Soviet Foreign Office on our part would be desirable.'

However, Söderblom, in his 'strictly confidential' letter to Foreign Office Under-Secretary Fallenius on 19 April, said that he 'presumed that the American representation in Hungary has been approached through the State Department. The US embassy in Moscow is otherwise hardly likely to feel that anything was to be done for America's part.' This confused and turgid quotation was released to the Swedish news media in February 1965, after a Swedish television programme had raised serious questions about the failure of Söderblom to act on America's offer of help.

As a US embassy official observed in a report to the State

---

* This was the date of President Roosevelt's death. Obviously, Ambassador Harriman had matters other than Wallenberg on his mind.

Department, 'the fact that the Foreign Office press release used a partial and confusing quote of Minister Söderblom's without publication of the full text of the message . . . has aroused the suspicions of the Swedish press.' It certainly had. The matter was taken up editorially in *Dagens Nyheter*. 'One must ask why that telegram was not quoted in full. The customary secretiveness? . . . The negative Swedish attitude caused the American interest to decline. The fact is that a Swedish *démarche* concerning Raoul Wallenberg was made shortly afterwards in Moscow. But would not an American action have carried much more weight at that time?'

The *Göteborgs-Handelstidningen* expressed a similar view: 'Unfortunately one has reason to suspect that the Swedish version was doctored. The Americans were eager, but it is doubtful whether the same could be said about the Swedish legation.'

Fifteen years after these disclosures, the story of Söderblom's second major blunder came to light with the release, at the end of January 1980, of 1900 pages of hitherto secret Swedish Foreign Office documents relating to the Wallenberg affair.* Among these – and quite the most remarkable – were Ambassador Söderblom's notes on a meeting he had with Stalin on 15 June 1946, before he left Moscow to take up a new appointment.

Söderblom was obviously bowled over by the honour of being received by the Soviet leader, who usually saw only the American and British ambassadors, and then only if they were bringing personal messages from their heads of government, at that time Harry Truman and Clement Attlee.

'Stalin seemed fit and in vigorous good health,' wrote Söderblom. 'His short but well-proportioned body and his regular features made an especially agreeable impression. His tone of voice and demeanor gave an impression of friendliness.'

In the course of their conversation, Stalin asked Söderblom if

---

* According to Foreign Office Secretary-General Leif Leifland, twenty-five pages were omitted from the document collection for legal reasons. Leifland insisted that nothing which might embarrass the government had been suppressed.

there was anything he could do for him. Söderblom mentioned the case of Wallenberg. 'You say his name was Wallenberg?' asked Stalin.

'Yes, Wallenberg,' said Söderblom, and spelt it out for the Soviet dictator, who wrote the name on a pad in front of him.

After Söderblom had recounted briefly how, according to Dekanosov, Wallenberg had been taken under Soviet protection, to be seen later leaving for Debrecen under escort, Stalin said: 'I suppose you know that we gave orders for the Swedes [in Budapest] to be protected.'

'Yes,' Söderblom replied, 'and I am personally convinced that Wallenberg fell victim either to a road accident or bandits.'

'Have you not had any definite information on the matter from our side?' inquired Stalin.

'No,' answered Söderblom, 'but I assume that the Soviet military authorities do not have any further reliable information about what happened after that.'

After this astonishing exchange, Söderblom went on to ask for an official statement from the Russians saying that all possible action had been taken to find Wallenberg, though without success, and an assurance that if further information came to light this would be passed on. 'This would be in your own interests,' said Söderblom, 'as there are people who, in the absence of an explanation, would draw the wrong conclusions.'

'I promise you,' Stalin replied, 'that the matter will be investigated and cleared up. I shall see to it personally.'*

If Stalin took Söderblom's remarks as meaning that the Swedish government no longer had any real interest in the Wallenberg affair, this would not be surprising. It may be no coincidence that at about

---

* Stalin's cynical indifference to the fate of Wallenberg – and his refusal even to authorize answers to Maj von Dardel's impassioned appeals to him – contrasts interestingly with the agonies he is said to have suffered at the uncertainty surrounding the fate of his own son, Yakov, a Red Air Force pilot known to have been taken prisoner by the Germans but never found after the war. The British knew Yakov had committed suicide in a POW camp but kept the news from Stalin to spare his feelings.

this very time, according to evidence later accepted by the Swedes as authentic, an NKVD commissar told Wallenberg in the Lefortovo Prison: 'Nobody cares about you.'

After the release of the Söderblom–Stalin document in 1980, the Swedish media challenged Söderblom, then aged seventy-nine and living in comfortable retirement at Uppsala, north of Stockholm, to explain himself. 'I didn't want to make a direct accusation to the Russians that they had killed Wallenberg or something of that kind,' he said. 'It would have made the whole situation more difficult if such an unsuitable suggestion had been made.'

In an interview with *Dagens Nyheter* he denied he had 'declared Wallenberg dead' at his meeting with Stalin. 'The suggestion that he might have died in an accident was only one of the theories I put forward. It was, after all, quite possible given the state of affairs which then existed. Or he could have been robbed by people who thought he was carrying a good deal of money and jewellery.'

Söderblom maintained that it was 'inconceivable' for him to have suggested at that time that the Russians were responsible for Wallenberg's disappearance. Besides, he had believed they really wanted to discover the truth. 'I do not think my behaviour was weak or cowardly. I did what was appropriate under the circumstances: I carried the matter to the highest possible level.'

Söderblom expressed extreme scepticism about the witnesses who have appeared over the years with information that Wallenberg is still alive. 'They have heard about him, and every rumour about a Swede is built up into a fantasy about Raoul Wallenberg.' He did, however, allow that 'the Wallenberg affair is something that haunts one . . . One never stops thinking about it.'

In the view of Tage Erlander, who was Social Democratic prime minister in 1946 and for many years subsequently, 'it was a very dangerous conversation between Söderblom and Stalin, dangerous and perhaps disastrous. It would have been better if it had never taken place.'

Erlander was none too happy about the timing of the release of the documents, which occurred when there was East–West tension over the Soviet invasion of Afghanistan. 'It may be regarded as

Sweden's small contribution to increasing that tension,' he said.*
'On the other hand, it should be remembered that the release of the
documents had been planned for some time. International opinion is
increasingly demanding an explanation of the Wallenberg affair, but
right now the Russians are not too concerned about world opinion.'

At about the time of Söderblom's fateful conversation with Stalin,
a Swedish journalist, Edward af Sandeberg, was released from Soviet
custody. He had been based in Berlin during the war as the
correspondent of a now-defunct Stockholm daily and arrested as a
spy by the Russians. After he got home, in June 1946, and first told
his story to the Swedish Foreign Office, he mentioned something
that one might have supposed would have electrified them. In the
course of his de-briefing he said that during his imprisonment he
had met a Rumanian and a German prisoner, each of whom had told
him independently that they had met a Swedish diplomat named
Wallenberg in prison. Not yet having heard about the Wallenberg
affair, Sandeberg did not realize the significance of this news.
Neither, it seems, did the Swedish Foreign Office; they made no
attempt to follow up his information. Later, when he had discovered
that Wallenberg was a *cause célèbre*, he published newspaper articles
on the matter, but they still ignored him.

The Rumanian mentioned by Sandeberg never turned up, but the
German, Erhard Hille, did after a mass release of Axis prisoners in
mid-1955. What Hille had to say then confirmed exactly what
Sandeberg had reported nine years earlier. Sandeberg believes the
reason for the Foreign Office's indifference was that Foreign Minister
Östen Undén thought he was a Nazi sympathizer, trying to stir up
trouble between Sweden and the Soviet Union. Indeed, Undén is on
record as having later described Sandeberg as 'that Nazi.' According
to Sandeberg, he 'never was, and that can be verified.' It was not
until May 1949, at the request of younger and more vigorous senior
officials at the Foreign Office, that Sandeberg was invited to make a
full statement.

* Sweden did not, however, follow President Jimmy Carter's lead and boycott
the Moscow Olympics, as partisans of Wallenberg had been urging long before
the invasion of Afghanistan.

Another opportunity that was missed occurred after Söderblom's departure from Moscow, when the chargé d'affaires, Ulf Barck-Holst, began pursuing a vigorous new line, hoping to undo the damage done by his former chief. Barck-Holst told the Foreign Office he was going to try for a further interview with Stalin and suggested that Foreign Minister Undén should take the matter up with Soviet Foreign Minister Vyacheslav Molotov at the United Nations in New York. Undén did not act on this suggestion; nor did he give approval to a further suggestion by Barck-Holst: that the Americans should be brought into play, in spite of the rebuff of the previous year.

Undeterred by the string of negative replies from Stockholm, Barck-Holst was suggesting in December 1946 that Undén might make some headway by 'sending a beautiful Christmas present to Mme Kollontai.' Where Söderblom had been over-cautious, Barck-Holst appears naïvely over-enthusiastic. However, he may have been right in believing that at that time some kind of exchange deal might have been struck with the Russians had they been handled correctly. On 30 December he cabled Stockholm to say that 'whenever the Wallenberg question has been raised, as a rule there has immediately been a question whether any favourable information has come in about Makarova, the Balts, or Granovsky.* In this way they have tried to use the Wallenberg case as a kind of basis for negotiations.'

On 14 January 1947 Barck-Holst suggested to Stockholm that they prevail on the Swedish press to stop publicity on the Wallenberg case for a while and prepare an exchange offer to make to the Russians. Barck-Holst said he 'perhaps over-optimistically has the impression that the case has begun to come under active consideration at last,' but could not do anything unless he soon received an acceptable offer to make to the Russians.

There is nothing in the documents released to show whether or not he received any encouragement, though the strong likelihood is

---

* Makarova, the daughter of a senior Red Army officer, had defected to Sweden in 1945, arriving with a group of refugees from the Baltic states annexed by the Soviets; Granovsky was another political refugee. The Russians wanted them all back.

(*Left*) Raoul Wallenberg, age three, with his mother and (*below*), at the same age, with his grandfather. (Photos courtesy of the Wallenberg family)

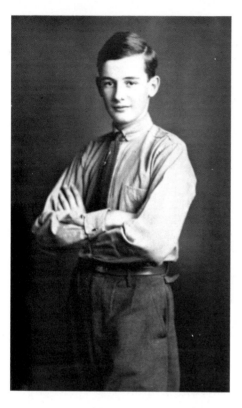

(*Above left*) Raoul Wallenberg, age fourteen.
(*Above*) Wallenberg in Florence, 9 April 1931.
(*Left*) Wallenberg with his mother on high school graduation day.
(Photos courtesy of the Wallenberg family)

A formal portrait, age twenty-four.
(Photo courtesy of the Wallenberg family)

(*Left*) Wallenberg in his
Swedish Army Reserve uniform.
(Photos courtesy of the Wallenberg
family)
(*Above*) Wallenberg (*seated*)
with the Jewish assistants in
his legation section.
(*Below*) Wallenberg (marked
with a cross) intervening
during a deportation at a
railway station.

SCHUTZ-PASS № 75 16

SCHWEDEN  SVÉDORSZÁG

(*Right*) A passport created by Wallenberg. (*Below right*) Jews wearing yellow stars cluster outside the Swedish Legation in Budapest.

Eva Heyman, whose diary is
quoted at length in the text.
(Photo courtesy of
Ghetto Fighters' House)

(*Above*) Women being
driven off at gunpoint
to a "death march".
(*Left*) Budapest Jews
read a notice ordering
them to leave their
homes and move to
the ghetto.
(*Below*) Jewish men
being marched through
Budapest, on their
way to forced labour.
Photograph taken
by Wallenberg.
(Photos courtesy of Ghetto
Fighters' House)

(*Above left*) Jewish community leaders lined up at a provincial concentration camp. (*Above*) A child murdered by the Arrow Cross in a raid on a Jewish children's home. (*Left*) Hungarian gendarmes execute an "uncooperative" Jewish community leader. (*Below*) Jewish women being marched through Budapest to a holding camp, prior to deportation. This photograph was taken by Wallenberg. (Photos courtesy of Ghetto Fighters' House)

(*Above*) Raoul Wallenberg with
his staff: Hugo Wohl, right;
Paul Hegedüs, left.
(*Right*) The last photograph
of Wallenberg, taken in
Budapest on 26 November 1944.
Sent by Raoul to his mother.
(Photos courtesy of the Wallenberg
family)

that the Swedes would never have considered handing over persons to whom political asylum had been granted. After this correspondence was released in 1980, ex-Premier Erlander said, 'The idea of an exchange was never brought up before me, nor would I have been agreeable.' He conceded that it might have been a different matter if the Swedes at that time had held a Soviet spy who could have been exchanged.*

Surveying the whole chapter of events in the two years after Wallenberg's disappearance, Erlander admitted that 'we failed to secure the release of one of our most notable countrymen, one of our greatest. In the continuing efforts to obtain certainty, one must presume that Wallenberg is still alive, otherwise it would be pointless to pursue the matter. It is very likely that he is alive.'

To Nina Lagergren 'it all makes terribly bitter reading. It's like a nightmare to learn how Raoul was abandoned to his fate.'

---

* In the 1960s no attempt was made to swap Colonel Stig Wennerström of the Swedish Air Force. He had been 'turned' by the Soviets when he was military attaché in Moscow in the 1950s and before becoming military attaché in Washington. At his trial in 1963 it was said he was a full-time Soviet agent, holding the rank of a major in the KGB. After serving his twelve-year sentence, with time off for good conduct, Wennerström retired to the country in Sweden. 'We couldn't have exchanged him,' commented a senior Swedish Foreign Office official in 1979. 'He's a Swedish citizen.' Another potential spy swap came to nothing in September 1979. Swedish Defence Ministry employee Stig Bergling, accused of spying for the Soviets, asked the Swedish government through his attorney if he could be exchanged for Wallenberg. According to the government, soundings were made in Moscow, but 'the Russians showed no interest.' Bergling was subsequently jailed for life.

# Chapter 13

After the departure of Söderblom and Barck-Holst from Moscow, more inquiries and memoranda were presented to the Soviet Foreign Ministry by the next ambassador, Gunnar Hägglöf. These received stalling replies until, on 18 August 1947, the Russians, obviously in an effort to put an end to this irritating business once and for all, brought in their senior deputy foreign minister, Andrei Vyshinsky, who up to then had not bothered himself personally with such a paltry matter.

One of the most difficult things to be explained away was the admission, originally made by Dekanosov* on 16 January 1945, that Wallenberg was under the 'protection' of the Soviet military. Vyshinsky dealt with this by saying that while his ministry had, indeed, received a brief message to that effect, 'based on indirect statements by one of the commanders of a military force fighting in Budapest,' it had been impossible to verify that information. The Russian officer who had made the statement had never been found. A search of prisoner-of-war camps and other establishments had turned up no trace of Wallenberg. In short, 'Wallenberg is not in the Soviet Union and is unknown to us.' The note concluded with the 'assump-

* Dekanosov was known as one of Stalin's top diplomatic hatchet men. He had been the Soviet ambassador in Berlin up to the time of the Nazi invasion of Russia in 1941.

tion' that Wallenberg had either been killed in the battle for Budapest or kidnapped and murdered by the Nazis or Hungarian Fascists.

For a while, Vyshinsky's reply silenced the Swedes. Certainly Foreign Minister Östen Undén could not find it in his heart to imagine – as he was to make plain later on – that so distinguished a Soviet luminary as Vyshinsky would tell a deliberate lie on such a matter. If there were any independent spirits in the Swedish Foreign Office who had their doubts they did not speak up. But the Swedish press were not so easily satisfied; nor were many Swedish parliamentarians. In December 1947 three members of the Riksdag put forward Wallenberg's name for the 1948 Nobel Peace Prize and this apparently stung the Soviets into their first public discussion of the Wallenberg affair.

On 21 January 1948 the semi-official Soviet weekly *New Times* fired off a broadside: 'A new campaign of slander against the Soviet Union has been unleashed in Sweden. Delving into the rubbish heap of anti-Soviet fabrications, the servitors of Swedish and foreign reaction have dragged out and revived the so-called Wallenberg affair . . .'

*New Times* said it was unknown whether Wallenberg had been killed 'by the frenzied Nazis or the bandits of Szálasi.' But then it added: 'Swedish right-wing papers gave this regrettable but by no means exceptional occurrence in wartime conditions, a sensational, even provocative character. Fables about the "Soviet secret police," which is allegedly holding Wallenberg in its fearsome clutches, were persistently disseminated by the press.'

The *New Times* article – a typical example of Soviet polemic, with not even a mention of Wallenberg's humanitarian activities in wartime Budapest – went on to denounce this 'filthy campaign,' describing the Wallenberg affair as 'less a mystery than the vilest of provocations,' the product of 'the despicable activities of the Swedish stepbrothers of the American warmongers.' It failed completely to touch on the substance of the affair.

Within a couple of months, as luck would have it, Wallenberg's friend and admiring colleague from Budapest, Per Anger, was transferred to the political department of the Swedish Foreign Office, where one of his functions was to take charge of the ever-growing

Wallenberg file. Going through the documents, Anger found confirmation of his belief that Wallenberg was alive and in Russian hands. He considered that Ambassador Söderblom's handling of the case had been disastrously weak-kneed and Vyshinsky's assurances that Wallenberg was 'unknown to us' totally unconvincing. The reports and rumours of Wallenberg's death at the end of the battle for Budapest, Anger believed, had been deliberately disseminated by the Russians to discourage further inquiries.

Anger knew from his own experience how suspicious the Russians had been about the activities of the Swedish legation and other foreign missions in Budapest after they took the city. He concluded that they would have been even more suspicious of Wallenberg since they found him on the Pest side of the Danube, cut off from his colleagues and claiming to be there to look after the Jews – a notion which Anger believed must have lacked credibility in Russian eyes.

He bore in mind that the Russians had arrested five Swiss diplomatic and consular officials in Budapest as a consequence of similar suspicions, and had held them for a year before exchanging them for two Russians who were in Swiss custody. Anger concluded that it was highly likely that Wallenberg had suffered a similar fate. Quite apart from these assumptions, disturbing if not yet conclusive stories were beginning to seep out via returning prisoners of Wallenberg having been seen in Moscow's Lubianka and Lefortovo prisons at different times. Not the least of these witnesses was the Swedish correspondent Sandeberg; it was on Anger's initiative in 1949 that Sandeberg was finally invited – three years after returning from Russian captivity – to tell his story to the Foreign Office. It was some time before direct testimony could corroborate this kind of evidence and thus warrant further diplomatic action, but it all added to Anger's conviction that Wallenberg was still alive, or had been until at least mid-1947.

As for Anger's political boss, Foreign Minister Undén, 'one almost got the feeling that he willingly accepted Vyshinsky's reply that Wallenberg was not on Soviet territory,' as Anger commented in his memoirs many years later.

Rudolf Philipp was, like Anger, convinced – and passionately so – that Wallenberg was alive. Philipp, an Austrian–Jewish journalist, had fled to Sweden after Hitler's Anschluss and now lived in Stockholm. After going through all the known facts about the Wallenberg affair, and dredging up a lot more through his own efforts, Philipp had gone to Maj and Fredrik von Dardel in 1946 to tell them he was certain Raoul was alive. They needed no convincing and they gratefully accepted him as a valuable ally.

In the same year, a Stockholm publisher brought out a book by Philipp that recounted Wallenberg's exploits in Budapest and impressively marshalled all the evidence indicating he was alive and in captivity. A hitherto sceptical Swedish public was largely convinced by Philipp's passionate and persuasive advocacy. A citizens' action committee on behalf of Wallenberg was formed to prod the government into more positive action and to conduct its own inquiries. This represented twenty-six social and political organizations with a total membership of over one million, and Philipp was to play a leading role in it.

Dogmatic, outspoken, obsessed with the idea that this saviour of the Budapest Jews must himself be saved, Philipp created such a stir that in 1947 the sluggish Foreign Office felt compelled to set up a special committee of experts to review the evidence being presented by Philipp and the citizens' committee. None of this made Philipp popular with the Foreign Office mandarins. One of them, Sven Dahlman, wrote in an internal memorandum: 'Even under normal circumstances Philipp is nervous, unbalanced, aggressive, and suspicious. One has to add, though, that his reputation in general is good and that among journalists he is regarded as an authority on Central European affairs.'

In November 1947 Foreign Minister Undén and senior officials of his ministry met members of the Wallenberg Committee for an exchange of views. It was a heated encounter, with voices raised and faces flushed with anger. Undén said he still believed Wallenberg had been killed in or near Budapest. Guy von Dardel countered that the evidence convinced him his half-brother was alive and in Russian hands. Undén scoffed. What possible reason, he asked, could the Russians have for holding him? Mrs Birgitta de Wylder-Bellander, one of the most active members of the committee, intervened to say that obviously they thought he was a spy.

'What!' asked the incredulous Undén. 'Do you believe that Mr Vyshinsky is lying?'

'Yes, I do,' replied the lady.

Undén was outraged. 'This is unheard of,' he exclaimed, 'absolutely unheard of!'

Undén's outrage was no doubt genuine. He was, by all accounts, one of those idealists who found it impossible to believe that leaders of great nations would tell lies in public – especially if they happened to be 'Socialists.' The deceit and double-dealing practised by Vyshinsky over the years, especially his role in the purges and show trials of the 1930s and in the conclusion of the Nazi–Soviet Pact in 1939, had apparently made no adverse impression on Undén.

During the late 1940s Per Anger found himself increasingly caught in the crossfire between his own ministry and the Wallenberg Committee, his sympathies and convictions drawing him towards the latter but his professional loyalties towards the former. Many times, he recalls, he felt on the point of asking to be relieved of responsibility for the case. Towards the end of 1950 he got an opportunity to talk frankly, face to face, with Undén about the Wallenberg case. They were travelling together to Oslo by rail for talks with the Norwegian Foreign Ministry. *En route*, Undén invited Anger to expound his views on the matter. After summarizing his reasons for believing Wallenberg to be alive and in captivity, Anger told Undén what he felt should be done to secure his release.

'I told him that in my view the only language the Russians understood in such a situation was either force or a *quid pro quo*. I pointed out that the Swiss and the Italians had regained their diplomats by exchanging them for Soviet citizens, while a Dane who had spent six years in captivity in the Soviet Union had been exchanged for a Russian held in Denmark. There had been numerous cases in Sweden in which Soviet citizens had been involved. Would it not be possible, instead of expelling the next spy, to keep him in case he could be exchanged for Wallenberg? After listening to my proposal Undén replied curtly: "The Swedish government does not do such things."'

Soon after this encounter, convinced that it was impossible to change Undén's attitude, Anger went to the head of his department and asked to be taken off the case. At the same time the Wallenberg Committee also finally lost patience with the government. Until then it had been avoiding publicity, in the hope that more could be achieved by working quietly. In December 1950 they decided this approach was leading nowhere and that henceforth they would actively seek the help of the Swedish press.

Things took a turn for the better during 1951, when an unusually energetic and determined official, Arne Lundberg, who had a strong interest in the Wallenberg case, took over as secretary-general of the Foreign Office. His arrival coincided with the receipt of crucial evidence from an Italian diplomat who had recently returned from captivity in the Soviet Union. So disturbing was this evidence that in February 1952 the Swedish government sent a strong new note to the Kremlin. They stated that their investigations now positively confirmed that Wallenberg had been in Soviet prisons, they urged that this information should now enable the Russians to establish his whereabouts, and they demanded that he be returned as soon as possible. It seemed that after a four-year period of relative inactivity the Wallenberg case was very much a live issue once more in Russo-Swedish relations.

The evidence that had spurred the apathetic Swedish government into renewed activity on behalf of Wallenberg came from Claudio de Mohr, cultural attaché at the Italian embassy in Madrid. During the latter days of the war he had been serving in the Italian embassy in Sofia, and had been captured by Soviet troops in Bulgaria in September 1944. In mid-1951 he and five other Italians had been exchanged by the Russians for six Italian Communists jailed in Italy. At a cocktail party in Rome after his return, de Mohr told a Polish émigrée that he had been in the cell next to a Swede named Wallenberg, with whom he had communicated by tapping code messages on the wall between them.

The Polish woman passed this information on to a compatriot living in Stockholm, who in turn passed it on to Wallenberg's family. Guy von Dardel immediately set off for Rome to get more detailed information from de Mohr. What he learned there took him to the Swedish Foreign Office, which in turn sent a senior police official, Otto Danielsson, to Rome to question de Mohr officially.

The Italian told how one night towards the end of April 1945 he and two other diplomats who were sharing cell 152 in the Lefortovo Prison heard the sound of new prisoners being put into the cell next door.

'Very early one morning, not long afterwards, we heard our new neighbours in cell 151 communicating with another cell by tapping in code. We understood the latter half of the message, learning from it that one of the new prisoners had been taken by the Russians in Budapest in January 1945. Later we got into direct contact with the prisoners in 151 and learned from them that one was a German diplomat named Willi Roedl and the other a Swedish diplomat named Raoul Wallenberg. We were very much surprised that a Swedish diplomat had been taken prisoner. We asked several times for confirmation of this to make absolutely sure.'

After that, said de Mohr, he and his cell-mates were in regular contact over a long period with Wallenberg and Roedl. Then there was a long break in communications before they resumed contact once more, this time with cell 203 on the floor above 151, into which the two diplomats had been moved. These contacts, said de Mohr, continued until April 1948.*

The *démarche* in February 1952, arising out of de Mohr's evidence, got the Swedes nowhere. No doubt the earlier, over-cautious approach had influenced the attitude of the Russians, whose reply on 16 April said simply that they had no further information beyond that contained in Vyshinsky's statement in 1947.

On 23 May the Swedes tried a new tactic. Would the Soviet authorities be willing to make further inquiries if the Swedes supplied them with the evidence obtained in the course of their own recent investigations? The Russians waited fifteen months before deigning to reply. On 5 August 1953 they told the Swedes once again that 'Wallenberg has not been and is not in the Soviet Union and is unknown to us.' With some asperity, Soviet Ambassador Konstantin Rodionov told the Swedish Foreign Office that over the years the

---

* De Mohr was almost certainly mistaken about this date; later evidence suggests strongly that Wallenberg was removed from Lefortovo Prison in the summer of 1947.

question of Wallenberg's fate had been 'shamelessly exploited' by circles hostile to the Soviet Union and that the Swedish press had been publishing 'invented articles' with the purpose of undermining relations between Sweden and the Soviet Union.

By 1955, ten years after the end of the war, large numbers of German and Austrian prisoners began returning from the Soviet Union. Alerted by de Mohr's evidence, Swedish Foreign Office investigators canvassed those returning, looking for any who might have seen or communicated with Wallenberg. Rigid procedures were established for interviewing all those who claimed such knowledge. Hearsay evidence was excluded. Only information deriving from direct contact with Wallenberg or his driver, Langfelder, was to be accepted. Each witness was to be kept in ignorance of the testimony of the others. Each interviewee was to confirm his statement under oath. All such statements were subjected to the sharp scrutiny of the veteran criminal investigator Otto Danielsson. Even the ultra-cautious Swedes concluded that the evidence of many of these witnesses was authentic.

• Gustav Richer was police attaché at the German legation in Bucharest until the Rumanians surrendered in August 1944 and the Russians took him prisoner. On 17 January 1945 he was taken to Moscow's Lubianka Prison and put into cell 123 with an Austrian lieutenant named Otto Scheuer. On 21 January Wallenberg was brought in to join them. Richter and Wallenberg became friendly. 'During the month we spent together he seemed in good spirits,' Richter testified. 'He told how he and his driver, Langfelder, had been brought to Moscow by train, but separated on their arrival at Lubianka. He gave me a piece of paper with his signature on it and his address at the Swedish Foreign Office, but this was later found by the Russians and taken from me.'

Richter said that at about the beginning of February Wallenberg drafted a written appeal to the prison director, protesting about his continued detention and asking to be allowed to contact the Swedish embassy. 'Wallenberg was taken for interrogation only once while he was sharing the cell with me,' Richter testified. 'He told me that one of his interrogators had said to him: "We know who you are. You belong to a big capitalist family in Sweden." Wallenberg said he had been accused of spying and he told me his interrogation had lasted an hour to an hour and a half.'

It seems clear from this evidence that when Wallenberg arrived at Lubianka he thought he would soon be released, hence the good spirits that Richter noticed. By the time he had been accused of spying he must have had serious misgivings.

On 1 March Richter was moved to cell 91 on the sixth floor of Lubianka Prison, while Scheuer remained in cell 123 with Wallenberg. Richter never saw Wallenberg, or had contact with him, after that.

But on 27 July 1947 something very strange happened. At about 10 p.m. he was taken from his cell for an interrogation, which was conducted by an NKVD colonel, with a lieutenant-colonel acting as interpreter. Richter was asked to name all the people with whom he had shared a cell since his capture. When he mentioned Wallenberg they appeared to have found the name they were looking for. 'They then asked me to give the names of all those to whom I had mentioned having met Wallenberg,' said Richter.

After he had done that Richter was put into solitary confinement, where he was kept for seven months, for no apparent reason. His solitude was broken by the arrival of two cell-mates, a German colonel named Horst Kitschmann and an admiral named Werner Tillesen. Kitschmann had at one time shared a cell with Langfelder. He told Richter that he too had been taken for interrogation on the night of 27 July, subjected to the same line of questioning, and then put into solitary.

Although three other prisoners – Otto Scheuer, Willi Roedl, and Hans Loyda – are known to have shared a cell with Wallenberg at different times in the Lubianka or Lefortovo prisons, Richter is the only one who returned to tell his story. Many others, however, communicated with Wallenberg by prison telegraph after his removal from Lubianka to Lefortovo in April 1945.

Since the prison telegraph is a vital element in the other testimony, something should be said about it and the conditions under which it operated. Lefortovo was a top-security jail. It held about six hundred prisoners, usually kept three to a cell. Every cell had a peep-hole, and every two or three minutes one of the four guards who patrolled each floor looked through the hole. Newspapers were forbidden, but library books were available, in Russian only. Prisoners were never given the opportunity to see anyone but their own cell-mates.

The prison courtyard was divided into small, walled-off sections, so that even during their twenty-minute exercise periods, once a day, prisoners remained isolated. Nor could they catch glimpses of each other as they entered and left their cells; the ground plan of the cell block was in the shape of a letter K to prevent this, and the guards used an elaborate system of flags when moving prisoners from their cells for exercise or interrogation to prevent accidental encounters with other prisoners *en route*. In addition, prisoners were forbidden to communicate with each other in any way. Despite this, the prison telegraph flourished – certainly in the time when Wallenberg was there. The most common method of telegraph, known to the prisoners as the 'idiot system,' consisted of spelling out messages by means of a simple but laborious code in which one tap meant A, two taps B, and so forth. A more sophisticated variant of this was the five-by-five system. In this, the letter W was dropped from the alphabet,* allowing the remaining twenty-five letters to be split up into a simple grid.

|   | 1 | 2 | 3 | 4 | 5 |
|---|---|---|---|---|---|
| 1 | A | B | C | D | E |
| 2 | F | G | H | I | J |
| 3 | K | L | M | N | O |
| 4 | P | Q | R | S | T |
| 5 | U | V | X | Y | Z |

By this method, one first tapped out a number in the horizontal

* In this context, the Latin alphabet, not the Cyrillic alphabet of the Russian language, which has thirty-three letters. Russian prisoners used a different method.

line and, after a pause, a number in the vertical line, to indicate the appropriate letter. Thus, four taps followed by three would mean N. Very occasionally, Morse code would be used.

Since all such communication was strictly banned, and the guards would look in through the Judas-hole every two or three minutes, great care had to be taken during transmission. To disguise what he was doing, the prisoner would sit on his bed with a book in one hand, apparently reading. In the other hand, behind his back, he would hold a suitable implement – usually a toothbrush – and tap with it on the wall. Often, the prisoner would remove his tapping arm from his sleeve and arrange the sleeve in a natural-looking way on his lap to deceive the guard.

There were other hazards. From time to time, the Soviet secret police placed spies in the cells to try to find out what was going on. A prisoner would never use the telegraph system unless he was sure of his cell-mates, and each cell had a call sign, so that the others would not be trapped into communicating with an informer. Tapping was, therefore, an extremely laborious and hazardous business. In a Soviet prison, however, one had plenty of time on one's hands. In his early days in captivity, Wallenberg was known to his fellow-prisoners as 'a keen tapper.'

• Karl Supprian, who was a scientific attaché at the German legation in Bucharest before his capture in August 1944, was among those who communicated with Wallenberg by these means. He shared a cell in Lefortovo with the Italian de Mohr and another Italian diplomat named Ronchi. After mid-April 1944 he regularly communicated with Willi Roedl, who was known to him from Bucharest, and Wallenberg, who was Roedl's cell-mate. Roedl first told him about Wallenberg. According to Supprian's testimony, 'I was very surprised to hear that a Swedish diplomat was in prison and asked Roedl to confirm this, so that there should be no mistake. Roedl repeated the message.'

• Heinz-Helmut Von Hinckeldey, a major on the German general staff, also captured in Bucharest, 'talked' to Roedl and Wallenberg by the same method. 'I communicated with Wallenberg in German,' von Hinckeldey testified after his return in 1955. 'Wallenberg gave the name of his family's bank in Stockholm as his address. Roedl told me the piece of paper bearing Wallenberg's signature and address, which he had hidden in the lining of his sleeve, was discovered by the guards and taken from him.' Von Hinckeldey said Wallenberg told him he had protested repeatedly about being kept prisoner and had asked in vain to be allowed to contact the Swedish embassy. 'He told me he had refused to make any statement to his interrogators, citing his diplomatic status.' Von Hinckeldey recalls the last message received from Wallenberg – 'We are being taken away' – but 'after such a long time I cannot exactly remember the date.'

• Ernst Wallenstein had been the scientific attaché at the German legation in Bucharest before he was captured on 1 September 1944. He said that he had had contact with Wallenberg and Roedl from the end of 1945, when they were sharing a cell one floor above his own in Lefortovo. He testified shortly after he was freed in 1955. 'I still remember very clearly that time as Wallenberg had the intention to send a written protest at his imprisonment, but was not sure to whom this should be addressed. By the knocking code, we agreed that it would be best to send it to Stalin himself and that the letter should be written in French. I suggested that he should use the form "*M. le Président*", and when Wallenberg asked for a polite form of closing, I suggested that a suitable phrase would be "*agréez, M. le Président, à l'expression de mes très hautes considérations.*"

'I know that Wallenberg wrote such an appeal and that he had it forwarded via the prison guard. I know from my own experience that such appeals were usually delivered.'

• Bernhard Rensinghoff, who was formerly economic counsellor at the German legation in Bucharest, shared cell 105 with Wallenstein, underneath and just to the right of Wallenberg and Roedl's cell 203.

He said: 'The contact between us was very lively. We exchanged messages daily. Roedl and Wallenberg were both enthusiastic knockers. Wallenberg told me in this way about his activities in Budapest and about his capture. For his address he gave "Stockholm."

'During our first exchange we spent most of the time composing a statement in French in which Wallenberg referred to his diplomatic status and asked to be granted an interview. Wallenberg had, in the summer of 1946, addressed this plea to Stalin,* requesting to be allowed to contact the Swedish legation in Moscow. After some time, Wallenberg got word that his letter had been forwarded.'

Shortly before Roedl and Wallenberg were removed from their cell, Wallenberg was taken for an interview. After the interview Wallenberg tapped out a message telling Rensinghoff that the commissar who interviewed him had said it was quite clear that his was 'a political case' and if he claimed to be innocent it was up to him to prove it.

According to what Rensinghoff said he was told by Wallenberg, the NKVD commissar said 'the best proof that Wallenberg was guilty was the fact that the Swedish legation in Moscow and the Swedish government had done nothing about his case. Wallenberg had asked to be put into contact with the Swedish embassy or Red Cross, or at least to be able to write to one of them, but they had not responded. "Nobody cares about you," said the commissar. "If the Swedish government or its embassy had any interest in you, they would have been in contact long ago."'

Whether this was part of the 'treatment,' or whether the commissar knew that the Swedish embassy had written off Wallenberg as dead, is impossible to say. Either way, the effect of such a remark on Wallenberg's morale must have been devastating.

According to Rensinghoff, Wallenberg on another occasion asked his interrogator if he would have a trial or not and was told that 'for political reasons you will never be sentenced.' The only other communication Rensinghoff had with Wallenberg – and as far as he could remember this was in the autumn of 1946 – was a brief message: 'We are being taken away.' This was followed by what sounded like fists being pounded on the wall before Wallenberg and his cell-mate were removed.

• Willi Bergemann, another former member of the Bucharest legation staff, was in cell 202 of the Lefortovo between September 1946 and May 1948. Next door, in cell 203, were Wallenberg and Roedl. Bergemann testified that he exchanged tapped messages with them until both of them were moved, which he thought happened

---

* Whether this was before or after Söderblom's disastrous interview with Stalin is not clear.

sometime between March and May 1947. 'Wallenberg was a very keen knocker,' Bergemann recalled. 'He knocked in perfect German. If he wanted to speak to us he would knock five times in succession before commencing.'

Although only one of Wallenberg's cell-mates came out of the Gulag to tell the tale, three men who shared cells with his driver Langfelder did get home.

• Horst Kitschmann, a Wehrmacht colonel, taken prisoner in May 1945, said Langfelder joined him in cell 105 in Lefortovo in November 1945 and stayed until he was moved in the beginning of December. In his testimony, given following his release in mid-1955, Kitschmann described Langfelder as a 'well-built man, about 172 centimetres tall, with red-blond hair, blue eyes, and a somewhat hooked nose. His age would have been between thirty and thirty-five. I remember he said that an aunt of his owned one of the biggest milling enterprises in Budapest ... Through Langfelder I learned for the first time about the Swedish diplomat Wallenberg.'

Like others who had been in direct contact with either Langfelder or Wallenberg, or who had heard about them from other prisoners, Kitschmann was called in for interrogation on 27 July 1947, as Richter had been. 'They asked me to name all the people I had shared cells with. When I mentioned Langfelder's name they asked me what he had told me. After I recounted what I had heard, the NKVD colonel in charge asked me whom I had told about Langfelder.' After his interrogation, Kitschmann was put into solitary confinement until 23 February 1948 'as a punishment for having told my cell-mates about Langfelder and Wallenberg.'

• Erhard Hille, a Wehrmacht corporal captured in January 1945, was in Lefortovo cell 105 on 22 March of that year when, as he testified in February 1956, 'the Hungarian citizen Vilmos Langfelder was moved into my cell.' He described Langfelder almost exactly as Kitschmann had done, saying the newcomer had told him he was a qualified engineer and that his family had owned a factory in Budapest. He told Hille about his and Wallenberg's exploits in wartime Budapest and about their arrest.

Hille said Langfelder had told him they were arrested by an

NKVD major three or four days after Wallenberg had reported himself to the Russians. 'Later they were brought by rail, via Rumania, to Moscow, where, as far as I can remember, they were brought to Lubianka Prison on 6 February 1945.' Langfelder had told him that he was moved to Lefortovo on 18 March, and that after three days alone in a cell he was moved to cell 105. He and Langfelder were cell-mates until 6 April, when Hille was moved to the Butyrka Prison. He had not seen Langfelder since, but, 'in later years, however, I met other prisoners who had been his cell-mates,' Hille said.

One of these had shared a cell with both Wallenberg and Langfelder, at different times. This was a prisoner named Hans Loyda, who told Hille in 1946, when they were both at a prison camp near Krasnogorsk, that after Langfelder had been taken on 18 March from the cell they shared in Lubianka he was replaced by Wallenberg. 'Wallenberg was a very good cell-mate,' Loyda had told Hille, 'and he asked the prison officer to pass his cigarette ration on to Langfelder.'

Loyda said Wallenberg was taken several times for interrogation. The Swede had complained to him that the Russians had no reason to hold him. He had told them he had represented their interests in Budapest, but they did not want to believe him. The interrogators had said Wallenberg was a rich Swedish capitalist, so why should he do anything for the Russians?

In mid-May 1945, Loyda said, he, Wallenberg, and Roedl (the third cell-mate) were taken from the Lubianka in a van. Loyda saw Wallenberg and Roedl taken off at Lefortovo, while he went on to Butyrka.

• Ernst Huber, a corporal telegraphist with German military intelligence in Rumania, who was taken prisoner in August 1944, said he shared a cell with Langfelder in Lefortovo during mid-April 1945. He gave a similar description of Langfelder to that given by Kitschmann and Hille, except that at this time he was wearing a beard.

Testifying in March 1956 Huber recalled the version Langfelder had given of the arrest of himself and Wallenberg. They wanted to contact the Soviet commander to organize help for the Budapest ghettos, and he and Wallenberg set out together by car. There was still shooting in the streets, so they had to proceed slowly, stopping every now and then to take cover in a house. Later they were stopped by some Russian soldiers who forced them to get out of the car and then slashed its tyres to stop them getting away. Wallenberg showed his diplomatic credentials and asked to be taken to the commanding officer. Instead, they were handed over to the NKVD and detained for a short time in a temporary prison in Budapest.

Then, escorted by an officer and four soldiers, they were taken by train to Moscow, via Rumania.* According to Huber, Langfelder added the detail that they stopped *en route* at a Rumanian town called Jassy, where they were allowed to go for a meal to a restaurant called Luther. In Moscow, as in Budapest, they were told they were not prisoners but in protective custody. On arrival in the Soviet capital they were even allowed a sightseeing trip to the famous Moscow subway system before going on foot to Lubianka Prison. On arrival there they were separated. Langfelder said he and Wallenberg were subsequently accused of spying for the United States, and possibly for Britain as well.

Like others who had been cell-mates of Langfelder or Wallenberg, Huber said he was suddenly called for interrogation 'one evening at the end of July 1947,' and asked to name all the prisoners with whom he had shared a cell. When he mentioned Langfelder the close questioning began. 'The rest of the interrogation concerned Wallenberg and what Langfelder had told me about him,' said Huber. After the interrogation, like the others, he was put into solitary confinement, where he remained until the following April.

Later during his imprisonment, Huber testified, he met Hille in the Butyrka Prison and also a Finn named Pelkonen. The latter, who had shared a cell with Langfelder in Lefortovo in 1945, was subsequently interrogated and then put into solitary confinement.

Though there are certain minor inconsistencies in the evidence gleaned from prisoners released by the Russians, they are mainly a

* Note that this information is the same as that given by Hille, above.

matter of discrepancies of dates. Far more significant than these discrepancies is the emergence, despite Russian endeavours, of a remarkably coherent account of Wallenberg's fate following his arrest. The interrogation of prisoners in July 1947 and their subsequent solitary confinement show, as a Swedish Foreign Office report noted, that 'the Russian authorities wished as far as possible to prevent information about Wallenberg from spreading.'

As a result of all this information, the Swedes felt able to assert flatly in a note to the Kremlin that 'complete evidence' existed and that it was now clear that the Soviets had held Wallenberg as a suspected spy. 'So the terrible tragedy occurred that Raoul Wallenberg, who made a heroic personal contribution to save people, including non-Jewish Socialists and Communists, from the Fascist terrorists, has been accused of spying and arrested.' The contents of this note, delivered personally to Soviet Deputy Foreign Minister Valerian Zorin, did not budge the Russians an inch.

A new Swedish note, dated 10 March 1956, contained a fresh element – a declaration signed by Supreme Court Justices Rudolf Eklund and Erik Lind to the effect that the evidence left no doubt that Wallenberg had been a prisoner in the Soviet Union after being taken into custody in 1945. At the urgent insistence of Rudolf Philipp the judges' declaration was amended in one important respect before it went to the Russians. Originally the two judges had said the testimony they had studied proved Wallenberg to have been alive up to February 1947. Philipp pointed out that it might prove dangerous to let the Russians know that their firm information went only as far as 1947. In other instances, he pointed out, the Russians had answered queries about missing prisoners with death certificates showing that the individual in question had died after the last sighting.

The 10 March note, with the judges' declaration attached, said that all the conditions seemed fulfilled to enable the Russians to trace Wallenberg and send him home, a tactful formulation that might have allowed the Russians to pretend that some terrible mistake had been made which could now be rectified. Instead, the Russians shot back a reply in the record time of nine days, and its tone and content were totally negative. Once more, it said, a 'thorough investigation' had been made which merely confirmed that Wallenberg was not and had never been in Russia. The Kremlin added that it was impossible to accept the testimony of 'war criminals,' whose information was in disagreement with the results of their own 'thorough investigation.'

But one must ask why such 'war criminals' were released – while Wallenberg and Langfelder were not – and why unregenerate Nazis wishing to slander the good name of the Soviet Union should do so by speaking up for a man who had, by his own account, thwarted Nazi plans by rescuing thousands of Jews.

# Chapter 14

At Easter 1956 Swedish Prime Minister Tage Erlander made an official visit to Moscow for talks with Stalin's successors, Communist Party Chairman Nikita Khrushchev, Premier Nikolai Bulganin, and Foreign Minister Vyacheslav Molotov. In his pocket he carried a letter from Maj von Dardel to her son. It is not known whether Erlander really believed that Wallenberg would ever receive it.

*Dear, beloved Raoul,*

*After many years of despair and infinite sorrow we have now advanced so far that the leaders of the governing parties, Prime Minister Erlander and Interior Minister [Gunnar] Hedlund, are going to Moscow to see to it that you may at last return. May they succeed and may your sufferings come to an end. We have never given up hope of seeing you again, despite the fact that all our efforts to contact you have, to our great sorrow, been unsuccessful. From other prisoners who have returned, and who have shared cells with you, we have got some information about your life in prison in Russia, and via Major Richter we have got greetings from you . . . There is a room waiting for you when you return with the Prime Minister.*

What made Maj von Dardel believe that Erlander would be able to bring Raoul back with him is not clear, but it was not to be. Even though, with the passing of the Stalin era, thousands more foreign prisoners – mostly Germans, and many of these with dubious war-crimes records – were being sent home, Wallenberg was not one of them.

Certainly Mrs von Dardel can have had little cause to believe the Russians would let him go. She had already appealed directly to Khrushchev without response. 'You who are yourself a father should be able to understand my feelings,' she had written, 'the sufferings that are tearing my heart to pieces. I ask you with all my heart to let my son return to his longing old mother.' She had also written to Khrushchev's wife, Nina: 'In my distress I turn to you, who are also a mother, with a plea for help to have my son allowed to return to his mother and his country.' Again, there was no reply.

When Erlander raised the matter with Khrushchev and company he got the stock reply; they stuck to the 1947 Vyshinsky version that Wallenberg was not and had never been in the Soviet Union. Erlander persisted, handing over to the Russians copies of some of the testimony they had gathered over the years. He carefully omitted the evidence of witnesses who still had friends or relatives behind the Iron Curtain, as well as other material that – should the Russians become aware of it – might cause serious consequences to individuals. Even without this material there was more than enough to make out a *prima facie* case. In a communiqué published on 5 April, at the end of the visit, it was stated that the Russians had agreed to study the documents handed over, adding that if it turned out that Wallenberg was in the Soviet Union, he would 'naturally' be allowed to return home.

On 14 July Soviet Ambassador Rodionov informed the Swedish Foreign Office that the results of new Soviet investigations could be expected 'shortly.' Two months passed; nothing happened. The Swedes sent a sharp reminder, pointing out that it was now six months since the Soviet leadership had promised an investigation of the latest evidence. Another two months passed and the Swedes sent yet another reminder, expressing 'surprise and great disappointment' that the Soviet pledge had not yet been implemented. Another two months went by – and finally the reply came. This response, delivered by Soviet Deputy Foreign Minister Andrei Gromyko on 2 February 1957, stunned Swedish officials.

In a complete reversal of all their previous denials, the Russians now admitted that Wallenberg *had* been a prisoner, but that, unfortunately, it appeared he had died ten years previously in Lubianka

Prison. The text of the Soviet statement, as released by the Swedish Foreign Office to the press the next day, said that in the course of a 'page-by-page search' of the archive documents from all wards on certain prisoners, 'a document has been found which there is good reason to consider as referring to Raoul Wallenberg.' This came from Lubianka Prison, and it took the form of a handwritten report addressed to the former minister of state security, Viktor Abakumov, and written by Colonel A. L. Smoltsov, the former head of the prison's health service.

The document, dated 17 July 1947, read, 'I report that the prisoner Walenberg [sic], who is well-known to you, died suddenly in his cell this night, probably as a result of a heart attack. Pursuant to the instructions given by you that I personally have Walenberg under my care, I request approval to make an autopsy with a view to establishing the cause of death.' In the same handwriting, an additional notation was scrawled across the bottom of the report: 'I have personally notified the minister and it has been ordered that the body be cremated without autopsy. 17 July. Smoltsov.'

The Soviet note went on: 'It has not been possible to find any other information whatsoever having the character of document or testimony, all the more so since the aforementioned A. L. Smoltsov died on 7 May 1953. On the strength of what has been cited above, the conclusion should be drawn that Wallenberg died in July 1947.'

Not only was the sole witness conveniently dead but so also was Abakumov, the minister to whom the report was addressed. The blame for the whole episode could be shifted on to him. 'It may be considered indisputable,' said the Gromyko note to the Swedes, 'that Wallenberg's detention in prison, as well as the incorrect information about him supplied by certain former leaders of the security organs to the Soviet Union's Foreign Ministry over a period of years, was a result of Abakumov's criminal activities. In connection with gross crimes committed by him, it will be recalled that Abakumov . . . was executed in accordance with the verdict handed down by the Supreme Court of the Soviet Union.'*

* Abakumov was liquidated in 1954 in the purge that followed the downfall and execution of Lavrenti Beria, Stalin's chief of secret police.

The Russian explanation ended on a conciliatory note: 'The Soviet government presents its sincere regrets for what has occurred and expresses its profound sympathy to the Swedish government as well as to Raoul Wallenberg's relatives.'

Flabbergasted though they were by the Soviet note, the Swedish government nevertheless made public an immediate comment 'strongly regretting' that the reply to their queries contained 'such meagre information. Nothing is said,' the note continued, 'about the motives for Wallenberg's arrest or about his fate during the years that followed. We expect that if any new material should appear in the Soviet Union we shall immediately have it communicated to us.'

Another week passed before the Swedes made a fully considered reply to the Soviets in the form of an unusually sharply worded note handed over to Gromyko by the Swedish Ambassador to Moscow, Rolf Sohlman, on 19 February. 'Swedish public opinion is justifiably shocked by what has occurred. If the Soviet security service was able to act in such an autocratic way as to make a diplomat of a neutral country a prisoner and keep him in prison for two and a half years without reporting the case to the Soviet government or the Foreign Ministry, this fact is not in itself a circumstance for which the Soviet government can disclaim responsibility. By expressing their regret the Soviet government have also admitted their responsibility.'

What was more, said the Swedish note, the Soviet government could not have been unable to obtain reliable information about Wallenberg 'if they had really undertaken the thorough investigations they have repeatedly assured the Swedish government that they had made.' In conclusion, the Swedish government found it difficult to believe that all the documentation concerning Wallenberg's imprisonment, except the note from Smoltsov, should have been 'completely obliterated.' They therefore expected any further material likely to clarify what happened to Wallenberg to be communicated to them, while reserving the right to press for continued investigations in the Soviet Union.

Quite apart from the altogether too convenient fact that everyone who might be held to blame was dead – all the way up to Beria and the mighty Stalin himself, who had scribbled Wallenberg's name on his desk pad that day with Söderblom in 1946 – the Soviet statement lacked credibility on almost every point. It was, to say the least, curious that the date of Wallenberg's supposed death was just ten days after he was last reported seen and ten days before all the prisoners who knew of him were called in for interrogation and then put into solitary confinement. Rudolf Philipp's earlier warning to the two Supreme Court judges not to draw attention to the date of the last reported evidence of Wallenberg appeared well-justified. Then there was the supposed cause of death – myocardial infarction. A heart attack was considered by Swedish specialists to be most unlikely in a man of thirty-five, on a prison diet and previously in good health.

But though it was clear that the Soviets were lying now, as they had lied all along, one thing in the statement might be true: Wallenberg might in fact be dead, even though the time and the cause of death alleged by the Russians were, to say the least, in question. However, it was not long before fresh evidence cast doubt on that possibility. Some time after July 1947, this evidence indicated, Wallenberg had been moved from Lubianka to Vladimir Prison, some 100 miles east of Moscow, where he was reportedly sighted into the mid-1950s.

This information, vetted with the same vigour as earlier evidence from returned prisoners, came from, among others, a Swiss named Brugger, who had spent a decade in Soviet prisons. He told the Swedish investigators that he and Wallenberg 'talked' to each other in prison code by tapping on the wall between their cells in the Corpus II hospital block of Vladimir Prison at the end of July and the beginning of August 1948. The Swede had identified himself as 'Wallenberg, First Secretary, Swedish Legation, Budapest, arrested 1945.' He asked Brugger, if he ever got out, to go to any Swedish embassy or consulate and say he had been in contact with him.

An Austrian, whose name was not disclosed because of possible reprisals,* said quite independently that he had actually shared a cell with Wallenberg for one night in Corpus II of Vladimir Prison around the end of January or the beginning of February 1955.

---

* He claimed the Russians threatened him with prison for life if he did not agree to spy for them after being released.

Wallenberg told him he had spent some years in solitary confinement and asked the Austrian, if he was released, to tell any Swedish diplomatic mission that he had met him. 'If you forget my name, just say a Swede from Budapest and they'll know who you mean.' When a prison political commissar came to the cell next morning and found Wallenberg had company, he had the Austrian transferred immediately to another cell. Afterwards, the Austrian testified, he had been warned not to talk to other prisoners about having seen Wallenberg on pain of imprisonment for the rest of his life.

A German named Mulle, who was sent to Vladimir Prison in 1956, told the Swedes he had met there a Georgian prisoner named Simon Gogoberidse, who had been in Vladimir since 1945 and was consequently considered very well-informed about what went on there and, in particular, about prominent prisoners. According to Gogoberidse, Wallenberg had been in solitary confinment for some years. He was not sure whether Wallenberg was in the hospital block because he was ill or for isolation purposes. Gogoberidse told Mulle that after the visit of the Swedish premier to the Soviet Union in 1956, a prison political officer had commented, 'They'll have to look for a long time to find Wallenberg.'

Another German prisoner, named Rehekampf, quite separately claimed to have been given similar information about Wallenberg by the same co-prisoner, the Georgian Gogoberidse. Both Mulle and Rehekampf, like a number of other ex-prisoners from Vladimir, characterized Gogoberidse as truthful and reliable.

This testimony sparked off a flood of fresh notes and memoranda from the Swedish Foreign Office to the Kremlin. The first, on 9 February, 1959, 'urges the Soviet Government to make a speedy investigation whether Wallenberg has been detained in Vladimir Prison.' Replying on 6 March, the Russians 'had the honour to state' that a new investigation in accordance with the latest Swedish request had shown that the information referred to 'has not been confirmed.'

On 27 June Ambassador Rodionov, now head of the Soviet Foreign Ministry's Scandinavian desk, sent for Sweden's Ambassador Sohlman and complained to him about 'items of information' in the Swedish press about Wallenberg's having been seen alive in Russian jails after 1947. This information, said Rodionov, was 'all made up' and added, 'The Foreign Ministry requests that what I have now said be reported to Mr Raoul Wallenberg's mother, Mrs von Dardel, who has turned to the Chairman of the Council of Ministers Khrushchev with an inquiry about the fate of her son. At the same time, on the part of the Soviet Union the hope is expressed that Sweden ... may assume an attitude that makes it impossible for certain elements in the future to use this question for the purpose of poisoning Soviet–Swedish relations.'

By now the Swedes were not so easily frightened by thinly veiled warnings of this kind. On 18 July, in a written memorandum, they refuted the suggestion that their actions were based on press reports, fabricated or otherwise, but were on the basis of evidence given by former prisoners from Vladimir Prison. 'Naturally,' said the memorandum, 'the Foreign Ministry must attach great importance to statements of such a detailed character. The Foreign Ministry does not believe that there is any reason to assume that these statements were made with the obvious intention of spreading untruthful information. Nor does it appear likely that all statements could be attributed to confusion of names or slip of memory.'

With respect to the Soviet wish that Sweden should not allow relations to be poisoned, the Swedes stressed that their only motive was to shed light on the fate of Wallenberg. 'If this happens it will remove a serious irritant in Swedish–Soviet relations.'

In early 1960 the Swedish government again brought two Supreme Court justices – Ragnar Gyllenswärd and Per Santesson – into the picture. They studied all the information so far received and on 25 April they produced a joint report saying that they were satisfied that 'the records are made with great care and do not give rise to the assumption that the statements were made after leading questions or in other circumstances which might have influenced the content. The statements contain a great amount of information, the correctness of which it was possible to check, and they support each other ... According to our opinion the present investigations must, according to Swedish law (although it does not include a full evidence in this respect), be considered to make it likely that Wallenberg was alive at least in the beginning of the 1950s and was then detained in Vladimir Prison.'

# Chapter 15

The next link in the chain of evidence was quite the most sensational thus far, although it was to be four and a half years before it became known to the Swedish public – the only people in the world, it seemed, who, by now, were concerned about Wallenberg's fate.

In January 1961 Professor Nanna Svartz, a distinguished physician from Stockholm's Karolinska Hospital* went to Moscow, as she had done many times previously, to attend a medical-scientific congress. There, she met several prominent Soviet colleagues, among them Professor Aleksandr Miashnikov. They had met before, in Moscow and elsewhere, and it was their habit to discuss matters of common interest, often of a highly technical nature, in German.

Sitting together in Miashnikov's office on 27 January, Professors Svartz and Miashnikov discussed the congress, certain lines of medical research, and similar topics. Professor Svartz then directed the conversation along other lines:

I asked him to pardon me if I brought up a question which was very close to my heart and to the heart of other Swedes. I gave him an account of the Raoul Wallenberg case, and asked whether he knew about it, whereupon he nodded in the affirmative.

* The hospital where Fredrik von Dardel was administrator. Dr Svartz and the von Dardels were friends and Maj von Dardel was her patient.

I asked him whether he could give me some advice on how I might go about finding where Wallenberg might be. I told him that we in Sweden had information to the effect that Wallenberg was alive only two years earlier and that his next of kin had received reports that indicated he was *still* alive. My informant then suddenly said that he knew about the case and that the person I was asking about was in poor condition.

He asked what I wanted, and I replied that the main thing was that Wallenberg be brought home, no matter in what condition. My informant then said in a very low voice that the person inquired about was in a mental hospital.

Professor Svartz was dumbfounded by this news. Realizing that she was on the very brink of solving the mystery that had so tantalized and disturbed her country for sixteen years, and of gaining the freedom of a man who had become a national hero, she was filled with an almost unbearable excitement. According to her account of the incident for the Swedish government, Professor Miashnikov then asked her to wait where she was while he went to fetch a colleague for consultations. After a while he returned with another Russian scientist (this man's name has never been disclosed), who remained with Dr Svartz when Miashnikov withdrew.

His colleague sat down, facing me. I asked him whether he had been briefed on what the matter was about and he confirmed that this was so. He asked me carefully about where Wallenberg had been serving and asked me to write his name on a piece of paper. I then wrote: Attaché Raoul Wallenberg.

I told him that Wallenberg's mother was one of my patients, and that she would be greatly relieved to have peace of mind and to be given full certainty. No matter how sick her son might be, it would be a blessing to her, as it would be for all of Sweden, if he could be given treatment in his home country. I asked him whether he could help us and he replied he would do everything within his power. I told him the entire Swedish nation would be grateful to the Soviet Union if Wallenberg were permitted to be brought home, even if he were seriously ill, both physically and mentally. This matter, I said, lies close to the heart of our government.

Dr Svartz mentioned to the Russian that she had made the personal acquaintance of the Soviet Deputy Foreign Minister Vladimir Semyonov during a visit he had made to Sweden. Her Russian colleague advised her to approach Semyonov directly. 'I further asked the colleague whether he considered it possible for me, as a doctor, to take Wallenberg home. He believed – "if he is still alive" – that such a procedure would not be impossible, but that I ought to talk to Semyonov about this.'

Dr Svartz hurried back to her hotel, got Semyonov's telephone number from the Swedish embassy, and phoned him – but his secretary said that he was abroad. That evening a banquet was held in connection with the medical congress. There, Dr Svartz spotted the Soviet colleague who had advised her to contact Semyonov and asked him if, as Semyonov was abroad, it would be a good idea to write to the deputy foreign minister. Her colleague advised that this would be the best course to follow.

'The colleague told me that after I had left them earlier in the day they had discussed the matter together . . . [and] both were of the opinion that a possible transportation to Sweden of the person in question – "if he is still alive" – naturally had to be organized through diplomatic channels . . .'

Immediately on her return to Stockholm a couple of days later, Dr Svartz telephoned the home of Prime Minister Erlander, with whom she was on terms of personal friendship. As soon as he had heard her account of what had transpired in Moscow, he asked her to come to his residence straight away and summoned Foreign Minister Undén.

Undén's reactions to Dr Svartz's astonishing story can only be guessed at; Erlander's are known. Having total confidence in Nanna Svartz's reliability, he lost no time in drafting a personal letter to Khrushchev, which was delivered to the Soviet party boss on 9 February by Ambassador Sohlman. It did not skate around the issue.

*I now wish to inform you that I have been informed by a Swedish physician, Professor Nanna Svartz, who visited Moscow at the end of January 1961 . . . that Wallenberg was alive at that time and that he was a patient at a mental hospital in Moscow. His health was not good. Mrs Svartz got this information from an internationally known, prominent representative of Soviet medical science.*

*Foreign Minister Undén and I have discussed the most suitable way of transferring Wallenberg to Sweden. We have found that the best would be if a*

Professor Svartz, still brimming with excitement at her discovery, could be forgiven for believing that her next trip to Moscow would be to collect Raoul Wallenberg and deliver him to his family. While she and Erlander waited for Khrushchev's reply, she wrote a personal letter to Miashnikov, expressing the hope that she would see him again very soon. She also wrote to Deputy Foreign Minister Semyonov, asking how far the investigation about Wallenberg had gone and about the possibilities of taking him home.

She received a reply from Miashnikov not long after. He wrote that he would be happy to see her again in Moscow. The following month – still without a reply from Khrushchev or Semyonov – Professor Svartz went again to the Soviet capital, where she went straight to see Miashnikov. In their first talk, with another Soviet scientist present, she asked Miashnikov if she might visit Wallenberg in hospital.

'He replied that this would have to be decided in higher quarters, and he added, "Unless he is dead." To this I rejoined, "But then he must have died quite recently."'

Professor Svartz began to sense that things were going badly wrong – a feeling which was accentuated when, at a second meeting with no third person present, Miashnikov told her she should not have told the Swedish government about their original conversation in January. 'He did not deny the conversation, but maintained that his poor German had led to a misunderstanding, and he declared now that he knew nothing about the Wallenberg case. He told me that he had been summoned to Minister President Khrushchev, who had been informed about our conversation and had been angered because of it.'*

Her earlier optimism waning fast, Professor Svartz tried again to contact Semyonov, this time dialling his private number, which she

---

* In a conversation with me in 1979, Professor Svartz recounted that Miashnikov told her Khrushchev was furious, pounding the desk with his fist and finally ordering Miashnikov out.

had been given by Miashnikov. Again she failed to find him. When she got back to Stockholm, Professor Svartz wrote to Semyonov again, asking for an appointment as soon as possible and declaring herself ready to travel to Moscow immediately. She never had a reply to either of her letters to Semyonov, not even an acknowledgement.

In May 1962 she was invited to another medical congress in Moscow. There, she met Miashnikov again, 'but when I tried to lead our conversation to the Wallenberg question, he merely declared that this question would have to be taken up through diplomatic channels and that no private talks between the two of us on this subject ought to be held.'

When Ambassador Sohlman had handed over his prime minister's letter to Khrushchev in February 1961, the Soviet leader had replied with obvious irritation that the Soviet Union had already given the Swedes all the information they had on Wallenberg and that there was nothing new to add. No further reply, either verbal or written, was forthcoming from the Soviet leadership in the next eighteen months. Then, on 17 August 1962, Erlander sent for Soviet Ambassador Feodor Gusev, who was about to leave for a new post, and delivered to him a crisp message to be transmitted to Khrushchev.

*As you may understand, Mr Ambassador, this situation causes me serious concern, and on your return to Moscow I ask you to convey this to the Soviet government and personally to its chief. When I speak about concern, I mean in the first place that the matter is of importance for Soviet–Swedish relations, in whose further development in a harmonious and friendly spirit I know you have a great interest.*

*What is involved is the question of a Swedish diplomat who was captured by Soviet troops more than seventeen years ago. You will certainly agree with me that no government in such a situation can refrain from demanding that the requests it makes, on the basis of information which it has received and found reliable, be given both thorough investigation and courteous treatment.*

Erlander went on to point out that it was a generally accepted principle of humane behaviour that all efforts should be made to reunite close relatives who have been separated by circumstances beyond their control. 'This principle is not only generally accepted in theory,' he said, 'it has also come to be put more and more into practice. I appeal urgently to your government and to the chairman of the Council of Ministers, Mr Khrushchev, personally also to take this into consideration in dealing with this matter. I make this appeal with the strong hope of a positive reply.'

But there was no reply. Neither did Professor Svartz succeed in numerous attempts between 1962 and 1964 to renew contact with Professor Miashnikov. In mid-March 1964 Soviet Foreign Minister Gromyko paid a visit to Stockholm, during which Erlander again pressed him for an answer and suggested a meeting between Professors Svartz and Miashnikov. Six weeks later, on 29 April, Professor Svartz at last received a letter from Miashnikov.

*I write to you in connection with new statements appearing in Stockholm concerning Mr Wallenberg's fate.\* I was cited in these statements in a way such as to indicate that I had given you some sort of information about him during your visit to Moscow in 1961.*

*As you will surely recall, I told you then that I knew nothing about Mr Wallenberg, had never heard his name, and had not the slightest idea whether or not he was alive.*

*I advised you to address yourself to our Foreign Ministry on this matter, through your ambassador or in person. Upon your request that I inquire about the fate of this person with our Chief of Government, N. S. Khrushchev, whose doctor I was according to your account, I replied to you that N. S. Khrushchev, as everyone knew full well, was in absolutely good health and that I was not his doctor.*

*Owing to some misunderstanding inconceivable to me, this short talk with you (it was carried on in the German language, of which I may not be fully master) has come to be erroneously interpreted in official Swedish quarters.*

Professor Svartz wrote a detailed reply on 28 May 1964, recapitulating their conversation of January 1961 as she remembered it, and replying to his suggestion that language difficulties must have caused a misunderstanding. 'I reminded him that the two of us at a number of conversations during the 1950s, when we first met, had always understood both questions and answers very well, as had also been

---

\* Despite the implication that these statements had been publicized, the fact is no public reference had yet been made to Professor Miashnikov's role in the Wallenberg affair. This was to remain secret for another seventeen months.

the case of our conversation of January 1961, as well as the conversations which followed.'

In July 1965 Professor Svartz had one last encounter with Miashnikov. As a result of further Swedish representations to the Soviet government, a meeting was arranged between the two doctors in Moscow, in the presence of Swedish Ambassador Gunnar Jarring and two representatives of the Soviet Foreign Ministry, one of whom acted as interpreter. The ensuing three-hour talk was conducted in Swedish and Russian. It produced nothing new.

Professor Svartz stuck to her version of what had passed between them, while Professor Miashnikov stuck to his, adding the fresh information that in any event he could not possibly have known about the Wallenberg affair before she mentioned it in January 1961, 'since he had nothing to do with prisons or prison hospitals or with prisoners of war ... Moreover, he had never been invited by any Soviet authorities to treat any foreign or other prisoners of war, therefore he could not have seen or heard of Wallenberg.'

Miashnikov claimed that during the January 1961 conversation he had said, '*If* Wallenberg is alive, *perhaps* he may be ill.' He added that by a misunderstanding of his syntax, Professor Svartz might have misinterpreted his words 'not as assumptions but as statements of fact.'

'He said he had been talking to me in a humane spirit and had not believed that I was on any official or semi-official errand. Had he believed so, he would naturally have summoned an interpreter who would have had to write down what was being said ...

'The discussions ended with a concluding declaration by my informant that he considered the question brought to an end between the two of us and that we had not come to the result that either one of us had wanted. To this I declared that neither did I believe that we could come any further and that testimony stood against testimony.'*

Four months after this last encounter between the two professors, Miashnikov died suddenly. 'He must have been in his early sixties

* From a written memorandum published in 1965 in a Swedish government White Book.

and had never appeared to me to be in poor health,' Nanna Svartz told me in 1979. 'I must admit I have often wondered whether it was really a case of natural death.'

# Chapter 16

If the Swedish public had known about Nanna Svartz's testimony and the Vladimir Prison sightings, there might well have been uncontrollable riots when Khrushchev paid a five-day official visit to Stockholm between 22 and 27 June 1964. As it was, there were huge demonstrations, and attempts were made to present the Soviet leader personally with a petition that contained over a million signatures demanding Wallenberg's release.

The day Khrushchev arrived in Stockholm, the daily newspaper *Expressen* covered its front page with an editorial in Russian, under the huge headline 'Where is Raoul Wallenberg?' The editorial, in the form of an open letter to Khrushchev, declared, 'Even if you have brought fifty people with you, it is one too few – you have not brought Raoul Wallenberg.'

In an attempt to ward off any unpleasantness over the Wallenberg affair, or indeed any discussion of it at all during the Khrushchev visit, the Russians had ten days before summoned Ambassador Jarring to the Foreign Ministry to receive an oral statement from Deputy Foreign Minister Aleksandr Orlov. Orlov stated firmly the official Soviet position that 'there was no doubt whatsoever' that Wallenberg had died in 1947 in Lubianka Prison.* Assertions that

---

* This phraseology suggested that the Soviets had now slammed closed the door they had previously left slightly ajar. The Gromyko memorandum of February 1957 had contained the formulation that 'the conclusion should be drawn' that Wallenberg had died in 1947.

he was alive after that were 'either due to mistakes or else they reflected the efforts of certain persons to complicate relations between the Soviet Union and Sweden.'

Since all possibilities for investigating the case had been 'completely exhausted,' said Orlov, the Soviet government saw 'no further reason for engaging itself any longer in this question.' This harsh, almost contemptuous, message ended with the thinly veiled warning that 'any return to a discussion on this regrettable fact belonging to the past could only cause harm to Soviet–Swedish relations.'

To his credit, Erlander ignored this warning. During Khrushchev's visit, he several times raised the embarrassing Wallenberg question, risking Khrushchev's notorious temper, which at one point reportedly exploded in a threat that if the name Wallenberg were mentioned once more he would cut short his visit and leave.

The main discussion of the question took place immediately after intergovernmental negotiations on trade and other matters on 23 June. The official Swedish account does little to disguise the sharpness of tone. After Erlander 'pointed to the necessity of at least bringing about clarity on this outstanding question,' Khrushchev declared that 'he could not have imagined the Wallenberg question would be brought up anew.' The fact that Wallenberg was not to be found alive in the Soviet Union had been 'already made sharply clear' to the Swedes.

'The Swedish government must realize that the Soviet Union naturally would extradite Wallenberg if he were alive, irrespective of his physical or mental status. The Soviet Union had expatriated and extradited all sorts of people. What interest would they have in keeping Wallenberg?' Despite Professor Svartz's evidence, which must all be a misunderstanding based on language difficulties, 'as far as the Soviet government was concerned the matter was closed.'

Khrushchev added that 'many deeply tragic things had happened during the Stalin period, and he did not wish to expose himself to this interrogation, as there were a number of questions which had been replied to long ago.' Erlander, however, stood his ground: 'Swedish public opinion would certainly find it very difficult to understand why the Soviet government objected to further investigations.' But all he was able to obtain from his guest was a grudging agreement not to prevent a further meeting between Professors Svartz and Miashnikov – which finally occurred more than a year later.

The next time Erlander raised the matter briefly, a couple of days later, Khrushchev adopted a slightly more conciliatory tone, and 'declared himself to be sincerely sorry that the Soviet government did not have access to any material whereby this regrettable subject of contention between the Soviet Union and Sweden could be brought to a close.'

At the end of the Khrushchev visit, Erlander issued a statement saying the Wallenberg affair had been raised without any result having been obtained, and added, 'We are deeply disappointed that the Soviet Union has not felt able to do more about the matter . . . We do not intend to give up our efforts.'

Little more than two months later Khrushchev fell from power, to be replaced by the partnership of Alexei Kosygin and Leonid Brezhnev. The Wallenberg affair had now been a *cause célèbre* through two Soviet dictatorships. Perhaps, the Swedes thought, a change of régime might bring about a change of attitude. They should have known better.

Erlander waited until Kosygin had been in office as prime minister four months before resuming the diplomatic offensive in a personal letter of 11 February 1965: 'As you certainly understand, I would not take up the matter if it had not been . . . of such great importance . . . and if I had not been convinced that an elucidation of this matter would remove disturbing factors in Soviet–Swedish relations.

'I know that you agree with me on the importance of Swedish– Soviet relations being further developed and that in this respect we have a joint goal. In this spirit I take the liberty of addressing an appeal to you that you personally make arrangements for an investigation into all aspects of the matter in question . . .'

Kosygin told Ambassador Jarring, who delivered the letter, that he had read the Wallenberg file carefully and could not reach any conclusion other than that Wallenberg had died, as stated by Gromyko, in July 1947. So far as a meeting between Professors Svartz and Miashnikov was concerned, he would not oppose it although he saw little point in it.

The tenacious Erlander was not to be put off. On 13 May 1965 he warned Soviet Ambassador Nikolai Belokhvostikov that he would raise the matter in person when he paid an official visit to Moscow in June. 'The Soviet government must realize that the Swedish government attached extraordinary importance to the affair and that Swedish public opinion demanded an account of it,' said an official summary of the Erlander-Belokhvostikov meeting.

True to his word, Erlander raised the irritating matter at two intergovernmental negotiating sessions, on 11 and 17 June. He told his hosts that it appeared from their more recent statements that the 'assumption' of Wallenberg's death in Gromyko's note of February 1957 had now become a 'certainty,' and added that 'it was important for the Swedish government to be given access to the investigations which had been made in recent years and which had obviously led to this change.' In addition, the question of whether Professor Svartz's testimony or that of Professor Miashnikov was correct 'must be clarified.'

Kosygin replied, with evident asperity, that 'there existed no further material and no personal file on Wallenberg; why, it was not known. Nor were there any Soviet witnesses. If Wallenberg were alive he would be found very soon; those who were in prisons and in hospitals were known. A chief of government could soon find a living man, but not a dead man. How could the Swedish government seriously believe that the Soviet authorities were keeping Wallenberg in the Soviet Union? Why should they keep him?'

Kosygin conceded that the affair was a difficult and complicated one for Sweden, but the Soviet government had done all it could 'and had no more to add.'

Erlander 'repeated with sharpness' his demands for all the evidence. He expressed satisfaction that there would be a meeting between Professors Svartz and Miashnikov 'but regretted that the replies to his other requests had been negative.'

Like Khrushchev's visit to Stockholm the year before, that of Erlander to Moscow ended on a somewhat discordant note and, after the totally unproductive meeting between Nanna Svartz and

Aleksandr Miashnikov the following month, Erlander decided the time had come to make the information at his disposal public. The Foreign Ministry was instructed to prepare a White Book containing the diplomatic exchanges and memoranda and the new evidence collected since the previous White Book of 1957. These were presented to the press and public on 16 September 1965, and predictably caused a sensation – especially the revelation about the Nanna Svartz affair and the evidence of Wallenberg's having been seen in Vladimir Prison into the mid-1950s.

The White Book was accompanied by a personal statement from Erlander, which Western diplomats in the Swedish capital considered to be a surprisingly strong condemnation of the Russians. 'The fate of Raoul Wallenberg has deeply engaged Swedish opinion,' he said. 'We have sought to convince the Soviet leadership of the extraordinary seriousness with which Swedish quarters look upon this question. An essential part of our negotiations with the Soviet leaders during this period has come to concern the Wallenberg case. Unfortunately the result has been negative . . .' Despite this, Erlander promised that 'as long as there is a possibility, this effort must continue.'

Erlander's brave last words notwithstanding, many Swedes took the publication of the White Book as a tacit admission that no successful resolution of the Wallenberg affair was now likely. If it did not succeed as a final effort to put public pressure on the Soviets, the White Book might at least answer opposition charges that successive Social Democratic governments had not pursued the case vigorously enough.

Certainly, both press and public were impressed by the tenacity Erlander had exercised in the years since 1957, as revealed in the White Book. They were outraged by the peremptory – at times downright contemptuous – attitude of the Russians. It is fair to speculate that if the Swedish government had been as persistent and purposeful in the early years of Wallenberg's captivity he might well have been returned long since.

# Chapter 17

Following the dramatic disclosures of the 1965 Swedish government White Book, the Wallenberg affair went into a long period of hibernation. For many years it seemed that the White Book had been the last gasp – that there was nothing more to be said or done about the perplexing and tragic fate of Raoul Wallenberg. True, his family remained active, especially his indomitable mother, Maj, loyally supported by her husband, Fredrik von Dardel, who, in his quietly meticulous way, kept a compendious private archive of every conceivable document and photograph pertaining to his stepson.

With the flow of post-war prisoners coming out of Russia now dried up, the late 1960s and early 1970s produced little in the way of reliable new evidence. Stories still seeped out of Russia from time to time about a mysterious Swedish prisoner, usually in a remote Siberian camp, but by now the Wallenberg story had acquired some of the aura of a romantic if tragic legend among the millions of inhabitants of the Gulag. If the von Dardel family, prompted by wishful thinking, occasionally displayed a degree of gullibility, the official Swedish investigators remained hard-headed and thorough. They discarded most of the 'evidence' that came their way between the mid-1960s and the late 1970s; the Wallenberg affair began to fade away for lack of nourishment.

What seemed like a major lead turned up in 1973 when a Russian Jew named Efim (Haim) Moshinsky surfaced in Tel Aviv with an

extraordinary tale. He claimed to be a former agent of SMERSH*
and the KGB who had fallen afoul of the Soviet system and had
himself ended up a prisoner. He said he first encountered Wallenberg
in Budapest in January 1945, after the Swede had been taken in by
the NKVD.

According to Moshinsky, the NKVD believed Wallenberg knew
the whereabouts of large amounts of gold and jewellery belonging to
wealthy Jews whom he had saved. The NKVD wanted to get their
hands on this loot and this, said Moshinsky, was why they arrested
him. For good measure, they also suspected him of having cooperated with the Gestapo and, said Moshinsky, they subjected him
to a brutal, nine-day interrogation – in which he, Moshinsky, did not
take part – before taking him to the airport and flying him to
Moscow.

Swedish investigators were immediately suspicious of this story as,
in several respects, it did not tally with what was already known.
There was no mention, for example, of Langfelder, who was certainly
arrested with Wallenberg. Furthermore, neither Wallenberg nor
Langfelder had ever mentioned to fellow-prisoners when they arrived
in Russia that either of them had been ill-treated. Also, both had
stated that they went to Russia by train, Langfelder adding the detail
of their having been allowed off the train to eat in the restaurant
Luther in the Rumanian town of Jassy.

Still, the Swedes allowed Moshinsky to continue his story. He
said that he saw Wallenberg again in 1961–62 on Wrangel Island, a
prison colony inside the Arctic Circle, where, according to both
Moshinsky and other more reliable sources, a number of foreign
prisoners were held, including a group of Italian military officers.
Moshinsky was himself a prisoner on Wrangel Island and he said
that although he recognized Wallenberg clearly, he was never able to
get closer to him than six feet because of an electric fence which
separated their two compounds. Moshinsky said he was unable to
communicate with Wallenberg in any way. This part of Moshinsky's
story, too, does not tally with more substantial evidence – such as

* The Soviet counter-intelligence agency, whose acronym means 'Death to
Spies.'

that of Nanna Svartz, according to whose account Wallenberg was in a Moscow hospital in 1961.

Other stories which cropped up during this period were not so easy to discount. In January 1970, on the twenty-fifth anniversary of Wallenberg's disappearance, a young Hungarian visiting Stockholm saw an account of the Wallenberg affair in a Swedish newspaper. He telephoned Maj von Dardel, who invited him to her home. The Hungarian, whose name remains a secret, told her that in Budapest he had a girl friend whose father was a senior Hungarian government official. While the young man was at lunch one day with the girl's family, her father mentioned that a Swedish diplomat named Raoul Wallenberg, who had been active in Budapest during the war, was at that time in a Soviet camp in Siberia.

The young Hungarian told Mrs von Dardel that until then he had never heard of Wallenberg and that he had not thought of the incident since – until he saw Wallenberg's name in the Swedish press that January day. His story was checked by Swedish officials as thoroughly as it was possible to do. They did at least ascertain that the Hungarian official and his daughter really existed.

What might have been confirmation of this story came from another informant, also unnamed, who said in 1974 that he had seen Wallenberg in the Vadivovo Camp, near the Siberian city of Irkutsk, in 1966–67. At that time, said the ex-prisoner, he was 'an old man with white and very thin hair, who said he had been very ill.' The other prisoners nicknamed him 'Roniboni.' Like so many reported sightings in recent years, this one could neither be accepted as authentic nor rejected as false.

The British ex-spy Greville Wynne* added another intriguing, if rather circumstantial, morsel of information. In March 1980, he recalled an incident which took place when he was in Moscow's

---

* Wynne was a key figure in the case in which Soviet senior scientific officer Oleg Penkovsky was executed for selling state secrets to the West. Wynne, the liaison between Penkovsky and British and US intelligence, was sentenced to eight years in prison in 1963 but was exchanged a year later for Soviet master-spy Konon Molody, alias Gordon Lonsdale, who was serving a twenty-five-year term in Britain.

Lubianka Prison. Prisoners there were customarily taken up to the roof for solitary 'exercise' periods in small pens, not much bigger than their cells below. They were taken up in one of a number of small lifts, which Wynne described as 'rusty iron cages.' He went on to say:

One day in early 1963, I was up on the roof when I heard a cage coming into the next pen. As the gate opened I heard a voice call out 'Taxi.' Given the filthy condition of the lifts, this struck me as a piece of defiant humour, which I greatly appreciated. About five days after that, the same thing happened – the cage came up and the same voice called out 'Taxi,' and this time I heard some conversation between the prisoner and his guard. I could tell from the accent that this was another foreigner, so I called out, 'Are you American?'

The voice answered 'No, I'm Swedish.'

That was all I could learn, because at that moment my guard put his hand over my mouth and shoved me against the corner of the pen. Prisoners were not allowed to communicate with each other.

The significance of this story is that, with the exception of Wallenberg (assuming he was still alive), there was no known Swede in Soviet captivity. If there were a Swedish prisoner of whom the authorities in Stockholm were unaware, he must have been held on purely criminal charges, in which case he would not have been in the Lubianka – a jail exclusively for political prisoners, traitors and foreign spies.

# Chapter 18

Gradually the Wallenberg case slipped from the headlines of the Swedish press and from the consciousness of the Swedish public. The committee that had worked so hard and effectively for so many years was eventually disbanded. Only the von Dardel family and a few fanatically loyal helpers, such as Rudolf Philipp, kept the flame alive. By the time the next substantial piece of evidence surfaced that flame had been all but extinguished.

The first element in this evidence was contained in a telephone call in November 1977 to Anna Bilder, a Russian Jew who had recently emigrated from the Soviet Union with her husband and thirteen-year-old daughter to the Israeli town of Jaffa. The caller, much to Anna Bilder's astonishment and delight, was her father, Jan Kaplan. In the last news she had had of him he was in a Soviet prison, serving a four-year sentence for 'economic crimes' connected with his own attempts to emigrate to Israel.

By Soviet standards, the Kaplan family had apparently lived in some style in Moscow, where Jan had been the administrator of an operatic studio. He was sixty-six and lived with his sixty-year-old wife, Evgenia, in an apartment on fashionable Gorki Street. He had been jailed in 1975 (two years after Anna and her family went to Israel) for currency offences and the illegal purchase of diamonds – economic crimes occasionally committed by would-be emigrants trying to get what wealth they possessed out of the Soviet Union.

Kaplan had a heart condition and now he was phoning his daughter from Moscow with the good news that, as a result of a medical certificate signed by five Soviet doctors, he had been freed from prison.

Anna was delighted to hear of her father's release but concerned about his health. To have been released after serving only eighteen months of a four-year sentence suggested to her that her father must be in very poor condition. But Kaplan brushed aside her anxious inquiries and assured her that prison conditions were not too rigorous. 'Why,' he said, 'when I was in Butyrka Prison hospital in 1975 I met a Swede who told me he had been in Soviet prisons for thirty years, and he seemed reasonably healthy to me.'

The significance of this remark was completely lost on Anna Bilder. She had never heard of Raoul Wallenberg and had no reason to believe that there was anything especially unusual about a foreigner having been jailed in Russia for thirty years. While passing on the good news of Kaplan's release to relatives in Israel, she happened to mention her father's encounter with the Swede. They, too, failed to recognize the significance of his remark.

At about the same time, other Kaplan relatives, also living in Moscow, wrote to members of the family in Detroit, Michigan, about Jan's release. 'He doesn't look at all in bad shape,' said the letter. 'He says that he met a Swede in the sick ward of Butyrka who had been a prisoner for thirty years then, but who doesn't look sick at all.' Like the members of the family in Israel, the relatives in Detroit also failed to realize the significance of the remark. It appears that Kaplan was doing all he could to get a message out, without its appearing too obvious to low-level state security officials who might be monitoring his mail and phone calls. But the message just was not getting through. It might never have got through but for the intervention of another recent arrival in Israel from the Soviet Union, a Polish-born Jew named Abraham Kalinski.

Kalinski claims to have served almost fifteen years in Soviet prisons, from 1945 until late 1959. After his release he remained in the Soviet Union until 1975, when he was granted a visa to emigrate to Israel. He brought with him a second wife and small stepdaughter and settled with them in an apartment in the Israeli coastal town of

Nahariya, close to the Lebanese border. Since Kalinski was largely instrumental in reviving the once-moribund Wallenberg affair, and since he is the only witness to surface in the West for many years with credible first-hand evidence, it may be worthwhile to take a closer look at him and his testimony.

Kalinski was a somewhat enigmatic figure. He seemed well aware that some suspected his motives and was almost over-anxious to establish his credentials and his credibility. At the same time, he seemed almost willing to create an aura of mystery around himself and his activities. In Israel, during the 1970s many Soviet émigrés seemed to live in, even to thrive on, an atmosphere of suspicion and intrigue, accusing and in turn being accused by each other. Given that the KGB had, almost certainly, infiltrated a number of agents among the scores of thousands of Jewish émigrés to Israel and the West, these suspicions were perhaps understandable. However, among the Russian Jews in Israel they sometimes appeared obsessive.

Kalinski claimed to be a former Polish Army officer who, during the latter stages of World War II, was attached to the Soviet Defence Ministry in Moscow as a liaison officer. He claimed that at the time he was married to a well-known Soviet film director, who committed suicide. He said he was arrested and jailed by the Soviets in 1945 after being betrayed by a Russian spy in the American embassy in Moscow who intercepted a letter, which he had addressed to the US government and sent via the Moscow embassy, about the Katyn Forest massacre.*

He claimed he first heard of Wallenberg in 1951, when he was in prison at a place called Verkhne Uralsk. He was told about the Swedish prisoner by David Vendrovsky, a Jewish author, who was moved into Kalinski's cell after previously sharing a cell with Wallenberg and a former Latvian cabinet minister, Wilhelm Munters.

---

* After the war, the remains of twelve thousand Polish officers were found buried in Katyn Forest in eastern Poland. The Russians claimed that the Nazis were responsible; the Germans maintained that the Russians carried out the massacre during their occupation of that part of Poland. After the collapse of the Soviet Union in 1991 the Russian government finally admitted Soviet responsibility for the crime.

'Vendrovsky told me that Wallenberg was a very interesting and exceedingly sympathetic man,' said Kalinski. He claimed that Vendrovsky told him in great detail about Wallenberg's version of his arrest and imprisonment as a spy.

Kalinski said Vendrovsky pointed Wallenberg out to him from their cell window as the Swede was exercising in a yard below.

'Several times a month until 1953 we saw them, Munters and the Swede, sometimes exercising in the yard, sometimes on the way to or from the bath-house, only this was by accident because we were not supposed to see other prisoners,' he said.

'In 1953, following the death of Stalin, Verkhne Uralsk was cleared to make room for the supporters of Beria and we were all transferred by rail to Alexandrov Central Prison. I was travelling alone, under heavy escort, as a dangerous state prisoner, but I saw Wallenberg and a group of other prisoners walk past my compartment. I never saw him at all in Alexandrov Central, though. It's an old tsarist prison and we were kept in separate blocks, but in 1955, when we were all being transferred to Vladimir Prison, I saw him again at the transit prison at Gorki, where all we prisoners were mustered in a big hall before continuing our journeys. He was in the same company, that is, with Munters and the others.'

Kalinski said his first two months in Vladimir Prison were spent in solitary confinement in cell 21 on the second floor of Corpus II. At the beginning of 1956 he acquired a cell-mate, the Georgian Social Democrat Simon Gogoberidse,* whom the KGB had kidnapped from Paris, where he was a political refugee. Gogoberidse told him he had just come from Corpus III, where he had been sharing a cell with Wallenberg and a former KGB general named Mamulov,† one of those who fell from grace with Beria. Gogoberidse said Wallenberg and Mamulov had also just been transferred to Corpus II and were in cell 23, on the same floor.

* Already mentioned in the testimony given by the witnesses Mulle and Rehekampf.

† It is a particularly grim irony that the humanitarian Wallenberg should have been forced to share a cell with Mamulov, of whom Aleksandr Solzhenitsyn has written, 'can anyone imagine a fouler butcher?'

'In fact, on that very day, after only a couple of hours, we saw Wallenberg and Mamulov from our cell window, exercising down in the yard,' said Kalinski. 'Afterwards I saw him many, many times when he was exercising either in Yard Four or Yard Five. These were the only two yards visible from my cell window.' Kalinski said he never got a chance to talk to Wallenberg. 'Towards the end of my time there I learned that Wallenberg was sharing a cell with a man named Shariyev, a former secretary of the Georgian Communist Party Central Committee. He was still there in cell 23 when I was released from Vladimir Prison on 29 October, 1959.'

Kalinski pointed out at this period that Wallenberg was always made to share a cell with Soviet citizens serving long sentences, never with foreigners. 'This was done to reduce the risk of evidence about him getting out. If he were to have shared a cell with a foreigner who was later released the Russians would find it impossible to keep it quiet.'

In answer to any suggestion that his story was a subsequent invention, Kalinski was able to produce interesting documentary evidence to support his assertion that he saw Wallenberg at the time stated. During his years in prison he sent out postcards regularly to his sister, who lived in the northern Israeli port city of Haifa. These cards were printed by the International Red Cross, in accordance with Soviet prison service specifications, and prisoners were allowed to send and receive one of these a month.* Each card included a perforated, tear-off bottom half for the return message. When Kalinski finally got to Israel in 1975 he found that his sister had kept all his postcards.

Among them is one from March 1959, written in Yiddish but in Hebrew characters, in which he tells his sister that all the Germans in the prison except two have been freed and the only foreigners left are now himself, one Italian, two Belgians, and a Swede. In another, which dates from August 1959 and is written in Polish, Kalinski tells his sister that the only foreigners now left in the prison, apart from

---

* Wallenberg obviously was not accorded this privilege.

himself, are one Italian and one Swede 'who saved many Jews in Rumania during the war.'

'Rumania' was a mistake, said Kalinski. 'Of course, I had heard from Gogoberidse and the others about what he had done in the war and just confused Hungary with Rumania.' Kalinski insisted that these postcards constitute convincing proof that he was telling the truth about Wallenberg. 'At that time I had no way of knowing that they were not going to let Wallenberg go eventually,' he said, 'and I had no idea that there was a great scandal about the Wallenberg affair. So why should I have mentioned him in those cards unless it was the truth?'

Kalinski handed these two postcards, and others out of the hundred or so in his sister's possession, to the Swedish Foreign Office in January 1980 so that they could be subjected to exhaustive scientific tests to establish their authenticity. After several weeks the Swedes let it be known that they were perfectly satisfied that the postcards were genuine.

So much for Kalinski's own testimony. How did he get so closely involved with that of Jan Kaplan?

In October 1978 he was flying from Tel Aviv to Vienna on business when his eye chanced to fall on a small item in *Nasha Strana*, a Russian-language Israeli newspaper. The story said that the noted Nazi-hunter Simon Wiesenthal, who took a personal interest in the Wallenberg case, had urged Sweden to boycott the 1980 Moscow Olympics if the Russians failed to disclose what they had done with Raoul Wallenberg.

As Kalinski told it later, this item transfixed him. 'Lord, I said to myself, isn't Wallenberg out yet? I would never have dreamed that he was still jailed in the Soviet Union. If I had only known, of course I would have told far earlier what I knew about him.'

In a state of high excitement, Kalinski called on Wiesenthal as soon as he arrived in Vienna. After this he appeared on West German television and as a result of this the Swedish Foreign Office got in touch with him. What Kalinski told the Swedes appeared to be important confirmation of their earlier information about Wallenberg having been in Vladimir Prison, and it brought forward the date of his last having been seen from mid-1955 to late 1959.

After Kalinski's return to Israel from that trip to Europe, he heard through the Russian émigré grapevine about Anna Bilder's telephone conversation with her father. He got in touch with her and she gave him a detailed account of it. Kaplan's mention of the unnamed Swede he had met in Butyrka Prison hospital excited Kalinski greatly. He decided to check further. On a trip to the United States in December 1978 he telephoned the Kaplan home in Moscow, having obtained the number from Anna. Evgenia Kaplan took the call. Her husband was 'not available,'* she told Kalinski. But she confirmed that he had told her about meeting a Swede in Butyrka in 1975.

Kalinski then contacted the Swedish embassy in Washington and arranged a meeting at their consulate in New York for 20 December. Swedish Foreigh Office Secretary-General Leif Leifland and East European Department Chief Sven Hirdman, then in charge of the Wallenberg case, were present when Kalinski again gave a detailed account of seeing Wallenberg in Soviet jails during the 1950s. He then added the astonishing information emanating from Jan Kaplan about the mysterious Swede in the Butyrka Prison hospital in 1975.

If the story were true, the unnamed Swede would have to be Wallenberg. Only he would have been a prisoner for thirty years at that time, and no other Swede was known or suspected to be in Soviet hands.

As a result of this information, the Swedish Foreign Office contacted their embassy in Tel Aviv and embassy counsellor Hakan Wilkens was instructed to invite Anna Bilder in for an interview. The normally cautious Swedes were so impressed by the evidence from both Anna Bilder and Abraham Kalinski that in January 1979 they formally reopened the moribund Wallenberg case.

On 3 January they sent a note to the Russian Foreign Ministry requesting the Soviets to investigate the new information 'in order to establish whether Wallenberg had been present in the above-mentioned prisons at the different dates indicated.' On 24 January the Russians replied: 'There is not, and cannot be, anything new regard-

* He was, in fact, in prison again by this time.

182

ing the fate of R. Wallenberg.' As already stated on innumerable occasions, he had died in July 1947, and the assertions that he was in the Soviet Union as late as 1975 'are not in accordance with the facts.'

Soon after the Swedes heard from the Russians, Anna Bilder learned that her ailing father was back in prison. What was more, she claims, she received anonymous phone calls – two from Russian-speaking women and one from an English-speaking man. One voice had said, 'Don't say anything about Wallenberg,' and had then hung up. Another said, 'I'm your friend. I think it's better for your father if you don't speak about Wallenberg.'

Then, in the second week of July, Anna received a letter from her mother, dated 14 June 1979. It had been brought out of Russia by a new immigrant to Israel.

*I write this letter to you though I am not sure that it will reach you and that the same thing will not happen as with Father's letter, because of which he is already a year and a half in prison again. But we have nothing to lose after what happened to Father.*

*All the time I didn't want and couldn't write, even more so because of your pregnancy and then after the delivery,\* but you cannot help Father. I lost all hope after I was called to Lubianka and learned that all this tragedy occurred because of the letter about this Swiss or Swede Wallberg [sic] whom he met in the prison infirmary when your father was sick with pneumonia and a heart attack. Father wrote a long letter about this Wallberg and for a long time he carried it around with him, looking for a chance to send it to you with a foreign tourist.*

*Every Saturday he went to the synagogue, where many tourists visit, but for a long time he had no success. He would come home very tired and say that everybody was afraid to take the letter through the border. Then one Saturday Father came home in a very good mood and told me that he had at last succeeded in giving the letter to a young foreign tourist who promised to send the letter to you in Israel from Vienna or Germany, I don't remember which.*

*A few days later, it was on Friday night, 3 February,† there was a thorough search of our home and they took Father away with them. Already about a year and a half he is in custody, sometimes in Lubianka, sometimes in Lefortovo. Now I have lost all hope of seeing you again some day.*

\* A reference to Anna's second daughter, Daniella, born in September 1978.
† Presumably 1978.

*When I was called in May\* to Lubianka, a very angry colonel screamed at me 'The Soviet authorities behaved humanely and because of his (Father's) sickness released him, but he ungratefully decided to send out illegally anti-Soviet spy letters to Israel through a foreigner. And your daughter,' he shouted, 'started up anti-Soviet propaganda there in Israel.'*

*Later he calmed down a bit and said, 'If your daughter wants to see her father again some day she should stop her agitation against her motherland.' About Father, he said, 'He is in good health, but his fate depends upon your daughter's behaviour in Israel – that is to say, he shouldn't make a fuss there.'*

*I don't know if it's better to keep quiet, as many people here advise, or the opposite, so that American senators and other big people should start campaigning for Father, because many people were released through complaints to American senators and even to the President himself. Some people say that only a fuss in the papers and on the radio will do any good. I don't know the answer myself. Here we are like blind puppies. You can see better there.*

*I'm afraid we won't ever see you again, or your little Daniella. Why did Father have to interfere in this business? He never had anything to do with politics, and wouldn't even listen to political jokes. Up to now I don't understand what happened to the letter your father gave to the young foreigner. Perhaps he was an agent of the Lubianka.†I don't know what went wrong, but I have no hope of anything.*

*Because of that letter about a poor prisoner they arrest a man and keep him for a year and a half. What good can you expect here? I know this letter must sound bitter. For a long time I didn't want to write and tell you all the truth, and now I've decided that to help him you should know all the truth. My dearest, write and tell me how little Daniella develops and how Marina does at school, and where you spend your holidays. I want to know everything, so write to me and don't be lazy. Let me know about them all the time.*

Anna Bilder agonized over the letter, wondering what to do for the best. She first disclosed the letter's contents to me on 23 July 1979. Then she consulted Abraham Kalinski, who urged her to turn it over immediately to the Swedish embassy in Tel Aviv. A couple of days later Kalinski and Anna went together to the embassy, where Evgenia Kaplan's letter was photo-copied and the original sent to Stockholm by diplomatic pouch. There it was minutely examined by police and Foreign Office Soviet experts.

---

\* Presumably 1979.

† 'An agent of the Lubianka' means a KGB man or an informer.

They were sufficiently convinced of the genuineness of the letter and Anna's verbal evidence to recommend to the foreign minister that grounds existed for a further *démarche* to the Kremlin. This time Prime Minister Ola Ullsten decided to intervene personally. On 22 August 1979 he sent a letter to his opposite number, Alexei Kosygin. Ullsten asked in strong terms for the Wallenberg case to be reopened in the light of the new evidence, and in particular that a Swedish embassy official be allowed to interview Kaplan, if necessary in the presence of a Soviet official.

On 28 August the Russians replied. They stuck to their old story that Wallenberg died in 1947, and that there was nothing more to add. No reference at all was made to the Swedish request for an interview with Kaplan.

The same day, Prime Minister Ullsten issued a statement calling the Soviet attitude 'deplorable.' 'Personally,' he added, 'I am convinced that the whole truth about the disappearance of Raoul Wallenberg is still not at hand ... We will continue our efforts to get a clarification of his fate. To this end we will, as we have done in the past, carefully test all new evidence that comes to our knowledge and take those measures we deem appropriate. The Wallenberg case remains an unsolved question ...'

# Chapter 19

Although the United States played no part in the attempts to locate and free Wallenberg after being rebuffed by the Swedes in April 1945, they retained an onlooker's interest in the case,* as a flow of cable traffic between the US embassy in Stockholm and the State Department in Washington indicates, if only because of its effect on Soviet–Swedish relations.

Thus, when Maj von Dardel addressed a letter to Secretary of State Henry Kissinger on 4 May 1973, seeking his help in the search for her son, US officials were already fully briefed on the ramifications of the Wallenberg affair. In her letter, Mrs von Dardel wrote: 'I have with the greatest admiration followed your patient and successful struggle for peace in the Far East. I turn now to you concerning my son Raoul Wallenberg, born in 1912. His father was the cousin of Jakob and Marcus Wallenberg, of whom you probably know.'

After outlining briefly her son's work in wartime Budapest and the unsuccessful attempts to obtain his release from Russia, Mrs von Dardel concluded: 'I ask you, who by virtue of your extraordinary efforts have liberated thousands of prisoners ... to undertake some-

* In July 1949 Secretary of State Dean Acheson, replying to an appeal from Guy von Dardel, pledged 'any assistance the United States can give.' There seems to have been no follow-up.

186

thing which can throw new light on my son's fate and if he is still alive to return him to liberty.'

When the letter reached Kissinger's desk at the White House, on 21 August 1973, it was accompanied by a confidential memorandum signed by Thomas R. Pickering,* executive secretary at the State Department. This senior official was recommending to Kissinger that the United States should officially take up the Wallenberg case after all these years. He said:

As Mrs von Dardel underlines in her letter, her son went to Budapest in 1944 on the request of the then US ambassador to Sweden to conduct a salvage operation for the Hungarian Jews, and his efforts saved thousands of Jews from death. As Mrs von Dardel is now eighty years old and in bad health, she probably wants to make a last attempt to ascertain the fate of her son before she dies. Against the background of the compassion one must feel in this case, and the fact that the American government was the driving force behind Wallenberg's mission in Hungary, we consider that we ought to take a positive stand on Mrs von Dardel's request and offer to make new inquiries at the Soviet Foreign Ministry, though without thereby giving her false hope that these attempts will be successful.

Pickering went on to recommend that Kissinger should approve an enclosed draft letter, to be signed by 'a State Department official at a suitable level.' The letter read:

*Dear Mrs von Dardel,*

  *Dr. Henry Kissinger has asked me to answer your letter and memorandum of May 4, 1973 ... Let me first state that I wholeheartedly support your desire to know definitely what happened to your son ... Against the background of the humanitarian nature of the case and your son's efforts for the Hungarian Jews during the last war, the United States government is prepared to ask the Soviet government, via the American embassy in Moscow, what has happened to your son. When an answer is obtained we will transmit it to you immediately, but considering the long period which has passed since your son disappeared and the previous unsuccessful attempts to get further information about his fate, I must ask you not to be too optimistic about the possibilities to obtain exact information*

---

* Pickering was merely the conduit through which the recommendation was passed on to Kissinger. The official mainly responsible for this effort was Walter J. Stoessel, Jr., at the time assistant secretary of state for European affairs.

*in his case. With the greatest compassion for your sufferings during all these years.*

*Very sincerely yours . . .*

This file included a detailed summary of the whole Wallenberg case for Kissinger's perusal, and a telex message ready for transmission to the US embassy in Moscow, instructing the ambassador to launch this new initiative, together with all the necessary background information. All that was required was Kissinger's approval on the file. He never gave it.

That file is available for study in the State Department's archives. Written across the top of Pickering's memorandum are the words 'Disapproved by Kissinger' and the date '15 October 1973.'

Kissinger offered an explanation of this episode when asked about it in 1979 by Mrs Lena Björck-Kaplan, chairman of the working group for the US Free Raoul Wallenberg Committee. As she recalls the conversation, the former secretary of state denied that he rejected the recommendation, claiming that he had never seen it. Could she really believe, he asked, that someone of his background – a German Jew who had escaped to the United States as a schoolboy – could have turned down such a suggestion? He could only suppose that a subordinate authorized to act on his behalf under certain circumstances must have done so on this occasion. In fairness to Kissinger, it should be pointed out that at the time the recommendation was rejected the calamitous October War was raging in the Middle East. It therefore seems quite possible that one of his senior aides took it upon himself to shunt such a comparatively 'minor' matter as the fate of an unknown Swede off his chief's agenda.

Nevertheless, in Sweden it is widely believed that Kissinger withheld his approval because he was still angry over the Swedes' condemnation of US policies in Vietnam and their harbouring of American draft-resisters.

Another world figure who might have helped Wallenberg but failed to was fellow-Swede Dag Hammarskjöld, secretary-general of the United Nations from 1953 until his death in an air crash in Northern Rhodesia in 1961.

According to Professor Carl-Fredrik Palmstierna,* private secretary to King Gustav VI (son of the monarch who had played a part in sending Wallenberg to Budapest), Hammarskjöld was asked three times in the 1950s by the Wallenberg Committee to raise the matter with the Russians. This was after he had promised that if direct Swedish representations failed he would work 'with heart and soul' for his countryman's release. According to Palmstierna's memoirs, when Hammarskjöld was asked to fulfil this promise – first in 1955, again in 1956, and finally in 1959 – he found reasons not to do so. In June 1956 it was Palmstierna himself who put the request to Hammarskjöld. In his memoirs he says:

He answered in a stream of crystal-clear phrases, saying the fact that he himself was a Swede made it doubly difficult to put the case of a compatriot to the Russians. If matters had been different he would, of course, etcetera, etcetera . . .

I wondered to myself how matters could have been different. If Hammarskjöld had taken up the case of a non-Swedish citizen he would presumably have been rebuffed with the argument that as secretary-general of the United Nations he had no right to meddle in the internal affairs of other countries. The indifference of Hammarskjöld did not surprise me. Again that damned Foreign Office outlook! Of course, there was no question of 'declaring war on Russia' as he said on a later occasion, quoting Undén. But was it not to be feared that the Russians would consider this lack of official interest in one of our own people, this anxiety to avoid any unpleasantness, as an indication of Swedish weakness?

Palmstierna also accuses the late King Gustav VI of indifference to the plight of Wallenberg.

When the case was brought to the fore again in the mid-1950s, I thought it advisable to draw the attention of my Royal master to the matter. This, however, proved far from easy . . . Our minister of foreign affairs, Östen Undén, a Marxist professor of law, followed with benevolent interest the Great Socialist Experiment in Russia and he allowed nothing to interfere with Sweden's friendly relations with Russia.

Out of loyalty – an elastic notion – the King had adopted the views of his foreign minister. I knew only too well that in the initial phase of the

---

* A distant relative of Wallenberg's mother and a friend of the family.

Wallenberg case Undén had committed many sins of omission, but criticizing his handling of the matter in front of His Majesty was like trying to get between the bark and the tree.

Palmstierna says his first conversation with the king on the subject took place in March 1955, during a visit to Stockholm by Gromyko, whom the king was about to receive in private audience.

This was, I hoped, an occasion . . . to open the matter directly with one of those responsible for detaining Wallenberg. It was, after all, a purely humanitarian case . . . I dashed to the King's study and suggested this to him. The King thanked me, admitting that he himself had thought of discussing the question with Gromyko. At last, I thought, maybe something will come of this. You never can tell how the Russians will react. Maybe they still feel some respect for a king.

But my optimism proved premature. In a quarter of an hour His Majesty returned, saying that having thought it over he felt he had better talk to Undén before raising the question with Gromyko. My disappointment was great. The outcome of that conversation [with Undén] was only too easy to predict.

Palmstierna recalls that the last time he tried to raise the Wallenberg question with the king, in the summer of 1959, Gustav appeared irritated:

'What do you expect me to do?' he demanded. 'Are we supposed to ransack the prisons of Russia or declare war for the sake of Wallenberg?'

Again those words of Undén's! Again I was told that never had so much been done for a Swede in distress as had been done in this case. This was, of course, no real answer, for the case was unique in Swedish history. With a shrug of his shoulders, the King made it clear he considered the responsibility was not his but that of the government. I contented myself by replying that posterity would concern itself deeply with the handling of this case. Another shrug, and His Majesty returned to the pile of papers on his desk.

Palmstierna believes that Queen Louise, as well as Undén, influenced the king against intervention:

I may be indiscreet, but in the name of historical truth I must state this. I do not know what persons could have persuaded her to believe that the Austrian Rudolf Philipp . . . who devoted years of research to revealing the Russian lies and subterfuges, was using the case of Raoul Wallenberg as a meal ticket, at the expense of the latter's family . . . Once when Her Majesty brought forth this accusation I replied in moderate terms that this was not the case; I knew exactly what reward Philipp had received for his endeavours. There was a somewhat confused reply.*

Palmstierna records that in 1972, at a press conference in Vienna, Undén's successor as foreign minister, Krister Wickman, declared that his government 'had consigned the case of Raoul Wallenberg to oblivion.' This, incidentally, was confirmed quite independently by Nazi-hunter Simon Wiesenthal, who was present and who in fact had asked the question which elicited this answer. 'He asked his secretary and the Swedish ambassador, "Who is this man who is asking this question?"' Wiesenthal recalls. 'And then he answered me. "This case has been closed for a long time. We are doing nothing more on this case."' In later years Wiesenthal was willing to concede that the Swedish government was once again pursuing the matter actively. 'When I was in Sweden recently,' he told me in late 1979, 'I was talking to the Deputy Foreign Minister and he said to me, "Now you will be content with us because we are active again."'†

Well into the 1980s Wiesenthal remained extremely active, persuaded as he was that Wallenberg might still be alive. In the summer of 1979, he was given air time on the Russian-language Service of the Voice of America, the US government-controlled overseas broadcasting organization, to transmit an appeal for anyone in the Soviet

* Philipp died in Stockholm in 1980. He was a lonely and embittered man and his only regular visitor seemed to have been Nina Lagergren, who, at his request, took possession of the mountains of documents – most of them relating to the Wallenberg affair – which cluttered his tiny apartment.

† Wiesenthal, as we have seen, was brought into the case at Maj von Dardel's request in the mid-1960s, although Soviet affairs are not, strictly speaking, his speciality. She sought his help because of his many remarkable successes in tracking down Nazi war criminals in remote parts of the globe, thanks to his private worldwide intelligence network and the exhaustive files of his documentation centre in Vienna. He is said to have played a part in the capture of, among others, Eichmann, though this is fiercely disputed by his free-lance and official rivals, including the Israeli secret service, Mossad. Wiesenthal has received no money from Wallenberg's family for his tireless efforts over the years.

Union who anything knew about Wallenberg's whereabouts to write to him – 'Simon Wiesenthal, Vienna, is enough of an address' – telling what they knew. 'We need little pieces of information so that we can build up a bigger picture,' he said. 'This is our duty as free people, not just my duty as a Jew, to help prove that this man is alive and to bring him back to the free world.

'We have so many Nobel Prize winners, you know, but I don't know of any other man whom I would rather nominate for the Peace Prize than Raoul Wallenberg.'

If Wiesenthal's use of the Voice of America to broadcast an appeal in Russian for information about Wallenberg suggests a degree of official US involvement once again, that indeed was the case.

In 1979, when the Kalinski and Kaplan testimonies first came to light, interest was suddenly kindled in the United States, where the Wallenberg story was virtually unknown. Annette Lantos, a Californián housewife of Hungarian–Jewish background, was moved to tears by a brief item in *The New York Times*. There was reason enough for her emotional reaction: she and her husband, Tom Lantos, then legal aide to Democratic Senator Joseph R. Biden, Jr., of Delaware, both owed their lives to their possession of 'Wallenberg' passports that, as teenagers, they had been able to obtain in Budapest in 1944. To both, Wallenberg had become a dim – if legendary – memory, someone they imagined had died many years before.

Annette Lantos threw herself energetically into writing letters, organizing committees, setting up press conferences, contacting potentially interested bodies – especially among the American Jewish community – and enlisting the support of prominent persons. Her husband's Washington connections helped. In July 1979 three influential senators – Frank Church of Idaho, Chairman of the Senate Foreign Relations Committee, Daniel Patrick Moynihan of New York, and Claiborne Pell of Rhode Island – plus Berlin-born freshman Senator Rudy Boschwitz of Minnesota became co-chairmen of the American Free Raoul Wallenberg Committee. The objectives of this committee were 'to gather and substantiate all information on the whereabouts of Wallenberg; to press the government of the Soviet Union to reveal all that it knows about Wallenberg and, if he is still alive, to free him; to enlist the support of governments, private groups, and individuals throughout the world in the committee's efforts on behalf of Raoul Wallenberg.'

When Nina Lagergren visited the United States soon afterwards, the tireless Annette Lantos helped to arrange widespread media coverage, which thus brought the Wallenberg affair to the notice of a wide American public. In the autumn of 1979, when Guy von Dardel was in the United States, Mrs Lantos and her senatorial supporters helped arrange a meeting with Secretary of State Cyrus Vance, who promised active American government support.

Soon after that Annette Lantos was selected to talk to President Carter on a radio phone-in programme. Naturally, she asked the president about the Wallenberg case – and he claimed that he had himself raised the issue with Soviet President Leonid Brezhnev when the two leaders met in Vienna, earlier that year. What response Carter got has not been disclosed.

In the autumn of 1980, just before the elections which swept President Carter out of office and cost Church his Senate seat, both Houses of the US Congress unanimously passed resolutions acknowledging Wallenberg's wartime achievements and calling on the State Department to take up his case with the Soviet government. The resolutions also called on the US delegation to the forthcoming Madrid conference on European security and co-operation – at which progress on the 1976 Helsinki Agreements on human rights was to be reviewed – to take up the issue with the Russian delegation.

The Swedes took the lead in an opening speech to the plenary session and in a further address before the conference's human rights committee. The US delegate to this committee followed up, saying:

'The United States heartily supports the intervention by the delegate of Sweden and his entreaty once and for all to ascertain the fate of Raoul Wallenberg. As the Swedish delegation said, there have been secret reports that he may still be alive. As you know, Mr Wallenberg's heroic actions in Budapest at the end of World War II were financed in part by the American government. The US delegation and the American people feel a special debt to Mr Wallenberg and his family. We would very much like to see the governments involved co-operate fully in order to determine the facts about his disappearance.'

The British delegate immediately followed, saying his country 'fully and wholeheartedly' supported the Swedish plea.

'Wallenberg's extraordinary work in helping refugees and the victims of oppression deserves special consideration,' he said. 'Renewed reports that he might be alive have aroused great hopes and deserve to be thoroughly investigated. In the confused post-war era when he disappeared strange things did happen. The possibility that he has somehow survived many vicissitudes cannot be dismissed.'

The Soviets, as usual, stonewalled. Their delegate said only that they would reply later in the conference to all the matters raised.

Ironically, the elections which swept Carter, Church, and so many others out of office brought to Congress the one man in American public life who owes his life directly to Raoul Wallenberg – Tom Lantos. Swimming against the political tide, he beat the incumbent conservative Republican to become the Democratic member of the US House of Representatives for the 11th District of California.

On 26 March 1981 Lantos introduced a resolution in the House of Representatives which would confer honorary US citizenship on Wallenberg, a distinction previously accorded only to one other foreigner, Sir Winston Churchill. His bill had 258 co-sponsors, guaranteeing it passage through the lower house. Lantos was confident that an identical resolution would pass swiftly through the Senate. The effect of making Wallenberg an honorary American, Lantos told a news conference before presenting his bill on the floor of the House, would be to 'give the State Department the legal basis to pursue the case of the ultimate American hostage.'

Lantos added: 'It is my considered judgement that the chances are even that Raoul Wallenberg is alive today.' But even if it turned out that he had died in captivity, by passing his joint resolution the US Congress, and people, will 'not only have honoured the man . . . but will have honoured ourselves and our profound commitment to human rights.'

Lantos's wife spoke with great emotion about Wallenberg. 'He was like a Moses from the north, who came to us in the most terrible days. His noble and courageous deeds truly shone like a bright light in that abysmal darkness. Just remembering his goodness and his sacrifice for our sake, somehow helped to heal my own emotional and spiritual wounds. If it is the only thing in my life I must spare no effort to help this man.'

Her colleague on the Wallenberg Committee's working group Elizabeth Moynihan, wife of the senator, took an equally strong if less emotional view. 'In the story of Raoul Wallenberg,' she said, 'two issues are tragically linked – the courage of a truly good man and his unjust fate. There are few comparable examples of a man facing evil to save his fellow-men.'

Nina Lagergren found a ray of hope in the upsurge of interest in her half-brother. 'If only my parents had remained alive long enough to see all these things happening – so many incredible things in the past few months. It's like a miracle really, this avalanche development, so many people having been moved about the fate of Raoul who had never heard of him before. It all seems to mean something. I firmly believe that all this couldn't be happening unless it means that we will get Raoul back.'


Throughout the long saga of the Wallenberg affair, the wealthy and influential brothers Marcus and Jakob Wallenberg, directors of the bank which used to bear the family name but is now the Skandinaviska Enskilda Bank, kept a remarkably low profile. Marcus, the older brother and head of the family, is known to have sent a letter to the Soviet ambassador, Mme Kollontai, regarding the fate of his cousin on 26 April 1945. The contents of the letter have never been disclosed, although Mme Kollontai – who had by that time been recalled to Moscow – is known to have replied that she would do what she could, although 'when one is no longer in charge it is not so easy.' This is the only known written exchange involving either of Raoul's two illustrious older cousins.

Marcus apparently knew Mme Kollontai well. It was reportedly on her advice that he flew to Finland in 1944 and was instrumental in getting the Finns to conclude an armistice with the Russians. A little later, during a period of strained relations between the Soviet Union and Sweden, it is known that Mme Kollontai suggested Marcus as a suitable Swedish ambassador to Moscow and that the

Soviet government let it be known that they would not object. Clearly, this head of 'a big capitalist family' was acceptable to the men in the Kremlin.

According to other members of the family, Jakob Wallenberg (who died in 1980) idolized Raoul's father. It may seem strange, therefore, that he and Marcus did not take a more public position on their cousin's behalf. Possibly, their interventions were very discreet. Maj von Dardel never liked to discuss the matter, although she is on record as having once said that 'whatever they have done, they have done behind the scenes.'

This appears to have been the case. In the 1970s they discreetly subsidized the Raoul Wallenberg Association in Stockholm through intermediaries and subsidiary companies, which have provided free office accommodation.

Their reluctance to champion their cousin's cause too openly was attributed by some to their fear of jeopardizing the business which their bank conducted with the Soviet Union. A more charitable explanation may be that they were aware of a certain amount of public resentment of the family, especially among the less affluent in Sweden, and that this made them unwilling to risk being accused of damaging Swedish–Soviet relations in pursuit of what might be seen as a family concern.

One family friend reflected sadly: 'It's ironic to think that if Raoul had been adopted by his stepfather and had taken the name von Dardel he might have been a free man many years ago.'

Like many powerful men, the Wallenberg brothers preferred to avoid publicity. Neither ever responded to questions by journalists about their role in the Wallenberg affair. This dislike of publicity apparently extends to the Enskilda Bank. In the winter of 1979, when a British television team wanted to film the entrance to the bank's headquarters to get pictures of portraits of the Wallenberg banking dynasty, there was some consternation among bank officials.

Told that the pictures were wanted for a documentary film about Raoul Wallenberg, a public-relations executive sniffed, 'That's not the kind of publicity we want.'

# Chapter 20

We have seen how Swedish weakness in the early years of Wallenberg's captivity led to a series of disastrous blunders that may have sealed his fate forever. We have seen how the Americans, rebuffed once by Ambassador Söderblom in Moscow in April 1945, made no further attempt to do anything about the man they were instrumental in sending to Budapest and how Henry Kissinger, given an opportunity to make amends in 1973, failed to take it. We have seen how other influential individuals who might have been able to help also failed to do so. What about the other two countries most intimately concerned – Hungary and Israel?

For a time, the Jews of Budapest – that is, those who refused to credit the Russian radio report of his death – believed either that Wallenberg was safely in Russian hands or that, if a prisoner, he would be released shortly. On 2 July 1945 the Israelite Congregation of Pest wrote to him, care of the Swedish Foreign Office, to convey the minutes of a board meeting of 21 June that 'solemnly commemorate your immortal achievement and heroic fight.'

The Budapest Central Jewish Hospital, they wanted to inform Wallenberg, was to have a pavilion named after him, though this would be 'but a paltry token of our gratitude, which we are unable to express in an adequate fashion.' They begged this 'great son of the noble Swedish nation . . . to keep us in kind remembrance and we pray that the Lord make your life happy and successful.'

As the months and then the years went by with no news of their saviour, the Budapest Jews came to the conclusion that he must be dead. He had come onto the scene out of nowhere and left in a legendary mist. One of their number, the historian and journalist Jenö Lévai, having discovered that Wallenberg had left extensive and well-documented records of his activities at the Swedish legation, embarked on his own memorial to Wallenberg – a book paying tribute to his heroic achievements.

The Jews of Budapest set up a Wallenberg Memorial Committee and began raising funds to put up a suitable monument to him. The noted sculptor Pál Patzai was given the commission. He submitted a design, which the committee quickly approved, for a heroic bronze figure, an athlete wrestling with a huge snake that bore the swastika on its head. It took Patzai two years to complete his memorial. It stood over eighteen feet high on its support, which bore a relief profile of Wallenberg and a poetic text in his honour. 'This monument,' it said, 'is our silent and eternal gratitude to him, and should always remind us of his enduring humanity in a period of inhumanity.' A site for the monument in Budapest's Saint Stephen's Park was approved by the Hungarian authorities.

The monument was put into place and covered with a tarpaulin, awaiting the day of its unveiling by the mayor of Budapest, Jószef Bognár. On the day of the inauguration – a Sunday in April 1948 – the entire Wallenberg Committee, representatives of the Swedish legation, hundreds of other Jewish and Gentile notables, and hundreds more ordinary citizens gathered to witness the ceremony. To their astonishment they found the statue was no longer there. During the night, Russian troops had arrived with ropes and horses and removed it.

Nobody knew where it had gone and nobody dared inquire. For some years the whereabouts of the statue remained a mystery. A minor civil servant, who had been a former pupil of the sculptor Patzai, told the artist that his work had been discovered in the cellar of an abandoned building in the capital. The support with the relief profile of Wallenberg and the inscription was not with it, and was in fact never found.

Some time after that the statue surfaced again, this time in the eastern city of Debrecen, where the thrifty Hungarian authorities –

long since completely reduced to Soviet-satellite status – had erected it in front of a state pharmaceutical factory. The swastika had been removed from the snake's head and the monument was now intended to symbolize man's struggle against disease.*

In Budapest meanwhile, Phoenix Street, one of the streets where Swedish-protected houses were located, close to the eastern bank of the Danube, had been re-named Wallenberg Street, and, despite official Hungarian attempts to turn him into a non-person, the street name has remained.

Jenö Lévai, the enthusiastic biographer of Wallenberg, was muzzled by stages. At the end of his otherwise excellent first book on Wallenberg he had accepted the Soviet version of his disappearance and death, perhaps in good faith – though if so with a good deal of gullibility. In a later volume on the terrible events of 1944 and early 1945, *Black Book on the Martyrdom of Hungarian Jewry*, he made scant mention of Wallenberg. In *Eichmann in Hungary*, published in 1961, he mentioned Wallenberg's name only once, *en passant*, and even quoted one of his reports in full without naming him.

When Lévai went to Stockholm in 1949 to deliver a eulogy on Wallenberg and pronounce him dead, he was involved in acrimonious exchanges with Rudolf Philipp, Wallenberg's other biographer, who insisted passionately that his hero was alive. When Lévai's book was translated into Swedish, his Stockholm publishers insisted that he re-write the chapter dealing with Wallenberg's disappearance to soften his assertion that Wallenberg had died in Budapest. Even with this amendment the book was withdrawn and virtually all copies pulped, possibly as a result of protests by the von Dardels.†

---

* Nevertheless, the local population seemed to know whom the statue was meant to represent. A Swedish journalist, Eric Sjöqvist, visited the site in 1964 and was told by his cab driver, 'Everybody knows it's Wallenberg.'

† Taken to task by an Israeli journalist, Naftali Kraus (see below), for his too ready acceptance of Wallenberg's 'death,' Lévai protested in a letter of 10 March 1975 that proofs of Wallenberg's survival did not appear until ten years after he wrote his Wallenberg biography and that 'I tried to imply the real truth.' This, of course, does not explain why he ignored Wallenberg's decisive intervention in his otherwise meticulously detailed *Eichmann in Hungary*, but, as he said in his letter to Kraus, 'Neither then nor now is it possible to write about it here.' Lévai was to outrage the Israelis in 1969 by delivering a lecture at Yad Vashem in

Despite Lévai's capitulation to Communist pressure, his book stands as an otherwise excellent and reliable source of information, and his summing up of Wallenberg's achievements is worth quoting: 'Of greatest importance is the fact that the Nazis and Arrow Cross men were not free to run amok. They had to take into consideration that all their moves were being watched by the young Swedish diplomat. There were no secrets from Wallenberg. The Arrow Cross were unable to delude him. They were unable to act with impunity . . . Wallenberg was the world's observing eye, the one who constantly demanded the criminals' conviction. This is the great significance of Wallenberg's struggle in Budapest.'

Just the same, thousands of Hungarian Jews who were small children at the end of the war and who owe their survival to Wallenberg grew up in Budapest only vaguely aware that there was such a person, and presuming him long dead. The Hungarian Communist leadership which arrived with the Red Army, having spent the war in Moscow, contained many Jews, such as Matyas Rákosy, Ernö Gerö, and Imre Nagy. The new government, however, accepted Marxist dogma about the nature of anti-Semitism and Soviet propaganda about the fate of Wallenberg and set about suppressing folk memories of him.

Right up to the collapse of the Soviet empire and the rebirth of Hungary as a Western-style democracy, the Hungarian authorities were at best ambivalent about Wallenberg, at worst dismissive. In the late 1970s the celebrated Budapest film director Peter Bacso made a movie about Wallenberg's wartime exploits, but at the last moment before its scheduled première in the autumn of 1978 the government withdrew permission for it to be shown. In the late 1980s, as the Kremlin began to loosen its grip on its satellites under Mikhail Gorbachev's reform programme, the authorities in Budapest, anxious for American investment, allowed the World Jewish Con-

---

which he argued that Szálasi and the Arrow Cross were not really anti-Semitic and that the real villain had been Horthy. This, of course, was in line with Marxist ideology, which holds that the 'masses' are not capable of anti-Semitism, only the bourgeoisie or the aristocracy, such as Horthy.

gress to commission Hungary's leading sculptor, Imre Varga, to make a statue of Wallenberg. It was made of Swedish granite and was sited on the edge of a small park in Buda where the Congress president, the Canadian–American distillery magnate Samuel Bronfman, dedicated it at a small and discreet public ceremony on May 2, 1987. No senior member of the Hungarian government attended and it was apparent that the régime was still unwilling to allow Marxist dogma about the causes of anti-Semitism to be challenged too openly. The statue bore an inscription in Latin of vaguely humanitarian import, which however made no mention of the Holocaust or Wallenberg's work to save the Jews, nor of his disappearance into the Soviet prison system.

In Israel disappointingly little has been done either to commemorate Wallenberg's extraordinarily selfless services to the Jewish people and humanity as a whole or to press for his release. In the entire country there was, until the early 1980s, only one street named after him. This was a grubby back street on the edge of what was the no-man's-land between the eastern and western sectors of Jerusalem at the time it was named. Until 1979 the plaque bearing the street name carried the dates 1912–1947. Then, learning belatedly that there was considerable doubt about it, the City Council had the date of Wallenberg's presumed death obliterated. Eventually, after Wallenberg's name had become something of a household word around the world, Jerusalem 'promoted' him and designated a street in the centre of the western half of the city as 'Rehov Wallenberg'. It scarcely does him justice. No grand avenue or leafy boulevard, it's a short one-way street, for use by buses and taxis only as they debouch into the bustling Jaffa Road. Tel Aviv did rather better than Jerusalem; due in part to Tommy Lapid's efforts, a handsome thoroughfare in the city's Kiryat Mada district now bears Wallenberg's name.

Wallenberg's name is also given to a pathology clinic attached to the big municipal hospital in Beersheba, a clinic conceived and paid for not by the Israelis but by a group of former Hungarian Jews living in Canada. It was formally opened in April 1971, but since then the hospital authorities, no doubt inadvertently, have built around the original clinic and obscured the commemorative plaque unveiled by the Canadian delegation.

But for the efforts of one Israeli journalist, Naftali Kraus – himself a Budapest ghetto survivor – Wallenberg might be virtually unknown to the Israeli public. Over the years Kraus plugged away at the Wallenberg story in the daily *Ma'ariv*. In 1974 Kraus wrote a monograph, *Raoul Wallenberg: The Man Who Died Many Times*, which was given strictly limited publication by Tel Aviv University's Institute for the Survey of the Diaspora. In Israel's only published work on the subject, Kraus writes harshly of his country's indifference:

The nation of Israel knows how to hold its martyr-heroes in its memory, but it does not deal as generously with the Righteous Gentiles who risked their lives to save Jews. Many of these – including some who laid down their lives in rescue operations – are forgotten. This is ingratitude . . . What do Jews know about Raoul Wallenberg, even the tens of thousands he saved from certain death? And what has been done in Israel to commemorate his memory? Nothing. Moreover, there is an embarrassing murkiness which borders on disgrace . . . In Israel there seems to be a conspiracy of silence . . . Even the material at Yad Vashem relates only to the period of his activities in Budapest and not to his later experiences. Yet this man is deserving of scrutiny until the end of his days.

Sadly, I can only confirm the impression so forthrightly conveyed by Kraus. Few Israelis, including those who owed him their lives, bothered to make the journey to Jerusalem's Holocaust memorial complex at Yad Vashem to be on hand when a tree was belatedly planted in Wallenberg's memory in the Avenue of the Righteous.

László Szamosi was an honourable exception, even though he owes his survival and that of his family more to his own remarkable efforts than Wallenberg's. Tommy Lapid turned up as one of the group officiating at the moving religious ceremony which preceded the tree-planting. So did Anna Bilder, whose father was consigned to the same fate as Wallenberg for daring to speak out about the Swede he met in prison in 1975. Tom Lantos and his wife were there from California, and it was thanks only to her spirited intervention that the American ambassador turned up with the Israeli interior minister, Dr Yosef Burg, and US roving envoy Sol Linowitz, who happened to be in Jerusalem for discussions with the Israeli government.

Nina Lagergren had stayed behind in Stockholm on business

connected with the Wallenberg Committee, and her brother Guy went as the representative of the family to perform the tree-planting, which had been delayed for so many years because his mother would never permit it. Maj von Dardel always felt that to allow a tree to commemorate Raoul's name in the Avenue of the Righteous would somehow signify that he was dead. After her death in February 1979 – followed within three days by that of her husband – Nina Lagergren and Guy von Dardel withdrew the family objections to the planting.

The ceremony received surprisingly little Israeli media publicity, both before and after the event. Presenting Wallenberg's Yad Vashem medal and certificate to Professor von Dardel, Prime Minister Menachem Begin declared in ringing tones: 'The Jewish people may forget its enemies and the wrongs done to it, but it never forgets a friend . . . We owe him an eternal debt of gratitude . . . We will continue to believe that he is alive, and we shall do whatever we can to try and save him.'

In fact, the Begin government and all the Israeli governments preceding it had done nothing about the Wallenberg affair. In the years from 1948 to 1967, when the Soviet Union recognized the Jewish State and each had full diplomatic representation in the other's capital, not a single query, note, or memorandum – verbal or written – appears to have been submitted by the Israelis about Wallenberg's fate. A senior Foreign Ministry official admitted to me in February 1980, after repeated inquiries, 'We have no file on Wallenberg.'

In 1982, the Begin government organized a week of events in honour of Wallenberg. These involved a tree-planting ceremony, the naming of a children's playground, the issuing of a postage stamp bearing Wallenberg's face, and a number of like events including a speech in which a tame Swedish politician invoked Wallenberg's name, none too subtly, in defence of Israel's invasion of Lebanon and against what he chose to call 'the new anti-Semitism' – i.e. the worldwide wave of criticism against Israel's aggressive Lebanon policy.

There were many, Israelis and foreigners alike, who found the use of Wallenberg's name in justification of the invasion deeply distasteful. It was at the very least arguable that, given his strength of feeling for the underdog, Wallenberg might have felt outrage at the random slaughter of civilians by Defence Minister Ariel Sharon's offensive.

If Wallenberg had been alive and inclined to add his voice to the condemnation, would he too have been dismissed as one of 'the new anti-Semites'?

To this sorry catalogue of official Israeli indifference to the memory of Raoul Wallenberg and his works, a small but telling postscript was provided not long before this revised edition went to press.

In April 1995, while in Jerusalem to film a television documentary, the author went with a camera crew to Yad Vashem. There he found that the carob tree he had seen planted in Wallenberg's honour some fifteen years before was looking decidedly sickly – its growth stunted, its leaves discoloured and diseased. The trees on either side, one named for Per Anger, the other for members of the Norwegian Resistance, were in a similar condition.

How could this be? The carob is a native of the Middle East, able to thrive on stony soil and with an absolute minimum of care and water. Carobs grow wild and flourish in the author's garden in Cyprus.

A Yad Vashem information officer conceded that the condition of Wallenberg's tree had been noticed. He said it had been found that the soil conditions in that particular sector of the Avenue of the Righteous were poor, owing to the presence beneath the surface of a large boulder. He said that the Yad Vashem authorities were considering what should be done to rectify this state of affairs, but were hampered by a shortage of funds.

It hardly seemed an adequate explanation. Why had it taken fifteen years to discover that the soil conditions were unsuitable? Had no one noticed that Wallenberg's sickly little tree had scarcely grown an inch since it was planted? As for the plea of poverty, Yad Vashem is funded directly, and quite generously, by the Israeli government. No one observing the size of its administrative and maintenance staff would conclude that it is starved of funds. As well, it receives generous donations for specific projects from Jewish organizations and individuals in the Diaspora.

Surely it is a bitter irony – although in keeping with the way he was abandoned and forgotten after his heroic performance in wartime Budapest – that of the 2000 trees in the Avenue of the Righteous the one dedicated to Wallenberg, of all people, should be so sickly and neglected.

# Chapter 21

Why did the Russians seize Raoul Wallenberg? Why did they never let him go? The first question is easier to answer than the second, for it is at least susceptible to logical explanation, however perverted the logic.

With hindsight it is perfectly easy to see how the Russians, especially in the atmosphere of paranoid hysteria that characterized the Stalinist period at the end of the war, should have thought Wallenberg to be a spy, for either the Americans or the Germans, or both. His explanation when found in the thick of the street fighting for Pest that he was looking after Jews must have seemed to the Russians incredible to the point of absurdity. To the average Russian, whose anti-Semitism was bred in the bone, such an explanation would seem an insult to the intelligence, all the more so coming from a Swedish capitalist who could have sat the war out in comfortable neutrality. Anti-Semitism apart, the concept of disinterested humanitarian work performed by volunteers – on behalf of whatever group – would be totally alien to Soviet perceptions of the real world.

When Budapest fell to the Russians they indulged in an orgy of looting, raping, and deporting to which friend, foe, and neutral alike fell victim. Jewish women who had survived the horrors of the death marches to the Austrian border had to yield their wasted bodies to the systematic violation of the 'liberating' Russian soldiery. Even young Jewish men were not exempted. Barrel-breasted Soviet women soldiers behaved little better than their male comrades.

Lars Berg, Wallenberg's fellow-secretary at the Swedish legation, tells in his memoir of the period how Russian troops entered the legation – officially sovereign Swedish territory – opened the safe, and emptied it of all the cash and valuables inside. He also tells how they completely cleared out the headquarters of the Hazai Bank, missing, however, a parcel left by Wallenberg in which Berg later found the enormous sum of 870,000 pengös in banknotes.*

As for deportations, a few experiences related by Jews saved by Wallenberg will give some idea of what went on in the early days of the Soviet occupation. 'Even Jews who were liberated by the Russians were taken to Siberia for up to ten years as prisoners,' recalls Tommy Lapid. 'They didn't distinguish between Jews whom they saved and Germans whom they captured. So that to think the Red Army would have distinguished between a blond [sic – he was dark] Swedish diplomat and a blond German officer disguised in civilian clothes would be altogether too optimistic.'

László Szamosi tells how five fellow-Jews who were helping him to run a children's home were taken off by the Russians and bundled aboard an east-bound train. Two of them escaped and told how they had been put together, quite indiscriminately, with a bunch of German prisoners and sent to a Soviet prison camp. This almost happened to Szamosi himself. He tells how he was rounded up with about 150 people, many of them Jews, and taken to the Hotel Britannia, where there were about 350 more prisoners.

The Russian interrogators ignored his plea that he was Jewish and totally disregarded his Swedish papers. Only the intervention of an official of the Soviet-sponsored Hungarian Provisional Government saved him from deportation. 'If not for that I might have suffered the same fate as Wallenberg,' says Szamosi.

Ferenc Hovarth, subsequently a professor of engineering at Beer-

---

* The parcel also contained a ring with 'an unusually big diamond' and an illustrated, hand-lettered pamphlet praising Wallenberg's efforts on behalf of the Jews. 'Probably a Christmas present from one of his assistants and admirers,' says Berg.

sheba in Israel, had a similar experience. He too was rescued by Wallenberg, only to fall later into the clutches of the Russians. 'I was taken by a very small Russian soldier, almost a child, and he took me to some very big Russian soldiers. When about twenty people had been rounded up they marched us to the courtyard of a building about a kilometre away, where we joined about a thousand other people. Nobody knew what was going to happen. We stood there for hours, wondering. Then, slowly, people were called up to a room for questioning by a Russian officer with an interpreter. I pulled out my Swedish passport and kept saying, "I'm a Swede, you must let me go." I refused to answer their questions, but kept saying, "I'm a Swede, it's written in Hungarian, it's written in English, and it's written in Russian, so please let me out. I'm not a Jew. I'm a Swede."

'It confused them so much that they finally said, "Okay, go to the devil – you're a Swede." So that's how I got out, but a lot of the people there that day were deported to Russia. Some came back after a year or two, but others never returned.'

Hovarth was doubly lucky. When, after a while, the Russians discovered that there were thousands of 'Swedes' in Budapest, they became, as Lars Berg recalls, acutely suspicious of all Swedish passport holders, and even more so of the Swedish legation which had issued them: 'They detained one after another of our local employees, especially Wallenberg's people. Most of them were re-leased but at least one of them never came back.

'The bravest among these told me what the Russians had been asking about. It was mostly about us Swedish diplomats, our work, our private lives, our friends. They wanted to know who was the head of espionage for the Germans, me or Wallenberg? Wallenberg seems to have been the one they suspected most. For the Russians, with their view – or rather, their lack of view – on humanitarian matters, it was completely unthinkable that the Swede Wallenberg should have come to Budapest to save Jews. He must have come on some other mission.'

Once Wallenberg had actually been taken in for questioning by the NKVD his danger would have been acute, especially if he had mentioned his plan for Hungarian economic recovery, which he may have been politically naïve enough to have done. His family name alone – as well-known in Northern Europe as Rockefeller in North America – might have been enough to condemn him. The Wallenbergs had owned property in pre-Revolutionary Russia and had actually been accused of backing White Russian forces in the Ukraine during the fighting which followed the October 1917 uprising.

Furthermore, it is entirely conceivable that Soviet intelligence knew all about the wartime links between one of his relatives and a group of Germans, mainly Prussian Junkers, who wanted to make a separate peace with the Western Allies and then join forces with the Anglo-Americans against the Russians.

Raoul's cousin Jakob was the main point of contact between these people and the Allies. During the war he was a member of the Swedish Government Commission on Economic Relations with Germany. In this role he travelled frequently to Berlin, where he was on close terms with Karl Goerdeler, former governing mayor of Leipzig. Goerdeler, a Prussian monarchist of the old school, was in turn closely connected with General Ludwig Beck, an ex-chief of the German general staff and leader of a group of senior Wehrmacht officers who, as the war began to turn against Germany, decided that Hitler must be got rid of. They organized several futile attempts on the Führer's life, culminating in the almost-successful 20 July bomb plot in 1944.

Had these attempts succeeded, Goerdeler would have been made chancellor in Hitler's place. From 1942 until Geordeler and his fellow-conspirators were arrested and hideously executed in 1944,* Jakob Wallenberg acted as a conduit for messages between the conspirators and the Western Allies, sending detailed proposals – all of which were rebuffed – to the British leader, Winston Churchill himself.

If Russian intelligence had known about this link between one member of the Wallenberg family and German 'reactionaries' on the one hand, and the Anglo-American leadership on the other, this knowledge certainly would have counted heavily against Raoul Wallenberg.

* On Hitler's orders the conspirators were hanged by piano wire from a row of butcher's hooks while a movie cameraman filmed their death agonies for the Führer's subsequent entertainment.

Among the many ways in which Soviet intelligence might have learned of the link was a disastrously indiscreet contact which members of the Goerdeler–Beck group made with the German Communist underground shortly before the 20 July attempt. Against the advice of Goerdeler and other older men among the plotters, the Socialist wing of their circle contacted the Communists in the hope of finding out what action they would take should the putsch succeed and to try to widen the basis of the Socialists' support.

Until then, there had been no links between the two mutually suspicious groups. The Communist underground considered Goerdeler, Beck, and company to be little better than the Nazis whom they wished to supplant. The success of such a reactionary group, they thought, might prevent a Communist Germany arising from the wreckage of the Third Reich. However, they agreed to the meeting, if only to find out what the other side was up to, and on 4 July the Socialists Julius Leber and Adolf Reichwein met the Communists Franz Jakob and Anton Saefkow, who brought along a third comrade, known as Rambow.*

The German Communist underground served chiefly as an espionage network for the Russians. One can only guess at how much information they were able to send back to Moscow about the Beck-Goerdeler group's activities, and whether this included any reference to Jakob Wallenberg's role as an intermediary.

In one sense, Raoul Wallenberg *was* an American agent, by virtue of the fact that he was reporting to and drawing funds from an agency of the US government. He may well have been ill-advised

---

* 'Rambow' turned out to be a Gestapo informer – one of a number of so-called V-men infiltrated into the Red underground by Gestapo chief Heinrich Müller, whom we have already met. Leber, Reichwein, Jakob, and Saefkow were all subsequently arrested and executed. Müller, a cold, dispassionate killer who was known to have a great respect for Soviet secret police methods, was never captured after the collapse of Nazi Germany. Neither was his body ever found. He was last seen in Hitler's bunker on 29 April 1945, and some surviving colleagues believe he went over to the Russians and joined the NKVD, which he so much admired. It is pure speculation, of course, but one can just imagine Müller finding that Wallenberg, the adversary of his former subordinate Eichmann, was now a captive of his new employers . . .

enough to tell this to the Russians. His captors are not likely to have taken much account of the fact that the Americans were supposed to be their allies or to have appreciated the distinction between a humanitarian agency and an intelligence agency.

Indeed, at least one official US document relating to Wallenberg's mission contains language dangerously redolent of cloak-and-dagger work, however innocent its intention. On 3 August 1944 Stettinius sent the following to the US embassy in Stockholm to be passed on to Ivar Olsen, representative of the War Refugee Board:

Please ask Wallenberg personally to contact Félix Szentirmay, 10 Szemlchegy Ut., Budapest, telephone 358–598, and orally tell him that through a friend in Los Angeles Wallenberg has heard from Eugene Bogdánnfy, whom Wallenberg does not (repeat not) know. As a means of verifying his statement as to the message, Wallenberg should refer to the following property held by Szentirmay: Bogdánnfy's ruby cuff-links and pocket watch, Mrs Bogdánnfy's fur coat, gold bracelet, and brooch with green stones. Wallenberg should also express Bogdánnfy's concern for Mikki's well-being. Wallenberg should tell Szentirmay that Bogdánnfy expects that Szentirmay will be asked to go to Switzerland soon and suggests that he apply for a visa immediately. Bogdánnfy wants Szentirmay to be sure that when he goes to Switzerland he has at his fingertips the cash position of all the enterprises. Szentirmay must of course treat this message with the highest confidence. Szentirmay should not (repeat not) be advised by Wallenberg of the reason why he is being asked to go to Switzerland, referred to below, or of the board's interest in the matter.

For your information, Bogdánnfy is a Hungarian residing in Los Angeles who has substantial interests in several large enterprises of which Szentirmay is manager. Union Bank of Switzerland acts as Bogdánnfy's trustee and will ask Szentirmay to go to Switzerland to discuss business problems. The purposes of the project are to secure adequate sources of supply of pengös against blocked francs or dollars and to have Szentirmay undertake to secure cooperation of individual named in Paragraph Three of Department's 1426 of July 17, WRB's 55,* and with whom Bogdánnfy and Szentirmay are well acquainted.

* This was one Otto Braun, who was described in the relevant dispatch as 'a German residing in Budapest, who is said to be in a position to aid escapes and concealments.'

If for any reason you do not (repeat not) believe that securing his or Szentirmay's cooperation is appropriate, advise the board thereof and do not (repeat not) ask Wallenberg to contact Szentirmay until the board has had an opportunity to consider such reason.

On 19 August Minister Johnson replied that the message would be delivered personally to Wallenberg by Per Anger, who was due to return to Budapest in a week, since 'it was not considered advisable to request Swedish Foreign Office to transmit message of this nature.' Indeed, it was not. Stockholm, like all neutral European capitals, was a hotbed of espionage during the war, and even an intelligence service less paranoid than the Soviets' might well have regarded the recipient of such a message with considerable interest.

According to Pavel Sudoplatov, a retired KGB hatchetman of high rank whose memoirs attracted considerable attention when they were published in 1994, there was yet another reason for the Soviets' particular interest in Wallenberg. Sudoplatov speculates that, having used Wallenberg's banker cousins as go-betweens in their peace negotiations with the Finns, Stalin and his henchmen viewed the captive Raoul as a similarly valuable asset, to be re-cruited as an agent of influence either by persuasion or coercion. Sudoplatov further speculates that when Wallenberg refused to be either persuaded or press-ganged the Soviet leadership had him executed.

Given all these factors, it is not surprising that Wallenberg was shipped off to Moscow by the NKVD. Given the apparent lack of interest in his fate in the early days of his incarceration, it is not surprising that the Russians were in no hurry to let him go, taking Swedish unconcern for tacit admission that they knew he had been up to no good. What is less easy to understand is why they should have hung on to him for so long after the Swedes had begun to show that they were, after all, seriously concerned, and long after the matter had become a considerable irritant to Russo-Swedish rela-tions. There is no obvious reason for the Russians to have deliberately wished to sour relations with Sweden; indeed, good relations might well have been to the advantage of the Soviet Union. Perhaps by that time it was impossible to put the machinery of the Gulag into reverse.

In any event, some Kremlinogists and most Soviet-era Russian dissidents and émigrés will tell you that to reason along those lines is to display a lack of understanding of the illogicality which characterized so much of Soviet behaviour. 'Don't look for logical explanations,' they say. 'Don't look for reasons why they should have kept him. Look rather for reasons why they should bother to let him go.' Perhaps Swedish displeasure alone never was a good enough reason, and it is a fact that, to cite just one illogicality, the Russians let thousands of highly qualified Jewish scientists and technicians – some of them formerly employed on sensitive government projects – emigrate to the United States and Israel, while refusing exit visas to others, such as humble tailors, shoemakers, and clerical workers.

But assuming that Wallenberg did not die in July 1947, as the Kremlin claimed – either from a heart attack, or under interrogation or by execution – why would his captors choose to keep him alive as an undeclared prisoner for decades, as so much perplexing evidence suggests? The answer might be that the Russians have a tradition, dating back to well before the Communist era, of burying people alive in their penal system rather than simply executing them, as a notable string of ex-prisoners from Dostoevsky to Solzhenitsyn can testify.

# Chapter 22

In August 1989 the Soviet authorities, of their own volition, at last brought themselves to utter the ten-letter word – Wallenberg – whose mention by others had been anathema to them for so many years.

In the full flush of *glasnost* the reforming Soviet president Mikhail Gorbachev instructed his ambassador in Stockholm to invite Nina Lagergren and Guy von Dardel to Moscow to discuss the case of their half-brother. The news created something of a media sensation, stirring speculation that a significant breakthrough was in the offing – perhaps even the reappearance of the principal actor himself.

Consequently, a swarm of journalists, representing both the Soviet and the international media, greeted the Wallenberg siblings when they arrived in Moscow on 15 October, accompanied by Per Anger and Sonia Sonnenfeldt, secretary of the Swedish Wallenberg Committee. The following day, the delegation met Gorbachev's deputy KGB chief, Vladimir Pirozhkov, and deputy foreign minister, Valentin Nikoforov. What the Russians had to offer was interesting, but ultimately disappointing. They handed over Wallenberg's diplomatic passport, some money that had been in his possession at the time of his arrest, a cigarette case and some notebooks. These items, the Soviets said, had been discovered by chance just a few weeks before, which must seem to sceptics to be a remarkable coincidence.

'It was quite incredible, handing me these items,' Nina said later.

'They gave me the feeling that they [the Russians] must have much more. Everyone told us the Russians never destroy files and documents. They must be somewhere in the KGB.'

The Russians also produced the original of the letter by the long-deceased prison doctor Smoltsov, reporting Wallenberg's death from a heart attack in July 1947. This was later to be subjected to forensic testing, witnessed by Swedish police experts, which established that the ink and paper were, indeed, from the 1940s. But there was no death certificate or other corroborating evidence, while the letter itself was penned not on official paper but a piece of scrap.

The delegation refused to accept it as evidence of Wallenberg's death and the Russians have since conceded that it hardly constitutes legal proof in the absence of more formal documentation. Indeed, some former KGB officers have privately expressed the view that the Smoltsov letter could have been an ordered forgery, and this seems quite likely for, at the very least, the stated cause of death in a young, healthy prisoner strains credibility. At the time, however, Gorbachev's spokesman, Gennadi Gerasimov, insisted that Wallenberg's death in 1947 was 'an irrefutable fact,' albeit 'a tragic mistake that has never been corrected.'

The delegation left Moscow determined, as before, that in the absence of convincing proof of his death Wallenberg must be considered still to be alive, and sensing that the Soviet authorities were unable, rather than unwilling, to produce him. That remains their position to this day. For what it is worth, it is also the official position of the Swedish and US governments, although it is difficult to imagine anyone in either bureaucracy seriously believing in the survival, somewhere in the depths of Russia, of a shambling octogenarian who once knew himself to be Raoul Gustav Wallenberg.

Despite the disappointing outcome of the Moscow visit, Wallenberg's partisans felt that the Russians were genuine in their desire to co-operate in finding a solution to the mystery. This was all the more so after the failed anti-Gorbachev coup of August 1991, which led to the final collapse of the Soviet Union. As Vadim Bakatin, subsequently head of the Interior Ministry, was to say: 'We do not know what the facts are concerning the fate of Raoul Wallenberg, but to prevent their investigation is to stand on the wrong side of history.'

After the Moscow meetings in October 1989, an international commission composed of five Russians and five Westerners was established to seek further evidence of Wallenberg's fate. The chairman was the Canadian civil-rights lawyer Irwin Cotler, while the one American member, Professor Marvin Makinen of Chicago University, had himself been a prisoner of the Soviets during the 1960s. The efforts of this commission have brought to light some more significant but inconclusive documents. One is a Moscow cremation list for the year 1947. Wallenberg's name does not appear on it.

Other documents include log-books from the Lubianka – inked over to conceal the names of Wallenberg and his driver, Vilmos Langfelder,* but restored after the collapse of the Soviet Union – which record three interrogations of Wallenberg and five of Langfelder.

Those logs were quoted in a dispatch to the London Sunday newspaper the *Observer* in October 1992, by the British historian Lord Nicholas Bethell, as evidence that Wallenberg did die, as the Soviets stated, in July 1947. They show that Wallenberg was interrogated in the summer of 1946 and spring of 1947 by an NKVD lieutenant-colonel named Dmitri Kopylyansky. Kopylyansky himself, tracked down by the *Observer* to an unlisted address in Moscow's up-market Tverskaya (formerly Gorki) Street district, insisted in a telephone interview that 'I never saw this man [Wallenberg] in my life.' And although the logs seem to give him the lie, the date they cite for Wallenberg's last interrogation by Kopylyansky, March 11, 1947, is more than four months before his purported death. So the connection is by no means clearly established and Bethell's claim that Kopylyansky 'may have been involved in [Wallenberg's] murder' cannot be more than speculation.

And speculation – albeit insider speculation – was all that any of

---

* In 1957, the Kremlin informed the Hungarian government that Langfelder died in the Lubianka in March 1948. As in the case of Wallenberg, the supposedly natural cause of death strains credibility. Before his arrest, Langfelder was known to be a particularly robust young man.

the Russian officials interviewed by Bethell was able to offer, because the file on Wallenberg had vanished and the only man who might have known the truth, Kopylyansky, wasn't telling. Nor, according to Bethell, was he being pressed by the powers-that-be to tell. As Alexei Kondaurov, spokesman for the Russian Security Ministry, told Bethell: 'We have no reason to believe that he can tell us anything more than he has said already.'

Intriguingly, Bethell reported that Kopylyansky was living under official protection. This may seem odd, since Kopylyansky was purged from the security services as long ago as 1952, apparently for the sin of having been born Jewish – another of the many ironies that enliven the Wallenberg affair. Why, after all these years, should he enjoy the protection of a régime that had supposedly turned its back on its Communist past and, in the process, had revealed the truth about many even more monstrous crimes, such as the Katyn Forest massacre? The *Observer* speculated, somewhat unconvincingly for this reader, that it was because Kopylyansky is the repository of 'the truth that Russia longs both to hide and reveal.'

At last report Kopylyansky was still alive, aged seventy-six and in poor health. He seems likely to take what he knows of the Wallenberg affair with him to the grave, unless his Jewish conscience should be sufficiently tormented by guilt to bring him to some kind of a death-bed confession.

Meanwhile, the Kremlin's bottom line seems to be encapsulated in the words of Alexei Kondaurov to Lord Bethell: 'I cannot deny that Wallenberg was murdered in the Lubianka. Indeed, I think it most likely that he was. But, as far as we know, there are no documents to confirm it.'

More insider speculation came in the 1994 memoirs of the old KGB hatchetman Pavel Sudoplatov. He devoted the best part of a chapter to the Wallenberg affair and also mentioned Kopylyansky as Wallenberg's interrogator, but did not lay Wallenberg's death at Kopylyansky's doorstep. Instead, in a passage that might have come from the pen of Ian Fleming, he introduced one Professor Grigori Moiseyevich Maironovsky, head of a super-secret installation known as Laboratory X. According to Sudoplatov, this was an NKVD toxicological research group and 'my best estimate is that Wallenberg was killed by Maironovsky, who was ordered to inject him with poison under the guise of medical treatment.'

It could be argued that the means by which Wallenberg was executed is irrelevant, but the arcane *modus operandi* described by Sudoplatov surely touches on his credibility. One has to wonder why it should be thought necessary to kill Wallenberg by poison injection when a bullet at the back of the head, the more usual method, would be simpler and a lot quicker. And since the body was to be cremated and the ashes tipped into a common grave, the usual procedure according to Sudoplatov, who would ever know the difference anyway?

A declassified but once top-secret document quoted by Sudoplatov as evidence that Wallenberg was executed in July 1947 is a letter from Soviet deputy foreign minister Vishinsky to his boss, Molotov, dated May 13, 1947. In it, Vishinsky requests Molotov to direct state security minister Abakumov 'to submit a summary of the substance of the [Wallenberg] case and suggestions for liquidation.'

This raises a tricky question of semantics. Did Vishinsky mean liquidation of the case or liquidation of the prisoner? Opinion is divided on this, even among Russians claiming to be familiar with the usages of Soviet officialdom. But Sudoplatov says that to him 'it is clear that this was not a suggestion to close the case, but one to eliminate Wallenberg.'

However that may be, it should be pointed out that in instances other than the Wallenberg case Sudoplatov has not been found an entirely credible witness. For instance, his sensation-stirring assertions that Robert Oppenheimer, Niels Bohr and other nuclear physicists involved in the World War II Manhattan Project gave atomic bomb secrets to Stalin have been comprehensively shot down. So far as the Wallenberg affair is concerned, Sudoplatov – like everyone else who has claimed to unravel the mystery – is unable to cite any documents to support his assertions. Still, while conceding that the file is missing, Sudoplatov says he is sure that here and there in the Kremlin – in the Molotov section of the Presidential Archives, in the Khrushchev Section of the Presidential Archives, in the Ministry of State Security Archives – there must be the odd letter that lays bare the truth.

In the event, all of Sudoplatov's signposts have been followed by independent researchers and none has led to the documents in question. When I instituted my own enquiries through a reliable Russian colleague in Moscow I was told: 'Don't waste your time and money. It's been checked out and there's nothing there.'

So what Sudoplatov's 'revelations' come down to at the end of the day, apart from a lot of detail that had already been published, is a 'best estimate' that Wallenberg was given a lethal injection by the sinister head of Laboratory X. His account is far from convincing.

Meanwhile, members of the international commission have been ploughing through scores of thousands of prison registration cards, hoping to trace Wallenberg's movements beyond his last officially acknowledged location, the Lubianka. In their research they have discovered that many foreign prisoners were given false names or else referred to only by a number. This makes their task infinitely more difficult. 'If this is what has occurred in Wallenberg's case,' the commissioners have said, 'it makes the discovery of his card – and of his fate – well-nigh impossible.'

What, then, are we to make of this tantalizing mystery? Setting aside the possibility that Wallenberg might still be alive as a notion to be entertained only by true believers, we surely have to conclude that he did not die when the Soviets said he did, and certainly not because of a heart attack. But the when, where and how of his death seem likely to remain unknown, as does the why of the destruction or removal of his file.

Surely, though, we owe it to Wallenberg's memory and to history to obtain the answers to these questions, which is why the unremitting efforts of those who persist in seeking the answers deserve our support and encouragement, even if we cannot share their belief in Wallenberg's survival.

And then, even for the sensibly sceptical, there is always the nagging thought that even if there is only a million-to-one chance that he is alive, Wallenberg has certainly earned the right to be given that chance.

As Palko Forgacz, one of the tens of thousands he saved from the gas chambers, said after the war: '*He was more of a hero than the heroes of old. He did good for the sake of doing good. He never made any demands and never expected any thanks for what he did. He knew that people are weak and miserable, but he did not want to make them better. He only wanted to help them.'*

# Bibliography

Anger, Per. *With Raoul Wallenberg in Budapest*. Stockholm, 1979.

Bauminger, Arieh L. *Roll of Honour*. Tel Aviv, 1971.

Berg, Lars. *What Happened in Budapest*. Stockholm, 1949.

Braham, Randolph L. *The Destruction of Hungarian Jewry: A Documentary Account*. New York, 1963.

Dardel, Fredrik von. *Raoul Wallenberg: Facts around a Fate*. Stockholm, 1970.

Dawidowicz, Lucy. *The War Against the Jews*. New York, 1975.

Dulles, Allen. *Germany's Underground*. New York, 1947.

Hausner, Gideon. *Justice in Jerusalem*. New York, 1966.

Heyman, Eva. *The Diary of Eva Heyman*. Jerusalem, 1974.

Hoess, Rudolf. *Commandant of Auschwitz: The Autobiography of Rudolf Hoess*. London, 1959.

Hungarian–Jewish Studies, Vol. 3. New York, 1973.

Lévai, Jenö. *Black Book on the Martyrdom of Hungarian Jewry*. Zurich, 1948.

—— *Raoul Wallenberg: His Fascinating Life, His Daring Struggles, and the Secret of His Mysterious Disappearance*. Budapest, 1948.

—— *Eichmann in Hungary*. Budapest, 1961.

Morse, Arthur D. *While Six Million Died*. New York, 1967.

Palmstierna, Carl-Fredrik. *The Feather in My Hand*. Stockholm, 1946.

Philipp, Rudolf. *Raoul Wallenberg: Fighter for Humanity*. Stockholm, 1946.

Reitlinger, Gerald. *The Final Solution: The Attempt to Exterminate the Jews of Europe, 1939–45*. New York, 1961.

*Rescue Attempts during the Holocaust*. Jerusalem, 1977.

Shirer, William, L. *The Rise and Fall of the Third Reich: A History of Nazi Germany*. New York, 1960.

Sjöqvist, Eric. *The Wallenberg Affair*. Stockholm, 1974.

Sudoplatov, Pavel and Anatoli, with Jerrold L. and Leona P. Schecter, *Special Tasks: The Memoirs of an Unwanted Witness – A Soviet Spymaster*. New York, 1994.

Swedish Foreign Office White Books. *Raoul Wallenberg*. Stockholm, 1957, 1965, 1980.

Wulf, Josef. *Wallenberg: He Was Their Hope*. Brussels, 1968.

Yad Vashem Studies, Vol. 5. Jerusalem, 1963.

• Much of the material relating to Adolf Eichmann and his part in the Final Solution originates from captured Nazi documents, from the transcript of his trial in Jerusalem (and Gideon Hausner's account of it, see above), and from Eichmann's own tape-recorded interviews, given to the Dutch journalist Willem Sassen in Buenos Aires before his capture and trial; which formed the basis for two articles in *Life* magazine, in January 1961.

• Much of the official material relating to Raoul Wallenberg's mission to Hungary originates from US State Department documents and from the War Refugee Board's archive at the Franklin D. Roosevelt Memorial Library in Hyde Park, New York, as well as from his own official reports and private letters.

# Discover more about our forthcoming books through Penguin's FREE newspaper...

# READ MORE IN PENGUIN

In every corner of the world, on every subject under the sun, Penguin represents quality and variety – the very best in publishing today.

For complete information about books available from Penguin – including Puffins, Penguin Classics and Arkana – and how to order them, write to us at the appropriate address below. Please note that for copyright reasons the selection of books varies from country to country.

**In the United Kingdom**: Please write to *Dept. JC, Penguin Books Ltd, FREEPOST, West Drayton, Middlesex UB7 OBR*.

If you have any difficulty in obtaining a title, please send your order with the correct money, plus ten per cent for postage and packaging, to *PO Box No. 11, West Drayton, Middlesex UB7 OBR*

**In the United States**: Please write to *Consumer Sales, Penguin USA, P.O. Box 999, Dept. 17109, Bergenfield, New Jersey 07621-0120.* VISA and MasterCard holders call 1-800-253-6476 to order all Penguin titles

**In Canada**: Please write to *Penguin Books Canada Ltd, 10 Alcorn Avenue, Suite 300, Toronto, Ontario M4V 3B2*

**In Australia**: Please write to *Penguin Books Australia Ltd, P.O. Box 257, Ringwood, Victoria 3134*

**In New Zealand**: Please write to *Penguin Books (NZ) Ltd, Private Bag 102902, North Shore Mail Centre, Auckland 10*

**In India**: Please write to *Penguin Books India Pvt Ltd, 706 Eros Apartments, 56 Nehru Place, New Delhi 110 019*

**In the Netherlands**: Please write to *Penguin Books Netherlands bv, Postbus 3507, NL-1001 AH Amsterdam*

**In Germany**: Please write to *Penguin Books Deutschland GmbH, Metzlerstrasse 26, 60594 Frankfurt am Main*

**In Spain**: Please write to *Penguin Books S. A., Bravo Murillo 19, 1° B, 28015 Madrid*

**In Italy**: Please write to *Penguin Italia s.r.l., Via Felice Casati 20, I–20124 Milano*

**In France**: Please write to *Penguin France S. A., 17 rue Lejeune, F–31000 Toulouse*

**In Japan**: Please write to *Penguin Books Japan, Ishikiribashi Building, 2–5–4, Suido, Bunkyo-ku, Tokyo 112*

**In Greece**: Please write to *Penguin Hellas Ltd, Dimocritou 3, GR–106 71 Athens*

**In South Africa**: Please write to *Longman Penguin Southern Africa (Pty) Ltd, Private Bag X08, Bertsham 2013*

# READ MORE IN PENGUIN

## HISTORY

**The Making of Europe**   Robert Bartlett

'Bartlett does more than anyone before him to bring out the way in which medieval Europe was shaped by [a] great wave of internal conquest, colonization and evangelization. He also stresses its consequences for the future history of the world' – *Guardian*

**The Somme Battlefields**   Martin and Mary Middlebrook

This evocative, original book provides a definitive guide to the cemeteries, memorials and battlefields from the age of Crécy and Agincourt to the great Allied sweep which drove the Germans back in 1944, concentrating above all on the scenes of ferocious fighting in 1916 and 1918.

**Ancient Slavery and Modern Ideology**   M. I. Finley

Few topics in the study of classical civilization could be more central – and more controversial – than slavery. In this magnificent book, M. I. Finley cuts through the thickets of modern ideology to get at the essential facts. 'A major creative achievement in historical interpretation' – *The Times Higher Education Supplement*

**The Penguin History of Greece**   A. R. Burn

Readable, erudite, enthusiastic and balanced, this one-volume history of Hellas sweeps the reader along from the days of Mycenae and the splendours of Athens to the conquests of Alexander and the final dark decades.

**The Laurel and the Ivy**   Robert Kee

'Parnell continues to haunt the Irish historical imagination a century after his death ... Robert Kee's patient and delicate probing enables him to reconstruct the workings of that elusive mind as persuasively, or at least as plausibly, as seems possible ... This splendid biography, which is as readable as it is rigorous, greatly enhances our understanding of both Parnell, and of the Ireland of his time' – *The Times Literary Supplement*

# READ MORE IN PENGUIN

## HISTORY

### A History of Wales   John Davies

'Outstanding . . . Dr Davies casts a coolly appraising eye upon myths, false premises and silver linings . . . He is impartial. He grasps the story of his country with immense confidence and tells it in vigorous and lucid prose . . . Its scope is unique. It is the history Wales needed' – *Daily Telegraph*

### Daily Life in Ancient Rome   Jerome Carcopino

This classic study, which includes a bibliography and notes by Professor Rowell, describes the streets, houses and multi-storeyed apartments of the city of over a million inhabitants, the social classes from senators to slaves, and the Roman family and the position of women, causing *The Times Literary Supplement* to hail it as a 'thorough, lively and readable book'.

### The Anglo-Saxons   Edited by James Campbell

'For anyone who wishes to understand the broad sweep of English history, Anglo-Saxon society is an important and fascinating subject. And Campbell's is an important and fascinating book. It is also a finely produced and, at times, a very beautiful book' – *London Review of Books*

### Customs in Common   E. P. Thompson

Eighteenth-century Britain saw a profound distancing between the culture of the patricians and the plebs. E. P. Thompson explains why in this series of brilliant essays on the customs of the working people, which, he argues, emerged as a culture of resistance towards an innovative market economy. 'One of the most eloquent, powerful and independent voices of our time' – *Observer*

### The Habsburg Monarchy 1809–1918   A J P Taylor

Dissolved in 1918, the Habsburg Empire 'had a unique character, out of time and out of place'. Scholarly and vividly accessible, this 'very good book indeed' (*Spectator*) elucidates the problems always inherent in the attempt to give peace, stability and a common loyalty to a heterogeneous population.

# RE

## HISTORY

**Citizens**  Simon Schama

The award-winning chronicle of the French Revolution. 'The most marvellous book I have read about the French Revolution in the last fifty years' – Richard Cobb in *The Times*

**To the Finland Station**  Edmund Wilson

In this authoritative work Edmund Wilson, considered by many to be America's greatest twentieth-century critic, turns his attention to Europe's revolutionary traditions, tracing the roots of nationalism, socialism and Marxism as these movements spread across the Continent creating unrest, revolt and widespread social change.

**The Tyranny of History**  W. J. F. Jenner

A fifth of the world's population lives within the boundaries of China, a vast empire barely under the control of the repressive ruling Communist regime. Beneath the economic boom China is in a state of crisis that goes far deeper than the problems of its current leaders to a value system that is rooted in the autocratic traditions of China's past.

**The English Bible and the Seventeenth-Century Revolution**
Christopher Hill

'What caused the English civil war? What brought Charles I to the scaffold?' Answer to both questions: the Bible. To sustain this provocative thesis, Christopher Hill's new book maps English intellectual history from the Reformation to 1660, showing how scripture dominated every department of thought from sexual relations to political theory ... 'His erudition is staggering' – *Sunday Times*

**Private Lives, Public Spirit: Britain 1870–1914**  Jose Harris

'Provides the most convincing – and demanding – synthesis yet available of these crowded and tumultuous years' – *Observer* Books of the Year. 'Remarkable ... it locates the origins of far-reaching social change as far back as the 1880s [and] goes on to challenge most of the popular assumptions made about the Victorian and Edwardian periods' – *Literary Review*